Palgrave Studies in Agricultural Economics and Food Policy

Series Editor
Christopher B. Barrett, Cornell University, Ithaca, NY, USA

Agricultural and food policy lies at the heart of many pressing societal issues today and economic analysis occupies a privileged place in contemporary policy debates. The global food price crises of 2008 and 2010 underscored the mounting challenge of meeting rapidly increasing food demand in the face of increasingly scarce land and water resources. The twin scourges of poverty and hunger quickly resurfaced as high-level policy concerns, partly because of food price riots and mounting insurgencies fomented by contestation over rural resources. Meanwhile, agriculture's heavy footprint on natural resources motivates heated environmental debates about climate change, water and land use, biodiversity conservation and chemical pollution. Agricultural technological change, especially associated with the introduction of genetically modified organisms, also introduces unprecedented questions surrounding intellectual property rights and consumer preferences regarding credence (i.e., unobservable by consumers) characteristics. Similar new agricultural commodity consumer behavior issues have emerged around issues such as local foods, organic agriculture and fair trade, even motivating broader social movements. Public health issues related to obesity, food safety, and zoonotic diseases such as avian or swine flu also have roots deep in agricultural and food policy. And agriculture has become inextricably linked to energy policy through biofuels production. Meanwhile, the agricultural and food economy is changing rapidly throughout the world, marked by continued consolidation at both farm production and retail distribution levels, elongating value chains, expanding international trade, and growing reliance on immigrant labor and information and communications technologies. In summary, a vast range of topics of widespread popular and scholarly interest revolve around agricultural and food policy and economics. The extensive list of prospective authors, titles and topics offers a partial, illustrative listing. Thus a series of topical volumes, featuring cutting-edge economic analysis by leading scholars has considerable prospect for both attracting attention and garnering sales. This series will feature leading global experts writing accessible summaries of the best current economics and related research on topics of widespread interest to both scholarly and lay audiences.

Donovan Stanberry · Lystra Fletcher-Paul

Food Security in the Caribbean

Historical Perspectives, Current Challenges, and Sustainable Solutions

palgrave
macmillan

Donovan Stanberry
University of the West Indies
Kingston, Jamaica

Lystra Fletcher-Paul
Saint James, Barbados

ISSN 2662-3889 ISSN 2662-3897 (electronic)
Palgrave Studies in Agricultural Economics and Food Policy
ISBN 978-3-031-66054-2 ISBN 978-3-031-66055-9 (eBook)
https://doi.org/10.1007/978-3-031-66055-9

Cover illustration: A display of fruits and vegetables at the Denbigh Agricultural, Industrial and Food Show/© Carlian Smith, Photo and Graphic Specialist, Ministry of Agriculture, Fisheries & Mining, Jamaica

This Palgrave Macmillan imprint is published by the registered company Springer Nature Switzerland AG
The registered company address is: Gewerbestrasse 11, 6330 Cham, Switzerland

Foreword

I am indeed pleased to have been asked to prepare a foreword for this seminal work on Food Security in the Caribbean by Dr. Donovan Stanberry and Dr. Lystra Fletcher-Paul. This work comes at a critical time in Caribbean development where we have been challenged by a set of events, comprised of three interconnected crises:

- a cost-of-living crisis stemming partly from the war in Ukraine and the COVID-19 pandemic.
- a developing country debt crisis following the COVID-19 pandemic and climate-related disasters and.
- the climate crisis as the glaciers melts and storms and droughts intensify.

Against the background of the above crises, this book is a welcome amplification of the cry from the Prime Minister of Barbados, Honourable Mia Motley, who, through the Bridgetown Agenda, has been championing the cause for new financial arrangements for developing countries to address the challenges of climate change and food security. Prime Minister Motley states *inter alia*, that,

"*The situation is compounded by tightening monetary policies in developed countries and a strengthening U.S. dollar. One in five countries is experiencing fiscal and financial stress. Unaddressed, there will be deepening hardship, debt defaults, widening inequality, political upheaval and a delayed shift to a low-carbon world. Global leaders are now experienced in managing crises. They know what to do and have the means necessary. We must act now. We cannot be good at rescuing banks but bad at saving countries*".

Prime Minister Mia Mottley further added:

"*If we allow the threats of climate and the pandemic, and of violence and of the digital divide and of food insecurity to crowd out the traditional ambition of development as captured by the sustainable development goals, then our people will come to suffer, and regrettably, the world is going to become a very inhospitable place for us to live*".

These pronouncements are expressions of the challenges that the Caribbean faces today. Specifically with respect to food security, the book amply and meticulously highlights the state of food security in the Caribbean region, accentuating the stark picture painted in a recent report prepared by the CARICOM Secretariat and the World Food Programme. According to the report,

> "An estimated 2.8 million people or nearly 40 percent of the population in the English-speaking Caribbean is food insecure, 1 million more than in April 2020. Severe food insecurity continues to increase in the region with the current figure 72 percent higher when compared to April 2020. Highlighting the lasting impact of the pandemic, two years in, the results demonstrate deteriorating food consumption and diets with 25 percent of respondents eating less preferred foods, 30 percent skipping meals or eating less than usual and 5 percent going an entire day without eating in the week leading up to the survey.
>
> High food prices continue to affect people's ability to afford a nutritious diet with 93 percent of respondents reporting higher prices for food compared to 59 percent in April 2020. The ongoing crisis in Ukraine is expected to create an even deeper impact on the cost of basic goods and services in the Caribbean".

Chapter 6 of the book not only highlights the fact that poor nutrition and poor food choices are contributing to the high incidence of diabetes, hypertension, cancers and obesity in the Caribbean; it also emphasizes the initiatives of regional leaders in drawing global attention to this quiet crisis of the explosion in non-communicable diseases. These chronic non-communicable diseases continue to be a threat to the development of the region. Poor quality imported food high in salt, sugars, trans fats and pesticides are known to contribute to the prevalence of these diseases. The threat is expressed in three forms: (a) increasing healthcare costs, (b) increasing loss of productivity and (c) increasing levels of poverty.

One in every three children in Barbados is overweight or obese and at risk of developing a chronic non-communicable disease as they get older. We are also increasingly seeing the effects of an unhealthy diet at younger ages. The current data show that 8 out of every 10 deaths and 4 out of every 10 premature deaths in Barbados are due to an NCD.

According to a recent report from the Caribbean Development Bank (CDB),

"*The economic costs of NCDs will not only further burden our countries but also undercut productivity and human capital investments in education and health*".

The Bank's Vice President, Operations, Mr Isaac Solomon, added that,

"*NCDs also result in loss of income; increased economic dependence and burden of care within households – the latter generally carried by women – and concurrent lifelong poverty traps. Failure to address NCDs undermines sustainable development and will also result in vulnerable and socially disadvantaged groups being left further behind*".

Over the period 2011–2030, NCDs will cost the global economy more than US$ 30 trillion, representing 48% of global GDP in 2010, and pushing millions of people below the poverty line. Mental health conditions alone will account for the loss of an additional US$ 16.1 trillion over this time span, with dramatic impact on productivity and quality of life (World Economic Forum)

These data suggest that NCDs will be a threat to the sustainable development of Caribbean economies.

The Healthy Caribbean Coalition and the Heart and Stroke Foundation are working hard to bring awareness to the people of the need for healthy life style and healthy eating habits. The Government of Barbados' new Nutrition policy for schools is a step in the right direction. But these initiatives must be supported by strategies for the production of healthy food and a National Nutrition Policy. It is noteworthy that Caribbean leaders through their initiative in bringing focus to this epidemic, inspired the international community to turn attention to this troubling issue, with the convening by the United Nations of a High-Level Meeting on Non-communicable Diseases in September 2011. This initiative elevated the fight against NCDs to the global level.

The fundamental question before us therefore, is—Will the next generation of Caribbean people be fit to confront the challenges of development and to take our region into the 22nd century if their health is compromised by chronic non-communicable diseases?

Food security, as defined by the FAO and the United Nations' Committee on World Food Security, means that all people, at all times, have physical, social and economic access to sufficient, safe and nutritious food that meets their food preferences and dietary needs for an active and healthy life.

Given this definition, it is clear that food security is much more than government actions to increase food supply because food insecurity undermines our national independence. Food dependence limits your independence and your capacity to take decisions in your own interest rather than in the interest of those who feed you.

Moving from a food insecure region to a food secure region, therefore, involves removing some of the last shackles of colonialism and using our God-given treasures of fertile lands to develop a new agriculture rooted in technology and innovation and driven by policies, plans and people committed to a new vision for the sector.

Food security *is not* and *should not* be a partisan political issue. Moreover, it is not good for our region to be at the mercy of another country for our food or energy supply. As long as we spend scarce foreign exchange to buy food, we will have less money to support healthcare, education and critical infrastructure projects.

Food security is essentially a multidimensional subject and we must, therefore, engage the entire society in a process of transformation through an integrated approach, if our efforts to improve our food security are going to be successful. In addition, we should avoid the consumption of processed foods and ready-to-serve meals that may be rich in trans-fats, saturated fats, salts, sugars and pesticides.

The enduring value of this seminal work, therefore, is not just the thorough enunciation of the state of food security in the region, but an elaboration of many concrete and practical solutions to different facets of the food security problem. Moreover, the book outlines the different roles of the respective stakeholders in implementing these solutions, reflecting the imperative of a multi-sectoral, multi-agency approach to what is an extremely complex and multi-dimensional problem. By highlighting case studies from across the region, the book will also contribute to boosting the confidence of our Caribbean people that we can find creative solutions to our own problems. Such an auspicious beginning certainly augurs well for the future.

This well-researched, expertly written volume should be an essential text and must read for students of agricultural economics, international relations and development studies; as well as academics, policymakers, operators in the agricultural sectors. Persons who are generally interested in issues relating to sustainable development and more specifically in tracing the implementation of the SDGs would also find this book very useful.

I have called for a Caribbean Food Security Agency that would coordinate regional actions on this issue, and I hope that this book will help students, policymakers and professionals of agricultural development to take a new look at food security and stimulate a new thrust to create a new platform for food security in the Caribbean.

Dr. Chelston Braithwaite
Former Director General,
Inter-American Institute for
Cooperation On Agriculture
2002–2010

Acknowledgements

Writing a book is never a solitary endeavour; it is the result of the collective effort, support and inspiration of many individuals and organizations. As we reflect on the completion of this work on Food Security in the Caribbean, we, the authors of this book, are deeply grateful to those who have contributed their expertise, encouragement and resources along this journey.

First and foremost, we thank Almighty God for inspiration and strength to carry out this project. Next, we extend my sincere gratitude to the farmers, agricultural workers, policymakers and community leaders across the Caribbean whose dedication to food production and security has been the driving force behind this project. Your resilience, knowledge and commitment to sustainable agriculture and food and nutrition security have been a constant source of inspiration.

We are indebted to the many colleagues whose insights and contributions have enriched the content of this book. Specifically, we would like to mention Dr. Gillian Smith who made useful suggestions on possible sources of information and data, Dr Arlington Chesney who shared his vast knowledge and experience from working in the field of agriculture and food security in the Caribbean for well over four decades, Dr. Chelston Braithwaite, former Director General of IICA who, like Dr Chesney, shared his vast knowledge and experience, but also provided helpful insights on policies applied in other regions of the world which may be applicable in the Caribbean. Drs. Deep Ford and Patrick Antoine and Mrs Sunita Daniel who share their thoughts on the future of food and nutrition security from the perspectives of the Private Sector, farmers and traders. Special thanks are also due to Mr. Barton Clarke, former Executive Director of CARDI, who liberally shared his experience and perspectives in terms of how the region needs to proceed with the food security mandate. Your expertise has helped to shed light on the complex challenges and opportunities facing the region in its pursuit of food security.

We would also like to express our appreciation to the various governmental, private sector and international agencies, whose support and collaboration have been instrumental in shaping the research and implementation of strategies discussed in this book. Special mention should be made of the contribution of the following persons in this regard, who provided important data—Mr. Michael Pryce, Kevin Condappa, Miss Nashima Davis, Mr. Joseph Gyles, Mrs. Joan Brown Morrison, Mrs. Michelle Sherwood and Mrs. Janet Conie of Jamaica's Ministry of Agriculture, Fisheries and Mining; Ms. Tisheecka Clarke from the Tourism Enhancement Fund; Mr. Terron Francis from the Ministry of Finance and the Public Service; and Mr. Shaun Baugh from the CARICOM Secretariat. Miss Marcia Thomas, International Trade Specialist, Mr. Richard Pandohie, CEO of SERPROD Group Jamaica Limited and Mr. Cedric Stephens, Insurance Specialist granted interviews, which provided important insights from their vantage points on the issue of Caribbean food security. Your commitment to fostering agricultural development and resilience in the Caribbean is commendable.

To our colleagues and mentors, thank you for your guidance, feedback and encouragement throughout this endeavour. Your wisdom and encouragement have been invaluable.

Most importantly, we deeply grateful to our families and friends for their unwavering support, understanding and patience during the writing process. Your love and encouragement have sustained us through the challenges and triumphs of bringing this book to fruition.

Lastly, we extend my heartfelt appreciation to the readers of this book. It is our hope that the insights and perspectives shared within these pages will contribute to a deeper understanding of the issues surrounding food security in the Caribbean and inspire meaningful action towards a more sustainable and equitable future.

Contents

Acronyms

ACP	African, Caribbean and Pacific
ADC	Agricultural Development Corporation
AMDR	Acceptable Macronutrient Distribution Range
BMI	Body Mass Index
CAHFSA	Caribbean Agricultural Health and Food Safety Agency
CARDI	Caribbean Agricultural Research and Development Institute
CARICOM	Caribbean Community
CARIFTA	Caribbean Free Trade Association
CARPHA	Caribbean Public Health Agency
CATCO	Caribbean Agricultural Trading Company Limited
CBI	Caribbean Basin Initiative
CCAP	Caribbean Community Agricultural Policy
CCPAD	Caribbean Community Programme for Agricultural Development
CCRIF	Caribbean Catastrophe Risk Insurance Facility
CDB	Caribbean Development Bank
CDEMA	Caribbean Disaster and Emergency Management Agency
CET	Common External Tariff
CFC	Caribbean Food Corporation
CFNI	Caribbean Food and Nutrition Institute
CIMH	Caribbean Institute of Meteorology and Hydrology
COTED	Council for Trade and Economic Development
CPSO	CARICOM Private Sector Organization
CRFM	Caribbean Regional Fisheries Mechanism
CROSQ	CARICOM Regional Organization for Standards and Quality
CSME	Caribbean Single Market and Economy
ECLAC	Economic Commission for Latin America and the Caribbean

EPA	Economic Partnership Agreement
EU	European Union
FAO	Food and Agriculture Organization
FBDR	Food-based Dietary Guidelines
FIES	Food Insecurity Experience Scale
GATT	General Agreement on Trade and Tariffs
GDP	Gross Domestic Product
HEART	Human Employment and Resource Training
IDB	Inter-American Development Bank
IFAD	International Fund for Agricultural Development
IICA	Inter-American Institute for Cooperation on Agriculture
ILO	International Labour Organization
IMF	International Monetary Fund
IOM	International Organization for Migration
LAC	Latin America and the Caribbean
MPCI	Multiple Peril Crop Insurance
NAITS	National Animal Identification and Traceability System
NCDs	Non-Communicable Diseases
NEPA	National Environment and Planning Agency
NGOs	Non-Governmental Organizations
NPCI	Named Peril Crop Insurance
OECD	Organization for Economic Cooperation and Development
OECS	Organization of Eastern Caribbean States
OTN	Office of Trade Negotiations
PAHO	Pan American Health Organization
RADA	Rural Agricultural Development Authority
REDI	Rural Economic Development Initiative
RFNS	Regional Food and Nutrition Strategy
RFNSP	Regional Food and Nutrition Security Policy
RFP	Regional Food Plan
SDGs	Sustainable Development Goals
SDT	Special and Differential Treatment
SIDS	Small Island Developing States
UNDESA	United Nations Department of Economic and Social Affairs
UNDP	United Nations Development Programme
UNICEF	United Nations Children's Fund
USAID	United States Agency for International Development
WFP	World Food Programme
WFS	World Food Summit
WTO	World Trade Organization

List of Figures

List of Tables

CHAPTER 1

Food Security: Definition, Scope and Influencing Factors

Introduction

Food is one of the necessities of life. It is the first priority of any civilization or society, underpinned by the physiological requirement for the sustenance of live. In earlier civilizations, the production of and hunting for food were not only the main economic activities, but was almost a whole-of-society effort, given low levels of technology and hence low productivity. As technology improved and productivity levels raised, society was able to release some of the human resources previously devoted to producing food, into other fields of endeavour. The ease of growing food, often related to the availability of water, would largely dictate where humans settle. The world has, therefore, always kept a keen watch on the capacity of the agriculture to sustain human populations. Shakeel (2018) traces concerns of food availability for the population to as far back as the Chinese Emperor Wen in 163 BC. Thomas Malthus in his 1798 *Essay on the Principle of Population* also raised concerns about the expanding human population and the inability of the then state of agriculture and availability of natural resources to sustain the burgeoning population with food. Scoones (2015) pointed to a repeat of these concerns during the oil crisis of the early 1970s, triggering the publication of critical works on the 'limits to growth', with potential catastrophic consequences. These publications include *Blueprint for Survival*

D. Stanberry and L. Fletcher-Paul, *Food Security in the Caribbean*, Palgrave Studies in Agricultural Economics and Food Policy, https://doi.org/10.1007/978-3-031-66055-9_1

by Goldsmith et al. appearing in *The Ecologist* in 1972 and the Club of Rome's *Limits to Growth* by Meadows et al. in 1972. The repeated record breaking high temperatures of 2023 have also raised issues of coral bleaching and the capacity of the oceans to sustain human life with these temperatures poised to continue rising in the near future.

Malthus' fear of widespread human hunger if deliberate measures were not initiated to reduce human population was however averted by advances in technology, rendering agriculture more productive. The explosion in scientific and technological advances ushered in by the industrial revolution of the eighteenth century, for instance, has changed the structure of society in a profound way, increasing agricultural productivity and simultaneously giving pre-eminence to industry over agriculture, with a diminishing contribution of agriculture to the total value of society's output. Typically therefore, as countries advance on the development continuum, agricultural production is modernized and the sector's contribution to Gross Domestic Product (GDP) diminishes in relative terms. In Jamaica for instance, agriculture's contribution to GDP was 40% in 1930, declining to 31% in 1950 and 10.2% in 1968, reflecting the emergence of bauxite mining, tourism and a robust manufacturing sector from the 1950s and onwards. In Guyana, the change in the structure of the economy has been even more dramatic. According to the Bureau of Statistics, agriculture's contribution to GDP fell from an average of approximately 22% per annum between 2012 and 2019 to 10% in 2022, thanks to the discovery and exploitation of huge oil reserves.

Notwithstanding the relative diminution of the agricultural sector in CARICOM States in the last few decades, the sector still remains critical to overall economic performance and food security. Jefferson (1972) posits that the failure of the agricultural sector to meet rising food demand will put a strain on scarce foreign exchange or alternatively cause food prices to rise. This in turn will drive up wages and generally increase the cost of goods produced in the economy. It is also the case that the relatively large numbers of people still engaged in the agricultural sector can help to stimulate economic growth if wages are rising in that sector, or cause a slowdown in aggregate demand if there is a stagnation in the agricultural sector.

While the explosion in science and technology has undeniably increased food production, with the level of world food production more than adequate to feed the world's population, there are paradoxically alarming levels of hunger and malnutrition in the world. This has been a preoccupation of the global community since the late nineteenth century. At the same time, the increase in the world food production and productivity has had a devastating impact on the physical environment, raising concerns about agricultural sustainability. In the Caribbean, despite the relative modernization of agriculture, a general rise in production and productivity, economic diversification and rise in per capita GDP that now renders most English-speaking Caribbean countries middle income developing countries, there are currently significant concerns about food insecurity and lack of purchasing power to afford a healthy diet. A survey conducted in 2022 by the World food Programme (WFP), in collaboration with CARICOM showed that 57% of the Region's population is food insecure. At the same time the Pan-American Health Organization (PAHO) reported that some 52% of the region's population cannot afford the US$4.23 per day required to procure food for a healthy diet. The Caribbean Public Health Agency (CARPHA) in 2021 reported that the Caribbean has some of the highest obesity rates in the Americas, while Rambaran et al. (2021) indicated that the prevalence of childhood overweight in 10 English-speaking Caribbean countries of between 28% and 44.5%, with obesity rates of between 14.3% and 19.8%.

Given the currency and actuality of the issues of food production, lack of economic access to food, issues of malnutrition, the sustainability of agrifood systems and the impact of external events on food supply and access, the issue of food security therefore remains relevant for the Caribbean and deserves focused attention. This chapter will therefore explore the concept of food security, examine how the concept has evolved over time, and what are the major factors influencing the state of food security in the region.

The Concept of Food Security—Its Definition and Constituent Pillars

With every succeeding food crisis (such as occurred in the early 1970s and more recently in the 2008), the term food security becomes more popular and mainstreamed in the lexicon of governments, policymakers and international development agencies. But what does the concept of food security entail? What is its definition? Dutta and Saikia (2018) and Smith et al. (1993) point to over 200 definitions of food security up to the 1990s. Hoddinott (1999) additionally referred to over 450 indicators of food security. The plethora of definitions and indicators of food security underlines the increasing focus that the issues of hunger, malnutrition and lack of access to food have received in the last 50 years. Indeed, Maxwell (1996) listed some 194 studies on the concept of food security. In tandem with the multiple definitions of food security, is the growing number of studies examining these many definitions, such as Mckeown (2006) and Shakeel (2018) identified the 1974 World Food Conference, organized by the FAO in response to the then world food crisis, as giving birth to the term 'food security'.

Amidst the myriad definitions of food security, there seems to a be consensus in the literature that the 1996 definition of food security, emerging out of the FAO World Food Summit, is the most comprehensive, capturing most of the dimensions of this complex phenomenon. This definition states that: "Food security exists when all people, at all times, have physical, social and economic access to sufficient, safe and nutritious food which meets their dietary needs and food preferences for an active and healthy life". This definition encapsulates several dimensions of food security. These are as follows:

Availability

The first pillar of food security captured in the definition relates to the physical availability of food for 'all people', that is, at the global, regional, national, community and even at the level of the family, regardless of colour, race, gender or class. The 'availability' dimension was the original focus of food security. For a long time it was assumed that once there was an appropriate supply side response to the issue of food security, that is, producing more food and addressing the issues of distribution and trade, then the problem of hunger would be solved (Dutta & Saikia, 2018). However, the problem of human hunger persisted despite the world producing more food than is required to eliminate world hunger. Food becomes available to nations through a mix of domestic production, imports of food, food aid or storage. It should be pointed out that no one country possesses the range of agro-climatic conditions nor the comparative advantage in every instance to be able to produce all the food it consumes. Food importation is therefore unavoidable. The key is to ensure that domestic production is maximised to supply the critical mass of food consumed in a given country. It is also critical that the agricultural sector produces enough food for exports, in those areas where there is a clear comparative advantage, so as to be able to afford to import foods, where this is desirable. A country's capacity to produce food can be disrupted in the short run by external shocks, such as the unavailability of critical imported inputs, as well as by natural disasters. In these instances food imports will rise temporarily. For strategic reasons, it might be necessary for a country to produce some critical food items to reduce its dependence on imports, particularly given the propensity of food exporting countries to ban or suspend exports in times of crisis. Sharma (2011), for instance, explored the prevalence of the use of export bans and other restrictive measures during the 2007–2010 period and recommended measures for disciplining these practices within a multilateral framework.

Access

The second pillar of food security embedded in the definition relates to access. Food availability is a necessary, but not sufficient condition for food security. Shakeel (2018, p. 62) points to the Green Revolution largely solving the issue of food availability through increased production and productivity of agriculture, yet "people were still hungry and food-insecure". Indeed, food can be abundant at the country/regional level, but individual households cannot access it due to impaired purchasing power. Popkin (1981) shows that aggregated data at the national and regional levels often mask the extent of food insecurity at the household level, and therefore disaggregation of these data at the household level reveals higher prevalence of food insecurity, hunger and malnutrition. Gittelsohn et al. (1998) therefore assert that physical availability of food is not a good and reliable indicator of food security. Access relates to households having the capacity to acquire food in sufficient quantities through their own production, purchases, bartering, from food aid or gifts. Access to food by households is therefore a factor of the general income levels in a country, levels of employment and the strength of government's social welfare systems.

In attempting to decipher the paradox of increased food availability co-existing with high levels of hunger and malnutrition, Indian Nobel Prize winner Amartya Sen made a seminal contribution to the issue of households' access to food. In his 1981 classic *Poverty and Famines: An Essay on Entitlement and Deprivation*, Sen relates the poor's lack of access to food to the issue of failure of 'entitlements'. For Sen, each person in society has an 'entitlement' to a range of combinations of goods and services to which he has access. These 'entitlements' however can fail due to a number of factors. In relation to food security, a poor household's 'entitlement' to food can fail due to high inflation or low demand for its labour, even under conditions where food is generally available in the society. Another factor causing a farmer to lose his 'entitlement' to food is crop failure or depressed prices of food, due to overproduction. Sen's observation arose principally from his study of the Bengal Famine of 1943, where thousands were suffering from hunger, even while food production in 1943 was higher than in the pre-famine years. Sen's work is credited for the inclusion of the notion of access in the 1996 definition of food security, which, according to Maxwell and Slater (2003), represents a paradigm shift in the understanding of food security at the national and international levels, largely through the lens of food availability.

As with food availability, access to food by households can also be challenged by shocks in the economy, crop failures and national disasters, which either disrupt the household's capacity to produce its own food, or its capacity to purchase food. To ensure access of households to food 'at all times', the State has a critical role to play in terms of crop insurance, controlling the economic variables of inflation, unemployment and economic growth, as well as a robust social protection system to provide temporary relief to households without access to food. The literature also speaks of the importance of households accessing food in 'socially accepted' ways, that is, without resorting to stealing or scavenging (Dutta & Saikia, 2018; Labadarios et al., 2011), as well as in a manner consistent with socio-cultural norms. In other words, people must be able to access the food they desire based on their religious beliefs or their lifestyle preferences. Abundance of pork and pork products, for instance, does not enhance the food security for Rastafarian, Muslims and Sabbatarians. Access therefore is physical, financial and socio-cultural (Simon, 2012).

Utilization

The phrase "safe and nutritious food which meets their dietary needs" in the definition of food security relates to the utilization dimension of food security. The ultimate purpose for consuming food by individuals must be to be healthy and able to function optimally. The fact is while there can be food availability and access, if food is not properly utilized, the consumer might not derive the nutritional benefits. It is also the case that if the food consumed is not safe from a hygiene perspective, or balanced based on its nutritional value, then the food consumed will not enhance the health of the consumer. Renzaho and Mellor (2010) commends the 1992 USAID definition of food utilization as being a condition when "food is properly used; proper food processing and storage techniques exist and are applied, and adequate health and sanitation services exist". To these considerations, the FAO adds "diversity in diet" and "intra-household distribution of food" as critical components of the concept of food utilization. The notion of food utilization is therefore a complex one intersecting the disciplines/concepts of biology, food safety, nutrition, access to water and sanitation. In summary, diets must be diverse to allow for the range of nutrients required for healthy growth and development; foods must be prepared, handled and stored under hygienic conditions; and food must be distributed within the household, so as to allow for every member to have access to safe nutritious food and from a biological standpoint, the body must be able to absorb the nutrients in the food consumed.

In the CARICOM absolute hunger in terms of the absence of the physical availability of foods is not a major issue. There are issues relating to access, given relatively low levels of per capita income and inefficient social protection programmes that do not always provide universal coverage of the poorest. Food utilization is however a far more significant consideration, manifested in the heavy caloric orientation of diets and the disproportionately high consumption of processed imported food, laced with sugars, salt and unhealthy fats/oil. This reality is reflected in comparatively high levels of obesity and high prevalence of non-communicable disease in the region.

Stability

The term "at all times" in the definition of food security speaks to the issue of stability, as a critical dimension of food security. This stability, as a temporal concept, is relevant to all the previously highlighted physical dimensions of food security, viz: availability, access and utilization, and applies to all levels of food security, that is, at the global, regional, national, community, household and individual levels. As long as human beings physiologically require food daily for sustenance and proper bodily functions, then food must be available, accessible and properly utilized in a consistent, uninterrupted manner.

The literature distinguishes between chronic and transitory food insecurity (Barrett & Sahn, 2001; Dutta & Saikia, 2018; Simon, 2012). Chronic food insecurity relates to a long term, ongoing inability of nations, households and individuals to meet or satisfy their minimum requirement for food. This inability could relate to persistent drought and wars, or at the individual/household level persistent unemployment due to the state of the economy or the loss of physical or mental capacity to earn a living. Transitionary food insecurity, on the other hand, refers to temporary, short term inability to satisfy the minimum demand for food. This short-term inability to access food could be cyclical, that is, related to the crop cycle where food is scarce after the harvesting period (Hart, 2009), or could simply relate to temporary factors such as natural disasters, man-made disasters or crop failure related to the sudden and temporary onset of diseases, as well as temporary spikes in food prices.

The Caribbean is particularly vulnerable to a number of factors capable of disrupting food supply and access. Chief among these factors are natural weather-related disasters, being exacerbated by climate change, manifested in more frequent and intense hurricanes and flooding, as well as more frequent and prolonged droughts. The widespread lack of agricultural insurance in the region poses a particular challenge to mitigate this factor, and governments have become the insurers of last resort, consistently supporting farmers to resume production after disasters. The challenge is for extension services and agricultural research to educate farmers on inexpensive techniques to mitigate disasters and crop losses, such as terracing, rain water harvesting, planting of varieties of crops that are drought resistant, drainage and so on.

Volatility of food prices on the international market and the growing propensity of net-food exporting countries to ban or restrict exports of good in times of crisis, and the deliberate efforts of Russia to disrupt grain exports from the Ukraine can also temporarily contribute to food insecurity. Strategically therefore, it might well be appropriate for countries to incentivize the domestic production of a critical threshold of the major staples consumed locally, regardless of lack of comparative advantage, so long as the natural conditions allow for the production of such foods.

Vulnerability and Risk

Closely associated with the dimension of food stability is the concept of vulnerability and risk in relation to food insecurity. Vulnerability in relation to food security refers to conditions/factors that render a nation, household or individual incapable of accessing the minimum quantity of food required for healthy living. This vulnerability relates to the nation's/household's/individual's exposure to these factors and their capacity to cope with or mitigate these factors/conditions (Fafchamps, 1999; Simon, 2012; World Food Programme, 2009). The coping capacity is a measure of resilience, and can either be proactive, minimising the condition before it occurs, or reactive, responding to the impact of the condition/hazard after its occurrence (Dutta & Saikia, 2018). Within the Caribbean context, the role of the State is critical in mitigating the impact of these hazards. In relation to droughts, for instance, installation of irrigation schemes by the State is critical, given the widespread dependence of farmers on rainfall and the fact that such infrastructures are public goods, as is cold storage, drainage and good farm roads.

Risk as it relates to food security is a measure of the likelihood of the inability of a country/household/individual to access minimum quantity of food required for healthy living in the future. This risk can be mitigated by availability of insurance, savings at the household/individual level and the state of the economy and national policies at the country level.

The Evolution of the Concept of Food Security as an International Concern

The comprehensive definition of food security elaborated above, and which was adopted at the 1996 FAO sponsored World Food Summit, represents the culmination of the evolution of the concept over the previous 60 years. Although Thomas Malthus in 1798 expressed concerns about the capacity of agriculture to feed the world, Shaw (2007) refers to the United States Department of Agriculture initiating food aid in 1896 to manage agricultural surplus and stabilize farmers' income, food security as an international concern emerged in the 1930s, within the frame of the League of Nations. The League of Nations was founded in 1920 in the aftermath of World War I (1914–1918), by the victorious allies, and is generally regarded as the forerunner of the United Nations. Although its objectives were to foster international peace and security and to promote international cooperation, its early focus seemed to be dominated by the issues relating to world peace and security.

Dr. John Shaw, in his 2007 classic *World Food Security—A History since 1945*, is undisputedly the leading authority on the evolution of the concept of food security and the international institution framework that has been built around it. Shaw (2007) segments this history into three distinct periods viz: 1945–1970, 1970–1990 and 1990s and beyond. Simon (2012) building on Shaw's account adds another period—1990–2005, which he dubs the "golden years of Food Security". According to Shaw (2007), initial concerns about food security surrounded the issue of over production of food in the global North in the pre-World War I period, resulting in lower prices and the consequential impact on farmers' income. The solution proffered at the time was the purchasing of surplus by governments, which was subsequently used as food aid to food insecure developing nations. The League of Nations, the forerunner of the United Nations, recognized the necessity "for some form of multilateral world food security arrangement … to rationalize food production, supply and trade for the benefit of both producers and consumers" (Shaw, 2007, p. 5). However, the overwhelming concern of developed nations within the League of Nations was with preserving the income of farmers in the North, while millions were facing hunger and malnutrition in the developing world.

In the period leading up to World War II and immediately thereafter, the focus of the international community was how to increase food production and maintain food self-sufficiency in the face of disruptions occasioned by the war. After the war, attention was focused on restoring food production capacity in the war ravaged Europe, and in the interim supply that continent and the developing world with food aid. FAO as an institution was established in this period, and became the global institution tasked with coordinating expansion of food production and distribution. The emphasis on food security up to this period was overwhelmingly on availability. Thanks to the Green Revolution, food production increased rapidly up to the 1970s.

The decade of the 1970s commenced with a series events which precipitated a world food crisis by 1973. These events include crop failures due to adverse weather in major grain exporting countries, spiralling increases in oil prices due to cut back in production by OPEC countries and a general reduction in available food aid due to production cuts in North America, in an attempt to manage over production. The convergence of these events resulted in spiralling prices for food and agricultural inputs, sharp increases in the cost of producing and importing food. This crisis led to the convening of 1974 World Food Conference by the FAO, which resulted in the establishment of the Fund for Agricultural Development (IFAD) and the Committee on Food Security in the FAO. In this conference the concept of food security was institutionalized within the FAO. By the 1980s other food crises emerged resulting from conflicts in Cambodia creating a refugee crisis in neighbouring countries, as well as famine in Ethiopia. Importantly, in this period Amartya Sen in his study of the Bengal crisis pointed to the importance of access as a critical pillar of food security, as abundance of food can coincide with high levels of hunger and starvation.

Simon (2012) dubs the period 1990–2005, (where his analysis stops), as the "golden years of food security". Beginning in the 1990s to early 2000s, a record number of conferences/international meetings were convened, partially or wholly addressing the issue of food security. The global community has never had such a concentrated focus on the issue of food security. Significantly also is the fact that whereas in the past attention was only paid to the 'availability' dimension of food security, beginning in this period a more multi-sectorial/multifaceted approach was adopted in dealing with food security. It is also somewhat paradoxical that as observed by both Shaw (2007) and Simon (2012), this multiplicity of meetings surrounding food security occurred at a time when the FAO was reporting considerable progress in reducing both the absolute number of people and the proportion of the world's population that was food insecure (FAO, 1994).

As the year 2000 approached, representing the beginning of a new millennium, the Secretary General of the United Nations, Kofi Annan, saw this as a unique opportunity for the global community to take stock of itself and reverse the trajectory the world was proceeding on in respect to food security, poverty and inequitable development and unsustainable use of the planet's resources to sustain life. In order to reverse these negative trends and build a world that is free from conflicts and poverty, and embracing sustainable development, Kofi envisioned a greater role for the United Nations itself, and therefore called for a Millennium Summit in September 2000 in New York. To guide the deliberations of the Summit, Annan prepared a report, which inter alia, outlined eight goals to eliminate poverty, disease and hunger, ensure environmental sustainability and achieve a global partnership for development. These goals had specific targets that were largely composed of targets already agreed by the plethora of international conferences which were convened in the decade of the 1990s.

These goals and targets were unanimously adopted by the 189 Member States, represented by over 150 Heads of State/Government, representing up to that time the greatest concentration of world leaders in any given assembly. Specific to food security, the declaration modified the target of the 1996 World Food Summit to halve the proportion (not number) of the world population suffering from hunger and malnutrition, between 1990 and 2015. A number of the other targets were inextricably linked to this second target. For instance the first target of halving the proportion of people whose income is less than one dollar a day is critical to achieving the target of halving the proportion of people suffering from hunger, as income is critical to access to food. The target of reducing the proportion of people suffering from hunger was in turn critical to achieving the target relative to achieving universal primary education, as hungry children cannot learn. Similarly, access to food is critical to reducing child mortality, as well as improving maternal health.

This period from 1990 to the present has not been without its fair share of food crises and emergencies. The food crisis in Niger, in Central Africa, in 2005, resulted in widespread famine and death from hunger. According to Simon (2012), this crisis resulted from decisions taken in neighbouring Nigeria, which supplied grains to Niger, and which caused sharp increases in the price of grains, rendering this food largely inaccessible to people in Niger. This highlighted the importance of the economic access dimension of the food security, and reinforced the paradox of availability of food coinciding and coexisting with hunger and malnutrition.

Following sharply on the heels of the Niger food crisis was the world food crisis of 2008, which saw astronomical increases in the prices of grains, energy and such agricultural inputs as fertilizer. This crisis was closely related to the global financial crisis of 2007. The world food crisis of 2008 had little to do with any appreciable reduction in food production, but was largely due to the financial crisis, which many analysts attributed to speculations in financial markets. Von Braun (2011) and Mittal (2009) linked the food crisis with food (commodity) markets. The sharp spikes in food prices were also linked to the rapid expansion of biofuel production, in the years preceding 2008, through continued diversion of grains for food to feedstock for bio fuel production. Von

Braun, for instance, asserts that between 2004 and 2008, the amount of grains diverted to ethanol production more than tripled, 'fuelled' by increasing energy subsides provided by developed countries. Similar trends in diversion of food to fuel are also observed by Trostle (2005) with respect to the United States.

The poor in net food importing countries bore the brunt of these sharp increases in prices, as they neither had the resources to purchase the more expensive grains, neither could local agriculture in these countries adequately respond due to similar sharp increases in the price of imported fertilizers and other inputs, as well as the longstanding under-investment in agriculture. Higher prices for food commodities and agricultural inputs further worsened the fiscal position of many net food importing developing countries. The situation was further compounded by the institution of export restrictions in grain exporting countries, and even outright export bans (Mittal, 2009) and (Sharma, 2011). The crisis therefore precipitated widespread riots and social unrest across the world. Von Braun (2011), for instance, reported food riots in over 40 countries worldwide.

In the face of the 2008 world food crisis, the FAO convened a high-level conference on world food security in June 2008, attended by 181 States and the European Community. The conference bemoaned the fall in agricultural aid to poor countries from $8 billion in 1980 to $3.4 Billion in 2005, while agricultural subsidies in the OECD countries stood at $372 Billion in 2006. In the declaration, the high level conference "embrace food security as a matter of permanent national policy", and called upon all donors and the UN system to increase their assistance to developing countries, especially least developed countries affected by high food prices (FAO, 2008). The phenomenon of sharp increases in food prices globally was repeated in 2011, albeit on a comparatively more moderate level.

Food Security and the Sustainable Development Goals (SDGs)

As 2015 approached, the international community realized that the Millennium Development Goal #2 of halving the proportion of people suffering from hunger and malnutrition would not be achieved. In fact, at the World Food Summit plus 5 (WFS+5) in 2002, both the UN Secretary General and the Director General of the FAO bemoaned the slow progress towards the achievement of that goal (Shaw, 2007). The world food crisis of 2008 further retarded progress towards the achievement of the goal, and for many countries actually reversed earlier progress. In June 2012, 20 years after the Earth Summit, the international community once more converged in Rio de Janeiro for the United Nations Conference on Sustainable Development (Rio +20). The Conference adopted a document dubbed *The Future We Want*, in which a process to develop a set of sustainable development goals (SDGs) was launched to build on the millennium development goals. At the UN General Assembly the following year, a 30-member open working group was set up to develop proposals on the SDGs. The UN Sustainable Development Summit of September 2015 in New York adopted the *2030 Agenda for Sustainable Development*, with some 17 SDGs, the second of which is to attain zero hunger in the world by 2030.

Like the MGDs, there is a strong association between the zero hunger goal and other goals, notably:

1. Goal #1—No Poverty
2. Goal #3—Good Health and Well-being
3. Goal #4—Quality Education
4. Goal #6—Clean Water and Sanitation
5. Goal #7—Affordable and Clean Energy
6. Goal # 13—Climate Action
7. Goal #14—Life Below Water
8. Goal #15—Life on Land

9. Goal # 17—Partnerships for the Goals.

The attainment of goals 1, 6, 7, 13, 14, 15 and 17 is critical for the realization of a hunger free world, and goals 3 and 4 cannot be achieved if hunger and malnutrition persist in the world. A detailed breakdown of the targets associated with Goal #2—zero hunger by 2030 is given in the box below:

Box 1.1 SDG 2 Targets
SDG 2 Zero Hunger—Targets

2.1 By 2030, end hunger and ensure access by all people, in particular the poor and people in vulnerable situations, including infants, to safe, nutritious and sufficient food all year round.

2.2 By 2030, end all forms of malnutrition, including achieving, by 2025, the internationally agreed targets on stunting and wasting in children under 5 years of age, and address the nutritional needs of adolescent girls, pregnant and lactating women and older persons.

2.3 By 2030, double the agricultural productivity and incomes of small-scale food producers, in particular women, indigenous peoples, family farmers, pastoralists and fishers, including through secure and equal access to land, other productive resources and inputs, knowledge, financial services, markets and opportunities for value addition and non-farm employment.

2.4 By 2030, ensure sustainable food production systems and implement resilient agricultural practices that increase productivity and production, that help maintain ecosystems, that strengthen capacity for adaptation to climate change, extreme weather, drought, flooding and other disasters and that progressively improve land and soil quality.

2.5 By 2020, maintain the genetic diversity of seeds, cultivated plants and farmed and domesticated animals and their related wild species, including through soundly managed and diversified seed and plant banks at the national, regional and international levels, and promote access to and fair and equitable sharing of benefits arising from the utilization of genetic resources and associated traditional knowledge, as internationally agreed.

2.A Increase investment, including through enhanced international cooperation, in rural infrastructure, agricultural research and extension services, technology development and plant and livestock gene banks in order to enhance agricultural productive capacity in developing countries, in particular least developed countries.

2.B Correct and prevent trade restrictions and distortions in world agricultural markets, including through the parallel elimination of all forms of agricultural export subsidies and all export measures with equivalent effect, in accordance with the mandate of the Doha Development Round.

2.C Adopt measures to ensure the proper functioning of food commodity markets and their derivatives and facilitate timely access to market information, including on food reserves, in order to help limit extreme food price volatility.

The UN System has invested heavily in a sophisticated system of monitoring and measuring countries' progress in the attainment of these goals and an SDG progress report is produced and debated in the annual Sustainable Development Summits. As indicated in Chapter 3, the progress in attaining the SDG#2 has been less than satisfactory. The SDGs however serve as a rallying point, focusing and galvanizing all nations into action. In Jamaica for instance, the government promulgated a Vision 2030 Plan, before the SDGs were established, with economic, social and environmental goals and targets, basically mirroring the SDGs.

The Covid-19 Pandemic, the Russian/Ukraine Conflict and Their Impact on Food Security

The most significant events impacting food security since the SDGs are the twin occurrences of the COVID-19 pandemic and the Russian/Ukraine War. In response to the pandemic control measures were instituted worldwide, including widespread lockdowns, suspension of international travel and curtailment in the movement of goods. These measures, while deemed necessary to check the spread of the disease and reduce deaths and illness, also had the effect of curtailing economic activities and the loss of productivity within countries and the slowing down of trade between countries. All of this resulted in significant numbers of people losing employment and income, slowdown of the economy, disruptions in supply chains, increased in poverty and inflation getting out of hand.

The slowdown of economic activities in the Caribbean was particularly acute, given the region's high dependence on tourism, and the disproportionate impact of the lockdowns and restriction on air and cruise travels

(Ali, 2023a, 2023b; Simpson, 2022). Economic slowdown in the region is evidenced by negative GDP growth in 2020 relative to 2019 ranging from 2.7% in St. Vincent and the Grenadines to 20.2% in St. Lucia, according to World Bank data. This scenario had a devastating impact on food security, particularly for net food importing developing countries. The disruption of supply chains meant that there was less physical food to import. Also, curtailment of production of food both from the exporting countries and internally in the importing countries meant that there was less food available overall. This on the one hand reduced farmers' income and on the other hand caused the prices of food to spike. Access therefore became a major issue.

The economic slowdown precipitated by the responses to the pandemic necessitated a significant response from governments the world over, through huge stimulus spending to provide short-term relief to the poor and vulnerable, to prop up struggling businesses, to encourage businesses to keep as many people employed as possible and to incentivize farmers to quickly expand production. These unprecedented levels of public expenditure at a time when economies were shrinking had devastating fiscal impacts, driving up public debts. Ali (2023b) reported a general increase in the debt-to-GDP levels across the English-speaking Caribbean, with the increases in Bahamas, Barbados, Suriname and Jamaica moving to 75%, 139.8%, 143.8% and 109.7% respectively in 2020 from 59.7%, 123%, 80.8% and 94.3%, respectively, in 2019.

Due to the impact of climate change, low investment in agriculture in the developing world and continued volatility in commodity markets, the world was already at risk of not achieving the SDG #2 goal of a 'zero hunger' world by 2030. *The Sustainable Development Goals Report, 2020* (UN, 2020), indicated that in 2019, the year before the onset of the COVID-19 pandemic, some 25.9% of the world's population was being affected by moderate or severe food insecurity, compared to 22.4% in 2014, the year before the SDGs were adopted. UN (2022) reported that the impact of the COVID-19 pandemic "exacerbated an already deteriorating situation, with about 150 million more people facing hunger in 2021 than in 2019". Filho et al. (2020) also point to the threat the pandemic posed to the achievement of the SDGs.

In the Caribbean, the negative impact of the COVID-19 pandemic on food security is reflected in the increased dependence on imported foods within one year of the pandemic. Ali (2023a) shows that food imports as a percentage of total merchandise trade moved from approximately

19% in 2019 to approximately 23% in 2020, and to 25% in 2021. In absolute terms food imports increased to $4.9 billion in 2021 or by over $600 million compared to 2020. Interestingly, this increase in the food import bill was occurring at a time when the tourism sector, the mainstay of most Caribbean economies, declined precipitously, due to restrictions in global travel. In fact Ali (2023b) indicates over 50% decline in tourist arrivals in 2020 compared to 2019. Since a sizable portion of the region's food import bill represents food destined for the tourism sector, the sharp increases in the size of the food import bill may well have been reflecting spikes in the price of imported food, rather than an increase in quantum of food imported.

As if the impact of climate change, high food prices and the COVID-19 pandemic were not enough, on 2022 February 24 Russia invaded Ukraine, commencing a war that has been waging to the present time. A number of western countries, led by the United States, imposed sanctions on Russia and the war itself apart from taking many lives, have destroyed significant infrastructure in Ukraine and disrupted agricultural production and trade. Although Russia and Ukraine combined only account for 2% of global GDP, the war has been having a significant impact on global production, consumption and trade of food and energy, because of these countries' disproportionate share of global cereal, grain, sunflower oil, fertilizer and energy production and exports (Ben Hassen & El Bilali, 2022; OECD, 2022; UNDP, 2022). According to Ben Hassen and El Bilali (2022), Russia and Ukraine account for 34.1% of wheat exports, 26.8% of barley exports, 17.4% of the international trade in maize and 72.7% of sunflower exports. The disproportionate share of these two countries in the production and trade of these commodities renders them the 'global food baskets'. In relation to fertilizer and energy, again a significant share of the world's production is concentrated in these two countries. For instance, attributes 37% of global exports of potassium to Russia and Belarus, with the corresponding share of exports of nitrogen and phosphorus being 17% and 14%, respectively. In terms of energy, Russia and Ukraine together accounts for 12% of oil global exports and 9% of gas exports (Cardenas & Hernandez, 2022), thereby triggering panic in Europe at the onset of the war, as many of the larger economies in Western Europe sourced their oil and gas from Russia.

The disproportionate share of Russia and Ukraine in the global trade of grain, cereal, sunflower oil, fertilizer and energy means that any disruption of production in and export from these countries has the potential of triggering sharp increases in the prices of these commodities. This in turn has a direct impact on food security through reduced supply of these commodities, increased prices of food and fertilizer, and lower yields of crops in developing countries, as a result of lower fertilizer usage due to increased prices. The disruption of production and exports from Ukraine, caused by destruction of port facilities and the inability of farmers to fully engage production, has had a massive impact on world's food security from the early days of the war (Welch, 2023). Ben Hassen and El Bilali (2022) for instance, citing World Food Programme estimates, indicate that some 47 million people have been added to the 276 million people suffering from acute hunger before the onset of the Russia/Ukraine War. Net food importing developing countries in the Middle East and North Africa have been particularly affected, due to their high dependence on imports of grains from Russia and Ukraine (FAO, 2022).

The English-speaking Caribbean has comparatively little trade with Russia and the Ukraine, with less than 1% of its imports sourced from Russia and Ukraine (Ali, 2023b). Notwithstanding the region's low direct trade with these two countries, it has not been spared the negative impact of the war on its food security. Ben Hassen and El Bilali (2022) highlight a number of indirect impacts of the war, which singularly and collectively served to tighten global trade in foods, resulting in overall increased food prices, thus impacting food security across the globe, including in countries with little trade in food with Russia and Ukraine. With higher input prices attributable to the war, large food producers in the developed world were forced to substitute the growing of high fertilizer intensive crops such as wheat and maize with crops requiring smaller amounts of fertilizer such as soybeans. By the same token, in the developing world, faced with higher fertilizer prices, usage of this input was curtailed. The combined impact of these two developments has been less production of critical foods in both developed and developing worlds, which sharply impacted prices. Both availability of foods and economic access to food were impacted (Hebebrand & Laborde, 2022).

Given the general reduction in the production of critical food items, some major producers and exports of wheat, grains and vegetable oils resorted to export restrictions, including outright ban, exacerbating the already critical food insecurity situation in net food importing countries (Glauber et al., 2022). With curtailment of supply in the food trade, prices went up, further raising issues of access. The *Food Security Portal Food and Fertilizer Export Restrictions Tracker* for instance shows that since the war the number of countries instituting export restrictions moved from 3 to 26, covering a significant proportion of the exports of critical commodities such as wheat, maize, sunflower and palm oil. This of course goes against the grain of initiatives to liberalize agricultural trade under the WTO. Export restrictions in net food exporting countries have been accompanied by 'panic buying' in some net food importing countries, both at the household and governmental levels. Ben Hassen and El Bilali (2022) cite numerous reports of panic buying and stockpiling by consumers in Europe at the onset of the war.

The high food, fertilizer and energy prices triggered by the Russian/ Ukraine War caused a general spike in inflation across the globe, pushing up interest rates, resulting in a slowing down of economic recovery from the COVID-19 pandemic. Higher food and energy prices depleted foreign exchange reserves, creating balance of payments issues for net food importing countries. The fiscal impact of reduced economic growth and higher import bills have severely compromised the capacity of food importing developing countries to roll out adequate social safety net programmes to cushion the food insecurity impacts of the war, especially coming on the heels of the large stimulus spending during the pandemic to cushion the unemployment blows and keep the economy going. The Russia/Ukraine war therefore will not only slow economic growth, but plunge more people into poverty, hunger and malnutrition, as well as disrupt and reverse progress with SDGs #1 and 2.

The indirect impacts of the Russia/Ukraine War outlined above have affected the Caribbean Region in very profound ways. Except for Trinidad and Tobago, and more recently Guyana, the countries of the region are highly dependent on imported crude oil and natural gas to keep their economy turning. World Bank data indicate that between the end of 2021 and 2022, the price of a barrel of oil moved from \$71.53 to a high of \$114.59. The corresponding figures for natural gas are \$38.03 and \$70.04. This sharp increase over a short period of time, within the context of shrinkage of these Economies (due largely to the fallout in tourism), had a devastating impact on the fiscal accounts, balance of payment and on the level of indebtedness.

By the onset of the Russia/Ukraine conflict, economies in the region were already recovering, but had not attained pre-COVID 19 levels. There was also some recovery in the debt-to-GDP ratios in Jamaica, Suriname and Barbados, due to the phasing out of heavy spending on stimulus packages. However, the war had a devastating impact on inflation in the

Caribbean, precipitated by record high prices for imported fuel, food and fertilizer in particular, and more generally on the prices of all imported goods, due to the increase of shipping and freight rates occasioned by the supply chain disruptions. Ali (2023b), citing data from a World Food Programme/CARICOM Report, points to a 10.2% rise in food inflation across 20 Caribbean countries. The IMF further estimated that inflation rates in the Caribbean in 2022 more than doubled the average rate over the 2010–2019 period.

The high inflation in 2022 caused by the Russia/Ukraine conflict, manifested in the high cost of imported food, twined with the inability of local agricultural production to expand appreciably due to high costs of fertilizer and other inputs, and the phasing out of COVID-19 social safety net payments due to fiscal limitations, all had a negative impact on the state of food security in the Caribbean. A survey conducted by CARICOM, CDEMA, WFP and UN Food and Agriculture Organization in August 2022 found that 57% of the English-speaking population of 5.7 million was food insecure, representing an additional 1.3 million people rendered food insecure since February 2022 (CARICOM; World Food Programme; CDEMA; UN FAO, 2022). The same report highlighted over 70% of respondents reportedly skipping meals, eating less, eating less preferred meals or going for an entire day without food, in the week prior to the survey. This of course is not surprising, as reported in Chapter 2, the report from PAHO that the Caribbean people during this period faced the high cost of a healthy diet of $4.23 per day.

Food Security and the Role of International Trade and International Development Agencies

The issue of international trade in foods, and its role in rationalizing food production and supply within a multilateral framework, has been the focus of the international community from as far back as the pre-World War II days of the League of Nations. Shaw (2007) points to the League of Nation's preoccupation with the twin issues of managing the fluctuations in global agricultural production and prices; and how to use surplus production in the developed North to provide food aid to the developing South, without compromising agricultural production in the later. These considerations of the international community were borne more out a concern for producers' welfare in the North, than the amelioration of hunger and malnutrition in the South. Developed countries were concerned that wild fluctuation of the prices of agricultural produce in the North was adversely affecting farmers' income, and exports of excess production and the use of surplus for food aid would stabilize farmers' income. By the time of Roosevelt's 1943 Hot Springs Conference on Food and Agriculture, where the concept of the FAO was born, the thinking of the international community shifted more to the role of international trade in the alleviation of poverty and hunger. The declaration from that Conference identified poverty as the cause of hunger and malnutrition and went on to state that "it is useless to produce more food unless men and nations provide the markets to absorb it" (FAO, 1943). This stance is consistent with the view that economic development and poverty eradication cannot be achieved by aid and donor funds solely, but ultimately and sustainably through production and trade.

The issue of trade between countries has been the focus of much discourse in classical economic theories, notably David Ricardo's (1772–1823), theory of comparative advantage. This theory posits that nations should concentrate on the production and export of those goods and services for which they have comparative advantage, that is, they can produce cheaper than the competition. Implicit in this theory are notions of specialization and international trade. In other words, nations must specialize in the production of only those goods for which they have comparative advantage, export those goods and in turn import those goods for which they do not possess comparative advantage.

Within the frame of this theory, countries in CARICOM historically were assigned the role of producing agricultural commodities, notably sugar, bananas, rice, cocoa, coffee and tobacco, by their colonial masters for 300 years, for the sole purpose of exporting said products to said European colonial masters. Best (1968) describes this export orientation of Caribbean economies, often revolving around the production of a single crop for export to the Metropole in Europe, while importing almost everything consumed in the colonies from said Metropole, as the Plantation Economy Model. Of course what gave the Caribbean the comparative advantage to enable it to specialize in the production of sugar was the transatlantic slave trade, supplying millions of slaves from West Africa to the Caribbean to work for free on the sugar plantations for over 300 years.

Quite apart from brutality of slavery and the psychological damage this arrangement inflicted on people of African descent in the Caribbean, this economic model entrenched poverty and dependency, and was markedly inimical to the objective of food security. Any system that focuses on the production of a single export crop and actively discourages domestic food production, in favour of satisfying all of a nation's food demand from imports, is structurally and decidedly contradictory to the notion of food security. The region has therefore been historically conditioned to be import dependent. This position has been reinforced by bilateral trade agreements with the region's former colonial masters which provided preferential access for agricultural commodities to these European markets on highly concessionary terms, while using high tariffs and other non-tariff barriers to keep out the exports of higher value processed goods. The English-speaking Caribbean for instance has been the beneficiary of the Commonwealth System of Preferences, which was established between the United Kingdom and her colonies, and under which Caribbean sugar and banana could enter the UK duty free and at remunerative prices. This arrangement would eventually evolve into the LOME Agreement signed in 1973 when the UK entered the European Economic Community. The United States and Canada concluded similar concessionary agreements with the Caribbean in the 1980s, dubbed the Caribbean Basin Initiative (CBI) and CARIBCAN respectively.

Mittal (2009) points to conditionalities associated with World Bank and IMF sponsored structural adjustment programmes forcing governments of developing countries to sharply cut support to local agriculture in the form of research, extension, marketing, input supply and public investments in critical infrastructure of a public goods nature, resulting in significant disinvestment in the sector, and a corresponding fall in food production in the 1970s, 1980s and 1990s. Under these structural adjustment models, developing countries were told to focus on services, such as tourism, and commodity exports, and import 'cheap foods' from the developed North. Mittal (2009) asserts that many of these structural adjustment programmes collapsed or were abandoned by governments, triggering a withdrawal of support from other international development partners, who act in syndicate with the World Bank and the IMF. There has been a significant reduction in the flow of grants and loans to developing countries for agricultural development by the World Bank and the United States Agency for International Development since the 1980s up to 2008. The combined underinvestment in agriculture by both national governments and the international donor community has undermined agricultural growth and rendered developing countries food import dependent and poor. Action Aid International (2008) showed that while developing countries in the 1960s had a net agricultural trade surplus of $7 billion, by 2001 they largely became net food importers with an agricultural trade deficit of some $11 billion.

Notwithstanding the role of preferential bilateral trade agreements, that cemented the role of many developing countries as producers and exporters of commodities and the structural adjustment programmes of the World Bank and the IMF, which undermined food security in the global South, the international community since World War II has consistently extolled the virtues of international trade as a means of promoting development and poverty eradication. For example, the General Agreement on Trade and Tariff, entered into by 23 countries in 1947, recognized the value of free trade in "raising standard of living, ensuring full employment and a large and steadily growing volume of real income and effective demand" (GATT, 1947). The Cotonou Agreement of 2000 between the European Union and the African, Caribbean and Pacific (ACP) countries has as its objective "reducing and eventually eradicating poverty consistent with the objectives of sustainable development and the gradual integration of the ACP countries into the world economy" (EU/ACP, 2000). The revised Treaty of Chaguaramas establishing the Caribbean Community including the CARICOM Single Market and Economy, has among its objectives "improved standards of living and work" and "accelerated, co-ordinated and sustained economic development" (CARICOM, 2002).

Despite the heralded virtues and promise of international trade to boost development and reduce poverty in developing countries, fulsome participation of these countries in liberalized international trade can be problematic. This is particularly so for small island developing states (SIDS), such as all the islands in the Caribbean, which are beset by the handicaps of underdevelopment, small size and extreme vulnerability. Bernal (2006) identified a number of characteristics of small developing nations that militate against their full participation in globalized free trade, without being negatively impacted. These characteristics include high degree of openness, export and export market concentration, acute vulnerability to natural disasters and external economic shocks, overdependence on revenue from trade taxes, remoteness and isolation, limited institutional capacity and small-sized firms. Small size, remoteness and isolation and high transaction costs relating to small scale of production render production in these countries uncompetitive. Opening up of their markets through lowering or elimination of tariffs has the potential to destroy local production and make these countries even more import dependent. Given the lack of diversification in these countries because of their narrow export orientation and the overdependence on trade taxes, lowering/elimination of tariffs on the part of these countries can be a fiscal disaster. At the same time, due to the small size of firms and limited institutional capacity, these countries are not agile enough to exploit the potential opportunities afforded by international trade for export expansion.

Given all of these realities, Bernal (2006) underlined the appropriateness of Special and Differential Treatment (SDT), for small developing nations in the multilateral trading system, as well as the need for development support for these countries to build their capacities to successfully participate in international trade. Indeed, the GATT and WTO, its successor, embrace the principle of SDT, particularly for least developed countries. However, the appropriateness of SDT for SIDS is highly contested, as many developed countries point to small nations such as Singapore and other Asian tigers attaining levels of development rivalling some developed countries. The reticence of developed countries to SDTs also relates to the fact that developing countries are not homogeneous, and they are opposed to large countries such as China and India receiving these benefits. Notwithstanding this reservation on the part of some developed economies, a range of SDTs has been accommodated in international trade agreements, such as preferential, non-reciprocal trade with developed countries, longer adjustment periods afforded developing countries in relation to reducing and eliminating tariffs and the use of subsidies.

There is perhaps no other area of international trade that impacts developing countries more than the trade in agricultural goods, given the general agrarian orientation of these countries' economy and their susceptibility to food insecurity. Therefore with the assumed benefits of trade in promoting development and the elimination of poverty in these countries, purported by developed countries, it was expected that every effort would be made to support these countries to maximise the benefits of trade, and to offer them SDT when warranted. Ironically however, the developed world for many years resisted every attempt to bring agricultural goods fully under the rubric of trade liberalization. Indeed, although agricultural trade was included in GATT from its inception in 1947, many aspects of agricultural trade were exempted. The leading industrialized countries in North America, Europe and Japan, for example, fiercely protected their farming sectors, which were the beneficiary of huge domestic support, export subsidies and protection from external competition through high tariffs and quantitative restrictions on imports. These measures were designed to provide income stability to the farming sector in those countries, which constitutes an important political constituency. However, these measures did more than that, they also distorted global trade. For instance, bolstered by huge exported subsidies, many producers in the developed North exported many agricultural products to developing countries at prices below their cost of production, and in the process destroyed domestic production of many commodities, which simply could not compete with the cheaper imports.

At the same time, these very large industrialized countries extended concessionary non-reciprocal market access to some developing countries for the exports of commodities, which were mostly not in competition with their domestic production. As noted above, these arrangements include the LOME Agreement between the EU and ACP, CBI between the United States and the Caribbean Islands (excluding Cuba), and CARIBCAN between Canada and the Caribbean. These arrangements were trade distorting in that they excluded other developing countries which were more efficient producers of all the goods these agreements covered. Additionally, these preferential agreements reinforced the position of the beneficiaries of these agreements as commodity producers in the international division of labour, as well as discouraged agricultural diversification.

It was at the insistence of large net food exporting developing countries which were locked out of these preferential agreements, that agriculture was comprehensively included in the Uruguay Round of the GATT negotiations. Australia and large agricultural producers in South America such as Brazil, Argentina and Chile, as well as Thailand, were the chief proponents of full liberalization of agricultural trade, as they wanted a share of the EU and US market for their exports. While this liberalization would undoubtedly enhance export earning, rural development and food security in these net food exporting countries, other developing countries, such as the English-speaking Caribbean islands which were beneficiaries of preferential arrangements, became extremely vulnerable, as these arrangements were now being challenged.

It was generally assumed by the EU, United States and Canada that their non-reciprocal preferential trade agreements with sections of the developing world were covered by the GATT Agreement on Development (Part IV). Therefore from 1947 to the 8th Round of GATT Negotiations (the Uruguay Round), which commenced in 1986, the benefits enjoyed by eligible developing countries under these preferential agreements were basically unchallenged. With the full inclusion of agriculture in the Uruguay Round these arrangements became subject to legal challenge by other developing countries which were not benefitting from these agreements. In the process, it became clear that these arrangements were not in fact covered by the GATT Development and Agreement. Hence the sponsors of these preferential agreements were constrained to seek waivers, as they were deemed to be incompatible with free trade. In the meanwhile, the EU announced its intention to negotiate reciprocal free trade agreements with its partners in the ACP, called Economic Partnership Agreements (EPAs).

The EU regime for banana imports from the ACP under the LOME Agreement was among the first of these agreements to be challenged. The challenge was mounted by prominent banana producers in Latin America—Ecuador, Nicaragua, Costa Rica, Columbia, Guatemala and Venezuela, aided and abetted by the United States, whose companies Dole and Chiquita have massive investments in the banana industry all over Latin America. These countries were determined to get a much larger share of the EU market, which was mainly served by Jamaica, Belize, Suriname, the Windward and Leeward Islands, Martinique and Guadeloupe in the Caribbean and Cameroon and Cote d'Ivoire in Africa, as well as Spanish and Portuguese islands in the Mediterranean and the North Atlantic. Thomas (2006) provides a detailed and comprehensive account of this long challenge, which started within GATT during the Uruguay Round and was eventually resolved in the WTO in 2008. Thomas (2006) also outlined the prominent place banana exports held in the economies of these ACP countries, and how the dismantling of the EU banana regime impacted rural development and food security in these countries, particularly Jamaica. Stanberry (2022) similarly described the successful challenge to the EU sugar regime in 2003 by Australia, Thailand and Brazil within the WTO, and the devastating impact this had on the economies of Caribbean sugar producers—Jamaica, Barbados, Trinidad, Guyana, Belize and St. Kitts. The impact transcended the economic and fiscal, and was more so deeply social, rendering sugar-dependent communities a shadow of themselves, due to their deep levels of dependence on the sugar industry.

With these challenges of their preferential trade agreements with the ACP, the EU not only agreed to reform their sugar and banana regimes, but also signalled their intention not to seek further waivers for these agreements from the WTO. Richardson (2009) opines that by this time the ACP countries (former colonies) had lost their strategic importance to the EU and the EU was no longer sentimental about them. Rather, the EU's aim was to penetrate the large markets of the very countries that were frowning on their preferential arrangements. Hence, the EU commenced negotiations of bilateral EPAs with several blocs of developing countries. The EPA between the EU and CARIFORUM (CARICOM plus the Dominican Republic) was signed in 2008.

The erosion of preferential access to the EU market for banana and sugar, doubtless had an impact on food security in the Caribbean. Apart from loss of export revenue for the countries, thousands of small independent farmers were driven out of business and into poverty, without adequate social safety net protection to cushion their loss of income. These crops were largely not replaced through diversification, and hundreds of acres of land formerly occupied by these crops have been left idle, and became prey to housing developments. At the same time, the evidence has shown that these countries were not made rich by these preferential arrangements, which did not incentivise innovation, diversification and a graduation from predominantly primary production to value added activities (Bernal, 2006; Richardson, 2009). While the EPA still offers duty free access to these commodities, it does not guarantee remunerative prices, and with its small size, Caribbean producers cannot compete with Latin American producers of sugar and banana, which now have similar duty free access to the EU market. The EPA however opens up large possibilities for market access to the EU for a wide range of goods and services, included value added products, which were formerly excluded under previous trading arrangements. The question is what development support is available to small developing countries to transform their economies to exploit these opportunities?

There is no doubt that the tide of liberalization of global agricultural trade is irreversible, since the full inclusion of agriculture in the Uruguay Round of GATT in 1986. Although unfettered free trade in agriculture can hurt the food security prospects of small developing countries by destroying sensitive infant industries and increase food imports, small developing countries cannot advance their development at the required pace if they are locked out of international trade. The truth is food security is not solely about import substitution. The economies of small developing countries are too small and sustainable wealth will never be created by focusing on their small markets. What is critical is for small developing countries to make the critical investments in infrastructure and policy to exploit the export potential liberalized international trade offers (Stanberry, 2020). In this way agricultural production can be maximised to satisfy domestic demand, export surplus and use the revenues thus generated to import those food items that cannot be produced competitively locally or due to limitations of agro-climatic conditions. The challenge to small developing countries is to continue the struggle for SDT within the WTO to provide the protection that is warranted due to the inherent disadvantages of size, while pressing for development support to take full advantage of the possibilities international trade offers for export growth.

The Agreement on Agriculture negotiated in the Uruguay Round of GATT (1986–1994), and became operational in January 1995 to coincide with the coming into being of the WTO, holds much promise to small developing countries, in terms of their full participation in world agricultural trade. The agreement firstly addresses the issue of market access, whereby developed countries reduced tariffs on imports by 36% on average to be implemented over 6 years from 1995. This will nominally provide greater access to small developing countries to these markets, particularly for higher value goods, which were hitherto locked out of these markets by high tariffs. Developing countries were required to set 'bound' tariffs ceilings for a range of agricultural goods and given a longer time (ten years) to implement these rates. The agreement further attempts to improve market access by eliminating the use of non-tariff barriers such as quantitative restrictions and outright import bans, through a process of 'tariffication', which converted these restrictions into tariffs, thus making trade more transparent and predictable. Notwithstanding the trust for improved market access through the lowering of tariffs, the agreement makes provision for safeguard measures, where countries can temporarily impose higher tariffs and quantitative restrictions where imports threaten to overwhelm infant industries and sensitive domestic production.

The widespread use of domestic support and export subsidies in developed countries before the Uruguay Round is comprehensively addressed in the Agreement on Agriculture. Domestic support and export subsidies which are deemed trade-distorting and leading to dumping were cut and are now regulated. A whole new framework now exists under the agreement regulating the kind of domestic support allowable, called "Green Box", "Blue Box", "Development Box" and "Amber Box". This dimension of the agreement is beneficial to small developing countries in that it minimises the possibility of unfair competition from goods imported from developed countries, and provides legal avenues for small developing to support domestic under the "Green Box", provided this support is not trade-distorting.

The agreement on agricultural also deals with other non-trade issues such as food security, rural development and environmental protection. Within this context, there are special provisions for net-food-importing developing countries and least developed countries. In parallel with the agreement on agriculture, there is a special agreement on sanitary and phytosanitary measures, covering food safety standards, which were previously used as non-trade barriers to trade.

Although the Agreement on Agriculture holds much promise for small developing countries to participate more fully in global trade, there are still hurdles to be overcome. The matter of SDT needs to be broadened for small developing countries, such as Caribbean countries, as size is still not recognized within the WTO as a factor of development warranting special and differential treatment, as universally acknowledged for least developed countries. Also, while the agreement, under the 'green box' provisions, provides a legal outlet for small developing countries to provide support to domestic agriculture of a non-trade distorting nature, most of these countries need development support to assist in positioning their agricultural sector to make use of the opportunities for export under the agreement. These lingering issues must be addressed within the frame of the Doha Development Round.

The Doha Development Round represents the 10th round of negotiations on trade liberalization since the establishment of GATT in 1947. Mandated by the 4th WTO Ministerial Conference in Doha, Qatar in November 2001, this latest round of negotiations among all 147 members of the WTO was intended to achieve further reform of the international trading system to achieve lowering of trade barriers and revise trade rules. The overwhelming concern of the Ministerial Conference however, which inspired its mandate, was the recognition of the importance of "well targeted, sustainably financed technical assistance and capacity building programme" to support developing countries in securing a greater share of world trade. A major objective of this round therefore is to improve the trading prospects of developing countries, including addressing problems they are facing in implementing current WTO agreements. Sustainable development financing and capacity building support are indeed critical for small developing countries to install critical infrastructure to raise agricultural productivity, meet food safety standards and improve research and extension to lift small farmers' productivity and to climate proof agriculture generally.

Unfortunately, the Doha Development Round negotiations have stalled, with progress only made in the area of trade facilitation. It is telling that the issue of greatest controversy in these negotiations has been the agreement on agriculture, with developed countries fiercely resisting further concessions on export subsidies and other support to their domestic agricultural sector. The declining trend of development support for agriculture from major international development partners is also troubling. Renewed efforts must now be made to revive these negotiations within the Doha Round, as the worsening food security situation in the developing world, what is required is not mere food aid, but sustainable solutions.

Drivers of Food Security into the Future

The current agrifood system will not be able to deliver on the SDG goal #2 to end hunger and malnutrition in the world by 2030. The United Nations Secretary General has declared that the world is "tremendously off-track" in meeting all the SDGs by 2030 (FAO, 2022, p. 21). The inability of the current arrangements to end hunger and malnutrition relates to the unsustainable nature of the agrifood system in terms of its use of natural resources, the massive environmental degradation it engenders, and the inequities inherent in the system with respect to distribution of and access to the world's food resources. To transform the existing agrifood system into one that is environmentally sustainable, socially just and equitable and economically efficient, one has to identify and interrogate the trends of the drivers of the agrifood system. Where these trends are negative, they have to be reversed by global, regional and local actions to create a resilient and sustainable agrifood system that can deliver on the promise, indeed imperative, of ending hunger.

The Food and Agriculture Organization's 2022 publication of *The future of food and agriculture—Drivers and triggers for transformation*, in its "The Future of Food and Agriculture" series, seeks to explore three overarching questions as it ponders the future of food and agriculture and the ability of the current agrifood system to eliminate global hunger:

- Will the global agrifood system be able to sustainably nourish humanity in the future, while also meeting the non-food demand for agricultural products and the demand for required environmental services?
- Will socioeconomic systems evolve in such a way that income-earning opportunities will be assured to everyone, and that enough income will be universally assured to afford healthy diets that comprise foods produced in a sustainable way?
- Will the emergence of a critical and informed civil society, and active citizenships, be able to determine governmental actions to set off effective triggers leading to transformative processes of agrifood systems?

These overarching questions are speaking directly to the issues of sustainable food availability, universal access to food and utilization of sustainably produced food, as well as a global governance framework to ensure consistent and effective action to transform global agrifood systems. In contemplating these questions, FAO (2022) identified some 18 drivers, whose trend into the future could militate against food security, and which therefore must be managed and reversed by appropriate actions. The identified drivers are: population dynamics and urbanization; economic growth—macro outlook; cross-country interdependences, big data—control, use and ownership; geopolitical instability; rural and urban poverty; inequalities; food prices; science and innovation; public investment; capital-info intensity; in-out market concentration; consumption and nutrition patterns; scarcity of natural resources; epidemics and ecosystems degradation; climate change; and sustainable ocean economies. Obviously all of these drivers do not impact the agrifood system and food security in equal measure and in the same way across regions and countries of the world. The issues of population and urbanization, economic growth—macro outlook, public investment, geopolitical instability, climate change and sustainable ocean economies probably impact the Caribbean in more profound ways than the other drivers.

From as early as the eighteenth century, the relatively faster pace of population growth vis-à-vis growth in agricultural productivity has been a matter of concern in relation to food security. Although massive increases in agricultural productivity have, thanks to technology, largely assuaged these fears, population growth remains a matter of concern in Southeast Asia and Sub-Saharan Africa. The developed world is facing a different kind of concern in relation to population, that is, very slow growth and a change in the demographic profile, with an ageing population. This will have major implications for availability of labour, including for the agrifood sector, and a shrinking working population having to bear the burden of an ageing population.

In the English-speaking Caribbean, the issue of low population growth rate is real, influenced largely by outward migration to the North and lower birth rates. This scenario is compounded by relatively high rates of urbanization in the region, which Mycoo (2022) estimates to be about 72% and Donovan and Turner-Jones (2017) project to reach 80% by 2050. These shifts in the population portend serious challenges for food security in the Caribbean. In the Bahamas for example, attempts by the government to boost local production and replace imports have been stymied by unavailability of agricultural labour, linked to the high level of urbanization in that country (estimated at 84% by the IDB). Rapid urbanization in the region places increased pressure on the rural population to feed the burgeoning urban population, particularly in a scenario where there is not a commensurate increase in agricultural productivity. Urbanization also engenders changes in consumption pattern from locally produced food to more imported, processed, convenient and fast food, which not only balloons the food import bill, but also contributes to alarming levels of non-communicable diseases in the region. To arrest this trend, emphasis must now be placed on promoting urban and peri-urban agriculture, such as containerized gardens, use of balconies and roofs to grow crops. In Jamaica increasing urbanization involves the expansion of the Kingston Metropolitan Area westward on some of the country's most fertile soils, in the plains of St. Catherine, formerly occupied by sugar cane. This will have serious implications for food security.

The prospects for economic growth for the English-speaking Caribbean are conditioned by the structure of these economies, that is, dominated by tourism, commodities export, mining in Jamaica and Guyana and petroleum processing in Trinidad and lately in Guyana. Largely due to lack of scale, these economies have not been competitive, and the possibility of graduating from commodities to more value added exports is stymied by limited infusion of technology and limited range of human resources required to transform the manufacturing sector. It is also the case that these economies are extremely vulnerable to external shocks related to the high import content of local industries, overdependence on a few markets for exports and on external financing to turn the wheels of the economy. Extreme vulnerability to natural weather-related disasters is also a factor that impacts the pace of and growth trajectory of these economies.

Due to these structural issues, regional economies have been experiencing anaemic growth. Average annual economic growth in the region stood at 0.8% between 2010 and 2017, compared with 4.7% for other small States (OECD et al., 2019; Ram et al., 2018). Of course the COVID-19 pandemic and Russia/Ukraine war would have triggered negative economic growth across the Caribbean, with these economies only now returning to pre- COVID growth levels. In 2020 every English-speaking Caribbean country experienced negative growth, averaging negative 6%, with the exception of Guyana, which grew 37.8%, thanks to its new found oil (Alleyne et al., 2021). Similarly, the region's growth in merchandise exports has been slow, increasing by 0.61% between 2005 and 2010 and by 0.36% between 2011 and 2015 (OECD et al., 2019).

Clearly economic growth is a driver of poverty reduction. Where there is lack of economic growth poverty increases and impairs economic access to food by the poor. Average prevalence of poverty across the Caribbean has been reported to be 25% between 2001 and 2009, with Bahamas at 9.3% and Belize at 41.3% (ECLAC, 2018). Equally, economic growth must be equitably distributed across different social strata in order for economic growth to reduce poverty. In this regard, the Gini coefficient for countries in the Caribbean ranges from a low of 32.2 in Barbados to a high of 43.8 in Suriname (Beurmann & Schwartz (eds), 2018). The prevailing indicators of inequality in the Caribbean lie in the medium range, compared with other countries of the World, although Suriname stands among the most inequitable countries of the world.

A critical strategy in reversing the low growth phenomenon in the Caribbean lies in the modernization of agriculture and increasing linkages with the burgeoning tourism sector, as well as the manufacturing sector. Notwithstanding the robustness of the region's tourism, the retention of earnings from the sector is low, because of lack of linkages with agriculture. A significant portion of the food import bill in Jamaica for instance is attributable to import of foods destined for the hotels (Stanberry, 2019). The manufacturing sector across the region is largely involved in food processing. However, huge amounts of the raw material processed are imported. Liberalization of agricultural trade internationally provides opportunities for the region to export more value added agricultural products and to diversify markets, both within and outside of the region. There is also ample opportunity for sustainable import substitution. These opportunities, if exploited, can increase agricultural production and income, contributing positively to both food availability and access.

In order to realize the potential of the region's agriculture, significant restructuring of the sector will be required. Among the issues to be addressed are infrastructure inclusive of installation of irrigation systems, build out of food safety and traceability architecture, land reform to put more lands in the hands of farmers, rapid multiplication systems to produce clean planting material and facilitate the expansion of the livestock sector, and 'softer' investments such as research and development, improved extension services, market intelligence, training in GLOBAL GAP, export readiness. Most of these facilities/services are public goods in nature, and will therefore require significant public investment. However, most countries of the region are heavily indebted. In 2015 four of the 25 most indebted countries of the world, (as measured by the debt-to-GDP ratio), were in the Caribbean—Antigua and Barbuda, Barbados, Grenada and Jamaica (OECD et al., 2019). Although there has been some reduction in the debt burden of the region since, particularly in Jamaica, OECD et al. (2019) assert that two thirds of all CARICOM countries have debt-to-GDP ratios above 60%. With this heavy debt burden, after servicing debts, Caribbean countries have little fiscal space to make the kinds of investments necessary to transform agriculture and enhance food security.

This situation has been further exacerbated by the decline in foreign direct investment and official development assistance to the region and the agriculture sector in particular, as reported by ECLAC (2018). The fact is, even within the strictures of the fiscal challenges of the region, more investment can be made in the sector, if agriculture and food security are deemed priority. The prowess of the region in respect to its tourism was not attained by chance, but rather by carefully crafted packages of fiscal incentives including tax holidays, exemption from import duties, world-class airport infrastructure, public expenditure on marketing and promotion, provisions for accelerated depreciation and a strong policy and institutional framework. The agricultural sector across the region has not enjoyed such focused and comprehensive incentives, even though there are ample provisions for such support within the WTO's Agreement on Agriculture. Caribbean governments must therefore be more creative and deliberate in formulating policies and incentives to support agriculture even within the context of the tight fiscal realities they face.

Apart from direct public investments, government can also use fiscal, trade and procurement policies to incentivise the private sector to invest in agriculture. The build out of the infrastructure for the emerging business processing outsourcing sector has been done almost entirely by the private sector in Jamaica, in response to government's stimuli. The private sector must be incentivised to make backward linkages to primary agriculture to secure raw material instead of importing. Farmers must be trained and supported to move produce into hotels, and governments must make it more difficult for hotels to import produce which can be competitively produced in the region. The government is the biggest player in most economies in the Caribbean and must therefore leverage its spending power to support local agriculture in school feeding programmes and procurement of food for state institutions. A greater effort must also be made to mobilize local savings, including pension funds, to finance large public infrastructure.

In recent years the main driver of food insecurity has shifted from crop failures caused by drought and other natural phenomena, as obtained in Niger in the mid-2000s or the great famine in Ireland in the mid-nineteenth century, to geopolitical conflicts. The impacts of the Russian/Ukraine War have been amply elaborated above. But there are several other hot spots including internal conflicts in Sudan, the Democratic Republic of Congo, Ethiopia and Myanmar, precipitating millions of refugees, hunger and displacement. These conflicts have placed considerable pressure on the World Food Programme and other humanitarian organizations to respond. The current Israel/Hamas war is posing similar challenges of food insecurity among the Palestinian people who are under siege. Quite apart from the famine among war victims, conflicts have a wider impact on global food security, particularly when the warring countries are themselves major food producers and exporters. Wars tend to disrupt trade, including trade in food and also disrupt supply chains, causing food prices to spiral out of control, impacting populations far removed from the conflicts, but which are dependent on food imports for survival. Conflicts therefore affect both food availability and access.

The Caribbean is a relatively safe and politically stable space, and is unlikely to be the arena of any major conflict in the foreseeable future. However, by virtue of its high dependence on imported food, the region is quite vulnerable in terms of increasing conflicts in the world impacting its food security. In the Bahamas, for example, 90% of the country's food consumption is satisfied by imports (Ali, 2023a). The region has benefited in the past by wars, when wars in Europe ravished beet sugar production, and lend some impetus to the expansion of cane sugar production after World War I (Stanberry, 2022). Increase in geopolitical conflicts into future is not likely to have such positive impacts because of the region's dependence on imported inputs and structural impediments in the region's economies that militate against the agility required to pivot. The region therefore has to make the necessary investments to restructure its agriculture to sustainably replace a critical mass of the food it imports in order to safeguard its food security in the face of mounting geopolitical conflicts.

One of the distinguishing features of Small Island Developing States (SIDS) is their extreme vulnerability to weather-related disasters. Increased greenhouse gas and carbon dioxide emissions, generated through the burning of fossil fuel, that powers the industrialization of the world, blanket the Earth and cause global warming. Increases in global temperatures over time cause climate change, often manifested in more frequent and intense rainfall/storms/hurricanes, more prolonged droughts and sea level rise resulting from the melting of ice caps and glaciers. These manifestations of climate change impact SIDS disproportionately, even though these countries contribute the least to global warming. Climate change impacts the natural habitat of plants and animals resulting in the loss of biodiversity, while weather-related disasters result in huge economic losses, as well as loss of life. Economic losses include damages to physical infrastructure, production and production capacity and livelihoods of millions. The agricultural sector is particularly vulnerable to climate change as significant crop and livestock production is lost due to flood and wind damage, as well as drought. The situation is further compounded by the general absence of agricultural insurance in SIDS, to ensure quick restoration of production after a disaster.

The small size of most SIDS, particularly those in the Caribbean, means that natural disasters typically affect the entire country at once. The location of most population centres, economic activities and major public infrastructure on the coasts of these countries magnify the impact of violent weather-related episodes, coastal erosion and sea level rise. All of these challenges are faced by Caribbean SIDS, which OECD et al. (2019) characterise as the second most environmental hazard-prone region in the world. Since the early 2000s the frequency of natural weather-related disasters has markedly increased, with devastating impacts on the economy on the whole, and the agricultural sector in particular. Hurricane Maria in 2017 for instance wreaked damages to Dominica equivalent to 226% of its GDP (World Bank, 2018). In 2004 Hurricane Ivan ravaged Grenada, with losses amounting to 200% of its GDP (Mohammed et al., 2022).

Given the subsistence nature of the region's agriculture, dominated by myriad of small farmers without any form of agricultural insurance, not only are livelihoods lost for thousands of farmers, but their capacity to restart is significantly impaired. With the government emerging as the insurer of last resort for the sector, one can imagine the enormity of the fiscal challenge, against the background of high levels of indebtedness in the first instance. Farmers are rendered poorer, threatening their access to food, agriculture production is temporarily displaced affecting food availability, and imports of food increases, impacting balance of payments and increasing indebtedness.

Despite the commitments made by all nations at the Paris Climate Change Conference in 2015 to keep global temperature rise this century well below 2 degrees Celsius above pre-industrial levels and to strive to limit the temperature increase even further to 1.5 degrees Celsius, every indication is that these goals will not be attained. This portends great challenge to the region's agriculture and food security. Sustained and deliberate investments will have to be made to climate proof the region's agriculture through appropriate mitigation and adaption measures. Irrigation has to be expanded to reduce reliance on rainfall amidst almost annual prolonged droughts, better management of water, use of drought resistant varieties of crops, increased crop insurance and greater use of protected agriculture.

The English-speaking Caribbean countries, being islands and territories washed by the Caribbean Sea (Suriname, Belize and Guyana), are well endowed with marine resources. Their territorial waters and Exclusive Economic Zones (EEZ) represent marine space under the control of these States, several times the size of their land mass. Due to lack of resources and the absence of technology and equipment to exploit the vast resources of their marine space for economic prosperity, most of the islands of the region focus mainly on near-shore reef fishes, and largely ignore the vast pelagic resources which lie in the further and deeper waters of their EEZ. As a result, there is considerable overfishing of reef resources and many countries, including Jamaica, have had to establish fish sanctuaries to assist in the replenishment of the stock in these waters. There are also widespread unsustainable fishing practices such as spear fishing, use of dynamite and other explosives to catch fish, as well as the use of small-sized mesh, which catches juvenile fishes. Safety at sea is also a big issue and in countries with highly developed mining sectors, contamination of rivers and the marine environment has also emerged as an issue of concern. Another emerging concern that will impact the fishing industry is the matter of deep-sea mining, now actively being deliberated within the International Seabed Authority. Lack of centralized properly functioning sewage treatment systems have also been a contributor to the pollution of the marine environment, threatening the livelihoods of fishers from time to time.

Except for Jamaica, with a well-developed industrial conch fishing industry, with exports to the European Union, and to a lesser extent the Bahamas, industrial fishing is almost non-existent in the region. Both countries have had issues with over-fishing of conch, and the industry in Jamaica was actually suspended in the 1990s to allow for the development of a management and regulatory regime for the industry. This regime formally came in existence in 1999. The industry in the Bahamas was less regulated, but the Government of the Bahamas has recently been paying greater attention to management and regulation. Despite the regulatory regime in Jamaica, there remain issues of sustainability relating to the widespread poaching of conch from Jamaican waters by fishers from the Central American mainland, notably Honduras. Unfortunately, Caribbean States do not possess the wherewithal to properly police their vast marine spaces. Climate change is also threatening both near-shore and off-shore fisheries. Higher temperatures in Caribbean waters are causing loss of habitat for many species, compounding the damage being caused by pollution.

The marine space provides livelihoods for thousands of fishers in the Caribbean. In Jamaica alone the industrial conch fishing sector employs over 5500 people, many of whom are from coastal villages and the inner city (NEPA, 2021). An additional 30,000 people are engaged in the fishing industry in Jamaica. Livelihoods are threatened by unsustainable practices, catches have become smaller and smaller, and fishers have to go further and further to get a good catch, often at extreme danger to themselves. This state of affairs is obviously impacting the region's food security. Paradoxically, the region with all its vast fishing resources imports a staggering quantum of fisheries resources. In Jamaica for instance, nearly six percent of the food import bill in 2018 comprised fish products consumed by the lower socio-economic strata of the society—salted cod fish, tinned mackerel and sardines, with a another sizable portion of the food import bill attributable to crustaceans and other exotic fish products destined for the hotel trade (Stanberry, 2019).

One of the keys to economic prosperity in the region and the enhancement of food security lies in the sustainable exploitation of the vast marine resources available to the region. There are many species in the Caribbean waters that are in high demand in the East Asia, notably China and Japan. These species include sea urchins, sea cucumbers, squids, etc. and a variety of marine plants. Investments in equipment, large boats, the training of the region's fishers and provision of safety equipment will be necessary to exploit these pelagic resources. Proper management and regulatory regimes, investment in food safety and traceability systems will also be necessary to ensure the sustainability of these efforts. While Caribbean people do not in the main consume these species, these products can be exported and the revenue from these exports assist in funding the importation of those foods we consume, but cannot produce.

Conclusion

The challenge of feeding the world's population has been the focus of society's attention from the beginning of civilization. Thomas Malthus brought scholarly and international focus to the food security problematic in the late eighteenth century, pointing to the mismatch in the pace of growth of food production, on the one hand, and population, on the other. The Industrial Revolution and subsequent advance in technology, notably the Green Revolution, substantially increased agricultural production and productivity, essentially averting the calamity envisioned by Malthus. However, international attention continues to be focused on the issue of food security, through such institutions as the League of Nations and the Food and Agriculture Organization, which has emerged as the focal point of global efforts to combat hunger and malnutrition. Over the last 80 years or so, a number of international meetings have been devoted to the issue of food security, in response to sporadic episodes of chronic food insecurity and famine. In the meanwhile the causes of food insecurity have been shifting from crop failures due to adverse weather, to conflicts and other man-made crises, to speculation and the increased trading of commodities in financial markets. Over this period the world also discovered that while much focus was placed on food availability, with considerable increase in food production, the issues of access, utilization and stability have emerged as important dimensions of the food security problematic.

The world is also learning that while increasing food availability is a necessary condition for improving food security, this must be done in a manner that is environmentally sustainable and socially equitable. Increased trading in food internationally has been identified as a critical means of increasing food security, and to this end the international community has been promoting increased trade in agricultural good and elimination of protectionism under banner of WTO. Small developing countries however could suffer great economic loss in this liberalization process, hence the call for special and differential treatment for these countries. In the meanwhile, gains made in reducing hunger and malnutrition, as enshrined in the SDGs, have been reversed due to the onslaught of the COVID-19 pandemic and the ongoing Russia/Ukraine conflict. Food insecurity will continue to be a challenge into the foreseeable future based on the trends of a number of critical drivers of food insecurity. The nations of the world must therefore collectively and individually take deliberate steps to reverse these negative trends and embrace those trends which will promote and facilitate greater food security.

References

Action Aid International. (2008). *Action Aid International Annual Report, 2008.*

Ali, M. (2023a). *From Crises to Opportunity, an Innovative Approach to Food Security in the Caribbean Region.*

Ali, M. (2023b). *Post COVID-19 Ukraine—Russia Crises Ticking Time Bomb for CARICOM.*

Alleyne, D., et al. (2021). *The Economic Survey of the Caribbean 2020: Facing the Challenge of COVID-19. Studies and Perspectives Series—ECLAC Sub Regional Headquarters for the Caribbean* (No. 99). Santiago, Economic Commission for Latin America and the Caribbean (ECLAC).

Barrett, C., & Sahn, D. (2001). *Food Policy in Crisis Management (Draft)*. Cornell University. http://aerus.cornell.edu/faculty_sites/cbb2/Papers/Worldbankpaper.pdf

Ben Hassen, T., & Bilali, H. (2022). Impacts of the Russia-Ukraine War on Global Food Security: Towards More Sustainable and Resilient Food Systems. *Foods, 11*(15), 2301. https://doi.org/10.3390/foods11152301

Bernal, R. (2006). Special and Differential Treatment for Small Developing Economics. In R. Grynberg (Ed.), *WTO at the Margins: Small States and Trade and the Multilateral Trading Systems*. Cambridge University Press.

Best, L. (1968). Outlines of a Model of Pure Plantation Economy. *Social and Economic Studies, 17*(3), 283–326.

Beurmann, D., & Schwartz, M. (Eds.). (2018). *Nurturing Institutions for a Resilient Caribbean*. IDB.

Cardenas, M., & Hernandez, A. (2022). *The Economic Impact of the War in Ukraine on Latin America and the Caribbean*. UNDP Latin America and the Caribbean Policy Documents Series.

CARICOM. (2002). *Revised Treaty of the Chaguaramas Establishing the Caribbean Community Including the CARICOM Single Market and Economy*. CARICOM Secretariat, Guyana.

CARICOM, World Food Programme, CDEMA, UN Food and Agricultural Organization. (2022). *Caribbean Food Security and Livelihoods Survey: Impacts of COVID-19 and the Cost of Living Crisis*. Regional Summary Report.

Donovan, M., & Turner-Jones, T. (2017). *Caribbean Housing Is Expensive and Scarce. Here's How to Change That*. https://www.americanquarterly.org/article/caribbean-housing-is-expensive-and-scarce-here's-how-to-change-that

Dutta, H., & Saikia, A. (2018). Food Security: A Review of Its Definition, Levels and Evolution. *Asian Journal of Multidimensional Research, 7*(7).

ECLAC. (2018). *Caribbean Outlook, 2018* (LC/SES. 37/14/Rev.1). Economic Commission for Latin America and the Caribbean, Santiago.

EU/ACP. (2000). *Partnership Agreement ACP-EC*. Cotonou, June 23, 2000.

European Commission. (2006). *Partnership Agreement ACP-EC*. Brussels.

Fafchamps, M. (1999). *Rural Poverty, Risk and Development*. Report Submitted to the Food and Agriculture Organization (FAO).

FAO. (1943, May 18–June 3). *United Nations Conference on Food and Agriculture*. Hot Springs, Virginia. Final Act and Section Reports.

FAO. (1994). *Assessment of the Current World Food Situation and Recent Policy Developments*. Document CFS:94/2. Rome.

FAO. (2008, June 3–5). *Declaration of the High Level Conference on World Food Security: The Challenges of Climate Change and Bioenergy*. Rome.

FAO. (2022). *The Future of Food and Agriculture in Drivers and Triggers for Transformation*. The Future of Food and Agriculture No. 3. Rome. https://doi.org/10.4060/cc0959en

Filho, W., Brandli, L., Salvia, A., Rayman-Bacchus, L., & Platje, J. (2020). COVID-19 and the UN Sustainable Development Goals: Threat to Solidarity or an Opportunity? *Sustainability, 12*(13), 5343. https://doi.org/10.3390/su12135343

Gittelsohn, J., Mookherji, S., & Pelto, G. (1998). Operationalizing Household Food Security in Rural Nepal. *The United Nation University, Food and Nutrition Bulletin, 19*(3), 210–222.

GATT. (1947). *General Agreement on Trade and Tariffs*. Geneva-October 30, 1947.

Glauber, J., Laborde, D., & Mamun, A. (2022). From bad to worse: How Russia-Ukraine war-related export restrictions exacerbate global food insecurity. In J. Glauber & D. Laborde (Eds.), *The Russia-Ukraine Conflict and Global Food Security*, Section Three, Chapter 18, Pp. 92–96. https://doi.org/10.2499/9780894394_18

Government of Guyana. (2023). *Bureau of Statistics*. Georgetown, Guyana.

Hart, T. (2009). Exploring Definitions of Food Insecurity and Vulnerability: Time to Refocus Assessment. *Agrekon, 48*(4).

Herbebrand, C., & Laborde, D. (2022). High Fertilizer Prices Contribute to Rising Global Food Security Concerns. In J. Glauber & D. Laborde Debucquet (Eds.), *The Russian-Ukraine Conflict and Global Food Security*. International Food Policy Research Institute. https://doi.org/10.2499/9780896294394

Hoddinott, J. (1999). *Choosing Outcome Indicators of Household Food Security*. International Food Policy Research Institute.

Jefferson, O. (1972). *The Post-War Economic Development of Jamaica*. University of the West Indies.

Labadarios, D., et al. (2011). Food Security in South Africa: A Review of National Survey. *Bulletin of the World Health Organization, 89*(12), 891–899. https://doi.org/10.2471/BLT.11.089243

Maxwell, S. (1996). Food Security: A Post-modern Perspective. *Food Policy, 21*(2), 153–170.

Maxwell, S., & Slater, R. (2003). Food Policy Old and New. *Development Policy Review, 21*(5–6), 531–553.

McKeown, D. (2006). *Food Security: Implications for the Early Years*. Public Health.

Mittal, A. (2009). *The 2008 Food Price Crisis: Rethinking Food Security Policies*. United Nations.

Mohammed, E., Singh, S., McCordic, C., & Pitman, J. (2022). Food Security Challenges and Options in the Caribbean: Insights from a Scoping Review. *Anthropocene Science, 1*, 91–108. https://doi.org/10.1007/s44177-021-00008-8

Mycoo, M. (2022). *Building Urban Resilience in the Caribbean: Policies, Priorities and Prospects*. 11SD/SDG Knowledge Hub.
National Environment and Planning Agency. (2021). *Jamaica's Non-Detriment Finding for Queen Conch (Strombus Gigas)*. Kingston.
OECD et al. (2019). *Latin American Economic Outlook 2019: Development in Transition*. OECD Publishing. https://doi.org/10.1787/g2g9ff18-en
OECD. (2022). *The impacts and policy implications of Russia's aggression against Ukraine on agricultural markets*. Retrieved from https://www.oecd-ilibrary.org/docserver/0030a4cd-en.pdf?expires=1676328157%3Aid=id%3Aaccname=guest&checksum=9D630E6CA5262A0423A3F85EDC98F291
Popkin, B. (1981). Community Level Considerations in Nutrition Planning in Low Income Nations. *Ecology of Food and Nutrition, 10*, 227–236.
Rambaran, K., Teelucksingh, S., Sankar, S., Boyne, M., Xuereb, G., & Zimmermann, M. (2021). High Prevalence of Childhood Overweight and Obesity in ten Caribbean Countries: 2018 Cross-Sectional Data and a Narrative Review of Trends in Trinidad and Tobago. *Child and Adolescent Obesity, 7*(7), 23–36.
Ram, J., et al. (2018). *A Policy Blueprint for Caribbean Economics*. CDB Working Paper No. CDB/WP/18/01.
Renzaho, M., & Mellor, D. (2010). Food Security Measurement in Cultural Pluralism: Missing the Point or Conceptual Misunderstanding? *Nutrition, 26*, 1–9.
Richardson, B. (2009). *Sugar: Refined Power in a Global Region*. Palgrave Macmillan.
Scoones, I. (2015). *Sustainable Livelihoods and Rural Development*. Practical Action Publishing.
Sen, A. (1981). *Poverty and Famines: An Essay on Entitlements and Deprivation*. Clarendon Press.
Shakeel, A. (2018). Food Security: Theorizing the Evolution and Involution of the Concept. *The Arab World Geographer, 21*(1), 58–62.
Sharma, R. (2011). *Food Export Restrictions: Review of the 2007–2010 Experience and Considerations for Disciplining Restrictive Measures*. FAO Commodity and Trade Policy Working Paper No. 32.
Shaw, D. (2007). *World Food Security: A History Since 1945*. Palgrave Macmillan.
Simon, G. (2012). *Food Security: Definition, Food Dimensions, History*. Basic Reading as an Introduction to Food Security for Students from the IPAD Master, SupAgro, Montpellier Attending a Joint Training Programme in Rome from 19–24 March 2012.
Simpson, J. (2022). *Travel and Tourism in the Caribbean: Prospects for Growth*. https://wttc.org/portals/o/Documents/Reports/2022/Travel-and-tourism-in-the-caribbean.pdf

Smith, M., Pointing, J., & Maxwell, S. (1993). *Household Food Security, Concepts and Definitions: An Annotated Bibliography*. Brighton, Institute of Development Studies.

Stanberry, D. (2019, December 22). *Deciphering the Food Import Bill (Part I)*. Sunday Gleaner.

Stanberry, D. (2020, January 26). *Reorienting Agriculture for Export and to Serve Manufacturing*. Sunday Gleaner.

Stanberry, D. (2022). *How Trade Liberalization Affects a Sugar-Dependent Community in Jamaica: Global Action*. Palgrave Macmillan.

Thomas, M. (2006). Jamaica and the Case in the WTO Against the Europeans Communities Regime for the Importations, Sale and Distribution of Bananas (1992–2001). In R. Grynberg (Ed.), *WTO at the Margins Small States and the Multilateral Trading System*. Cambridge University Press.

Trostle, R. (2005). *Global Agricultural Supply and Demand: Factors Contributing to the Recent Increase in Food Commodity Prices*. Economic Research Service, USDA.

United Nations. (2020). *Sustainable Development Goals Report 2020*.

United Nations. (2022). *Sustainable Development Goals Report 2022*.

Von Braun, J. (2011). *Commodity Markets and Food Security: The Global Food Crises of 2008–2011—Causes and Remedies*. icrier.org.pdf.Joachim-Session6-Paper.pdf

Welch, C. (2023). *Russia, Ukraine and Global Food Security: A One-Year Assessment*. Center for Strategic and International Studies, Washington D.C.

World Bank. (2018). *World Bank Provides US$65 Million for Dominica's Post-Maria Reconstruction*. https://www.worldbank.org/en/news/press-release/2018/04/13/world-bank-provides-US$65-million-for-dominicas-post-maria-reconstruction

World Food Programme. (2009). *Emergency Food Security Assessment Handbook*. World Food Programme. Food Security Analysis Service, United Nations.

CHAPTER 2

Regional and National Institutional and Policy Support for Food Security

Introduction

Member countries of the Caribbean Community (CARICOM), the area of focus of this book, constitute a series of small islands forming an archipelago, stretching from the Bahamas in the North to Trinidad and Tobago in the South, just above the South American continent. This group of territories also includes Belize in Central America and Guyana on the South American mainland. Suriname also in South America, though a Dutch-speaking former colony of the Netherlands, is also included in this analysis. What is common about these countries is that they were mostly colonized by Britain, washed wholly or partially by the Caribbean Sea and have attained independence from Britain, beginning with Jamaica in August 1962. Haiti, sharing an island with the Dominican Republic, a former French colony, attaining independence in 1791, and a member of CARICOM is also included in this work. Not considered in this book are the larger Spanish-speaking territories of Cuba, Dominican Republic and Puerto Rico in the Northern Caribbean formerly colonized by Spain as well as a plethora of smaller islands in the Eastern and Southern Caribbean, which remain colonies of the United States, France, the United Kingdom and the Netherlands.

The English-speaking Caribbean territories were under British rule for most of their colonial history, although they were all "discovered"

D. Stanberry and L. Fletcher-Paul, *Food Security in the Caribbean*, Palgrave Studies in Agricultural Economics and Food Policy, https://doi.org/10.1007/978-3-031-66055-9_2

by Christopher Columbus, on behalf of Spain during his four voyages, between 1492 and 1504. These islands however were long occupied by the Caribs and Tainos, who crossed the frozen Bering Strait from Siberia and trekked southwards through North, Central and South America, from where they crossed into the Caribbean, with the Caribs settling in the Southern and Eastern Caribbean and the Tainos in the larger islands of the Northern Caribbean (Sherlock & Bennett, 1998). These indigenous people established a strong and sustainable civilization in the Caribbean before the arrival of Columbus. Specifically in relation to food security, they cultivated such staples as cassava, maize and sweet potatoes, and fruits such as sweet and soursops, pineapple, naseberries (also known as sapodillas), guavas and cocoa. They secured protein through fishing and hunting of wild animals (Sherlock & Bennett, 1998). They also had their system of religion, recreation and governance. All of this was destroyed by the Spanish, who exploited, abused, overworked and infected these people with European diseases, so that within 50 years of the arrival of the Spanish, they were completely exterminated (Mintz, 1971).

The islands became the subject of intense European rivalry, as the English, French and Dutch challenged the Spanish claim of exclusivity over the newly 'discovered' Americas. The Spanish in their quest for gold, having not discovered any appreciable quantity in the Caribbean, shifted their focus to Central and South America, where the prospect of finding gold was more encouraging. Most of the Caribbean Islands were therefore never effectively occupied by the Spanish. They were therefore vulnerable and became easy prey for the other European powers (Stanberry, 2022). According to Mintz (1985), Britain emerged as the most aggressive and successful of all of Spain's rivals, capturing the most territories from Spain, and quickly setting out to establish sugar plantations. Mintz (1971) posits that these islands captured by the British were ideal for establishing plantations, with the presence of fairly large tracts of rich alluvial flood plains. This geographic advantage was complemented by the wide-scale importation of African slaves to provide cheap labour, following according to Mintz (1985), the prototype established by the Portuguese in using African slave labour in their sugar plantations in their Islands of Sao Tome and Madeira. The success of the sugar plantations established by the British was further guaranteed by the almost insatiable appetite for sugar, which in the seventeenth century was transitioning from a luxury item to a mainstream item in the diet of the proletariat in Europe (Mintz, 1985).

The process of establishing sugar plantations in its colonies would have serious implications for food security in the English-speaking Caribbean. The rapid growth and tremendous success of sugar in the English-speaking colonies both funded and formed the economic basis for the rise of capitalism in Britain in the mid-eighteenth century (Gillespie, 1920; Thomas & McCloskey, 1981; Williams, 1944) all point to the significant transfer of wealth from the Caribbean colonies to fuel capitalism and industrialization in Britain. According to Mintz (1985, p. 55), "the Caribbean plantations were a vital part of this process, embodying all the features, and providing both important commodities for European consumption and important markets for European production". Of the 'commodities' provided by the Caribbean for 'European consumption', sugar was the most important. Significantly, these Caribbean colonies served as markets for 'European production'.

In essence, the British colonies in the Caribbean were built on a model of producing sugar on a monoculture basis for consumption in Britain, while the colonies imported most of what they consumed from the Motherland. The monoculture nature of sugar production in the colonies largely ignored the cultivation of other crops, necessary to ensure the food security of the colonies, which largely depended on the importation of basic foods from Britain. In fact, the entire enterprise of producing sugar for export to Britain dominated and pervaded every aspect of life in the colonies, and has been described in detail by Best (1968) as the plantation system. Beckford (1972) speaks to the entrenched dependency that this system engendered, which was not only economic, but social, cultural and psychological Mintz (1971), Thompson (1957) and Wagley (1957). Through this plantation system therefore, the English-speaking Caribbean was historically conditioned to be food insecure—depending on imports for its staple, with its traditional export crops sector commanding the best lands, the best institutional support and the most sophisticated marketing and physical infrastructure, while the domestic food crop sector lagged behind.

Diversification and the Emergence of the Independent Caribbean States

With the growing industrialization of Britain and the rise of Capitalism, by the mid-nineteenth century, sugar's hegemony in the British Empire began to be challenged (Stanberry, 2022). The dominance of the sugar industry prior to these developments was bolstered by protectionism. With growing capitalism, the new thinking was that there was more wealth to be generated from free trade than the protected sugar industry, which only benefitted a few privileged planters. This tide of liberalization led to the enactment of the Sugar Duties Equalization Act in 1846, which effectively dismantled the monopoly of imperial sugar in the British market, by allowing beet sugar from Europe and cane sugar from French and Dutch colonies to enter the British market on the same terms as cane sugar from the Caribbean. The abolition of slavery in the British colonies in 1838, ahead of abolition in rival European colonies, rendered British imperial sugar uncompetitive, and further weakened the sugar industry in the English-speaking Caribbean. The rapid expansion of beet sugar production in continental Europe around this time also did not augur well for the sugar industry in British colonies.

The relative weakening of the sugar industry provided some impetus for advancing food security in the Caribbean. With the abolition of slavery, slaves who were allowed to cultivate cash crops (vegetables, spices and tubers) on Sundays, then had the opportunity to expand the cultivation of domestic food crops as free men and women. With the relative decline in sugar production; coffee, banana, rice and cattle production emerged as large-scale agricultural activities, and coupled with the rise of the peasantry, constituted the first wave of diversification of the economies of the colonies. This was a positive development for food security, as the colonies were now making a concerted effort to feed themselves from domestic production.

Notwithstanding this measure of diversification, the sugar industry after its slump in the second half of the nineteenth century, received a lifeline in the early twentieth century, with the outbreak of World War I in Europe, from 1914 to 1918. The war disrupted beet sugar production in Europe and provided an opportunity for the resurgence of the sugar industry in the Caribbean colonies. By 1929, the British Government instituted a system of preferential access of imperial sugar to the British market at low tariffs and remunerative prices. This concession was further enshrined in the Commomwealth Sugar Agreement of 1952, under which Britain provided preferential market access for commodities from its colonies through guaranteed quotas and high prices. It further contributed significantly to the rebound of the sugar industry in the Caribbean in the post-World War II period, with Jamaica, Guyana, Belize, Barbados, St. Kitts and Nevis and Trinidad and Tobago emerging as the major beneficiaries in respect to sugar. Similar concessional marketing arrangements also existed within the Commonwealth Agreement for banana, which benefitted the banana industry in the Windward Islands and Jamaica.

Even while the sugar industry was making a rebound in the post-World War I period, social conditions in the Caribbean were deteriorating. Since the abolition of slavery, the peasantry was not receiving the support it deserved from the Colonial Governments in the Caribbean. Bolland (1981) and Mintz (1985) point to the efforts of the planter class to lure back freed slaves to the plantation to work in the face of labour shortage. The efforts of freedmen and women to establish the peasantry were systematically undermined. Lack of access to lands by freed slaves and generally harsh economic conditions precipitated the Morant Bay Rebellion in 1865 in Jamaica. The 1897 Commission of Enquiry into the Sugar Industry of the Caribbean noted the deplorable conditions in the Caribbean and recommended land reforms to support local agriculture. By 1938 widespread protests broke out in Jamaica over low wages in the sugar industry and overall poor social and economic conditions in the island. These protests prompted the establishment of the Moyne Commission of Enquiry by the British Government to investigate social conditions in the West Indies. The Moyne Commission pointed to the development of agriculture as the solution to improve the social and economic conditions of the colonies. Land reform was again recommended.

The 1938 riots in Jamaica, the return to the Caribbean of men who fought in World War II, and who were now sensitized to notions of freedom and justice, triggered in the Caribbean an irreversible march to self-government, universal adult suffrage and independence. Starting with Jamaica in 1944, the Caribbean colonies were granted universal suffrage, with political parties vying for political power to manage the internal affairs of the colonies. Concomitantly, Caribbean people began to see their path to development through regional integration. The West Indies Federation was therefore established in 1958 with 10 members: Antigua and Barbuda, Barbados, Dominica, Grenada, Jamaica, Montserrat, St. Kitts and Nevis, St. Lucia, St. Vincent and Trinidad and Tobago. The Caribbean people were asserting themselves.

In parallel with the above political developments in the post-war period, there were also significant developments on the economic front. Bauxite mining emerged in Jamaica and Guyana, the exploitation of oil in Trinidad and the emergence of a tourism sector almost universally across the Caribbean. At the same time, inspired by Sir Arthur Lewis' industrialization by invitation economic theory, a number of Caribbean colonies began the process of institution building and economic incentives to birth and nurture a manufacturing sector. These developments further diversified the economies of the English-speaking territories and provided opportunities for the growth and expansion of agriculture to provide food to the tourism sector and raw material for manufacturing.

In relation to food security, governments turned their attention to the development of domestic agriculture, which was long ignored, to support food security through institutional building, land reforms, credit schemes and the building out of modern Ministries of Agriculture, focusing on research and extension. In Jamaica for instance, such critical institutions as the Agricultural Development Corporation (ADC) was established in 1952 to facilitate and promote the development of agriculture in strategic areas such as livestock development and non-export crops. The ADC was mandated to acquire lands for subdivision into land settlements and forge partnerships with small farmers within a 'mother farm/satellite farm' model. Between in 1940 and the 1950s, the Jamaican Government by statute established a number of Commodity Boards (citrus, coconut, banana, coffee and cocoa), to support small farmers to participate in the traditional export crop sectors, specifically providing research, marketing, extension support, as well as the provision of planting material. According to Jefferson (1972), between 1949 and independence in 1962, the Government of Jamaica through various development plans rolled out some critical agricultural development schemes, such as the Farm Improvement Scheme in 1949, the Farm Development Scheme 1955–1960 and the Agricultural Development Programme 1960–1965. Under these schemes small farmers were provided loans and subsidies by the government amounting to \$7.2 million and \$8.5 million respectively between 1955 and 1968. In the meanwhile, according to the *Five Year Independence Plan, 1963–1968*, (1963), between 1938 and 1962 some 191 land settlements were established by the Government of Jamaica, benefitting 26,325 settlers and involving 137,000 acres.

While there was a concerted and deliberate effort by governments of the English-speaking Caribbean to give primacy to domestic agriculture in the post-war period, within the frame of internal self-government, these countries remained colonies of Britain, ultimately governed by a foreign power. Independence was of course the ultimate objective, and the political leaders of time never lost sight of the goal of independence. Jamaica was first out of the block, attaining independence in 1962, followed shortly by Trinidad and Tobago, and ending with St. Kitts and Nevis in 1983. With Jamaica gaining independence in 1962, the federal experiment which subsisted since 1958 was unravelled. While the newly independent countries pursued their development objectives individually, they remained acutely conscious that due to their small size, population and limited endowment with natural resources, regional integration remained their best prospect of growing and developing within the global economic space. On 15 December 1965 therefore, Antigua and Barbuda, Guyana and Barbados formed the Caribbean Free Trade Association (CARIFTA). By 1973 Jamaica, Trinidad and Tobago, Guyana and Barbados came together and formed the Caribbean Community and Common Market (CARICOM), by the Treaty of Chaguaramas, which came into being on 1 August 1973, effectively succeeding CARIFTA.

CARICOM's Food Security Initiatives

The formation of CARICOM in 1973 coincided with the global oil crisis of 1973, when oil prices spiralled out of control, impacting the price of cereals and other agricultural commodities. This general increase in the prices of agricultural commodities exacerbated the food insecurity of already food deficit countries, restricting their capacity to import food, even as food aid for cereals plummeted from 17 to 7 million tons (Dutta & Saikia, 2018). The CARICOM therefore understandably focused on the issue of food security almost from its inception. CARICOM's first food security initiative was the formulation of the Regional Food Plan (RFP), in the 1970s. This was followed by the Regional Food and Nutrition Strategy (RFNS) of the early 1980s. These initiatives essentially promoted public sector investments in the production of critical food crops to replace imports of said commodities. The RFP identified the specific crops, with targeted levels of production in specific countries, and concrete projects were formulated to achieve this. The RFP therefore represented a sort of regional division of labour, where selected crops were to be cultivated in specific countries based on comparative advantage and then traded with other territories. Processing of agricultural produce was also a critical plank of the RFP.

The RFP and the RFNS were basically orientated towards import substitution, against the background of the region's continued high food import bill. It was contemplated that import replacement through expanded domestic production would proceed while continuing to hold on to the preferential markets for traditional exports. This strategy failed principally because the lucrative prices obtained for traditional exports in preferential markets did not provide the incentives required to shift resources to the expansion of domestic crops. Antoine (2009) also points to the misalignment of domestic and regional agricultural policies, limited infrastructure and technical capacity as factors that stymied the diversification objectives of these initiatives.

The next wave of food security initiatives in CARICOM therefore shifted from import substitution through the protection of domestic agriculture to "a fundamental transformation of agriculture towards market-oriented, internationally competitive and environmentally sound production of agricultural products" (Antoine, 2009, p. 8). In keeping with this new direction, the Caribbean Community Programme for Agricultural Development (CCPAD) and its accompanying Regional Action Plan (RAP) were promulgated in 1989. These policy initiatives were orientated to increasing the export competiveness of the region's agriculture, and were in keeping with the shift towards globalization and increased liberalization of agricultural trade globally, as well as the intensification of the assault on the preferential trade agreements to which CARICOM's traditional export sectors had come to rely. Consequently, a number of national and regional projects for expanded production of non-traditional crops for exports were conceived and implemented, with varying degree of success. These efforts were, however, not sustained due to lack of funding and the absence of critical infrastructure to support competitive production. By 1996 the region formulated the Regional Transformation Plan (RTP) for agriculture to address some of the structural issues that militated against the successful implementation of the CCPAD.

The next major development in the evolution of food security initiatives in the CARCOM took place within the framework of the deepening of the regional integration process to create the Single Market and Economy (CSME), through the revision of the Treaty of Chaguaramus in 2001. In the preamble to the revised Treaty, the parties expressed their determination "to effect a fundamental transformation of the agricultural sector of the Community by diversifying agricultural production, intensifying agro-industrial development, expanding agri-business, strengthening the linkages between the agricultural sector and other sectors of the CSME and generally conducting agricultural production on a market-orientated, internationally competitive and environmentally sound basis" (CARICOM, 2002). In keeping with this determination, the Revised Treaty of Chaguaramas in Part 2, Article 56, articulates the Community Agricultural Policy, with the goal of, inter alia, "improved income and employment opportunities, food and nutrition security, and poverty alleviation in the Community" (CARICOM, 2002, p. 38).

In order to support the implementation of the Community's Agricultural Policy, the Revised Treaty of Chaguaramus articulates an implementation strategy (Article 57), as well as specific provisions to bolster the Community's agricultural production and trade and enhance its food security. Article 57 (2) designates the Council for Trade and Economic Development (COTED), to "establish effective support measures" to assist Member States to implement the Agricultural Policy. This support includes strengthening the institutional framework to modernize agriculture and enhance its competitiveness, strengthening the capacity of Member States in policy analysis, agricultural trade analysis and negotiations, and promoting mechanisms for collaboration among farmers across the region. Importantly, the Revised Treaty commits CARICOM to establish an appropriate regime to protect regional agriculture from dumping, subsidization and other unfair practices in international trade. Commitments are also made to improve marketing of agricultural produce in the region, through the establishment of marketing information systems, support for niche marketing and promotion of producer associations and joint venture marketing enterprises to respond to and take advantage of existing and emerging marketing opportunities. Other important provisions to complement and support the development of agriculture in the Revised Treaty include natural resource management (Article 58), human resources management (Article 63), research and development (Article 64), environmental protection (Article 65), and standards and technical regulations (Article 67). Importantly, the Revised Treaty also speaks to the development, management and conservation of the region's fisheries (Article 60) and forestry (Article 61) resources.

In relation to trade, the Revised Treaty (Article 82) established the Common External Tariff (CET), to be levied on all goods imported into the Community extra-regionally. However, this CET can be altered or waived for goods not produced in the Community, or not in sufficient quantity or quality to satisfy Community demand. The CET can therefore afford Member States a level of protection from certain agricultural imports and support the production of agricultural produce in the region, where there is a comparative advantage. The Treaty forbids the imposition of import duties on goods imported from other Member States, and frowns on trade-restricting measures such as quantitative restrictions on imports from within the region, as well as imposition of export duties on goods destined for export to other Member States. In order to promote intra-regional trade, discourage and prevent trade deflection and promote the highest level value added to imported goods, Article 84 outlines the Community Rules of Origin regime. The Revised Treaty with all its provisions is meant to promote efficient, expanded and sustainable agricultural production, expansion of free trade among CARICOM States, import substitution, greater value added in agriculture and increase food and nutrition security. COTED is mandated to superintend the operation of the CET and rules of origin.

The provisions of the Revised Treaty of Chagauramas and the Community Agriculture Policy provide a good basis for the expansion of agricultural production, increased intra-regional trade and the attainment of a greater level of food security in the region. Unfortunately, despite these provisions, the management of the application of the CET and the suspension of the safeguard regimes have sometimes instead worked against the achievement of the objective of food security. Rather than Member Countries using the protection of the CET and the safeguard mechanisms to bolster local production and enhance regional trade and food security, Member States frequently and routinely apply for suspension of the CET and waiver of the safeguard regimes, in order to facilitate imports of extra-regional food. The products frequently applied for suspension of CET and waiver of safeguard measures to allow for their importation include raw, refined and hydrogenated oils derived from various plants, varying fruit purees, fruit and vegetable juices and concentrate, herbs and spices (cinnamon, ginger, turmeric, pimento, nutmeg, etc.), nuts (peanuts, cashew, hazel nuts and almonds), coconut products, refined sugar and coffee. These products are prime candidates for import substitution. The suspension of the CET and waiver of safeguards mechanisms, apart from militating against the advance of food security, has resulted in significant revenue loss to Member States, amounting to some US$2,237,385,924, between 2018 and 2022, according to data from the CARICOM Secretariat (see Table 2.1). It is also noteworthy that the consumption of many of these products is linked with the increase in overweight and obesity in the region and by extension, the increasing incidence of non-communicable diseases.

The Community Agricultural Policy outlined in Articles 56 and 57 represents only a framework, which must be properly elaborated with detailed strategies and actions at the level of Member States and involving harmonization of actions across Member States. It would take approximately a whole decade after the Revised Treaty of Chaguaramas of 2001, to formulate and promulgate a detailed Community Agricultural Policy in 2011. Along this journey, there were some important milestones in the policy formulation process. In an effort to lend some impetus to the operationalization of the RTP, President Bharrat Jagdeo, then President of Guyana and CARICOM Head responsible for agriculture, identified and elaborated some 10 'binding constraints', militating against the transformation of the region's agriculture, enhancement of intra-regional trade, expansion of non-traditional exports and ultimately the attainment of food security. Dubbed the 'Jagdeo Initiative', it was felt that addressing

Table 2.1 Revenue Foregone from Suspension of CET and Waiver of Safeguard Regime, 2018–2022

Member states	*2018*	*2019*	*2020*	*2021*	*2022*	*Total*
Barbados	1,061,790	14,383,955	28,242,232	22,358,178	29,661,318	95,707,473
Dominica	121,408	1,088,000	1,203,409	131,409	3,409	2,547,635
Grenada	975	790,938	–	–	0	791,913
Guyana	2,653,200	55,173,140	170,194,378	84,831,309	90,430,472	403,282,499
Jamaica	95,349,758	57,547,009	84,945,278	104,428,279	115,443,502	457,713,826
Saint Lucia	9,880,000	4,440,000	5,960,000	–	10,840,251	31,120,251
St Vincent and the Grenadines	129,000	2,064,135	2,162,807	124,820	2,304,863	6,785,625
Suriname	130,193	59,831,152	2,372,931	52,754,578	29,454,626	144,543,480
Trinidad and Tobago	121,441,236	95,938,336	111,029,646	376,846,060	389,637,944	1,094,893,222
Total (USD)	230,767,560	291,256,665	406,110,681	641,474,633	667,776,385	2,237,385,924

Source CARICOM Secretariat

these key binding constraints would facilitate the realization of the objectives of the transformation of the region's agriculture as set out in the RTP and the Community Agricultural Policy as per Articles 56 and 57 of the Revised Treaty. The concept of the Jagdeo Initiative was endorsed by the CARICOM Heads of Government Conference in Grand Anse in 2004, and formally approved by the Heads Conference in 2005. Fig. 2.1 presents the key binding constraints.

A former Head of the Caribbean Agricultural Research and Development Institute indicated that while the Jagdeo Initiative correctly highlighted the critical constraining factors inhibiting the development and modernization of the agricultural sector, the constraints were presented in "a vacuum", lacked "context" and "the details were never worked out". The Initiative should have also addressed the CARICOM countries that are best suited to produce critical crops and livestock based on comparative advantage, existence of infrastructure and an enabling environment. Clearly the Jagdeo Initiative did not achieve the intended objective, as the region's food import bill moved from US$2.08 Billion in 2000 to US$5.03 Billion in 2018. Intra-regional trade continues to be stymied by poor transportation networks, with the percentage contribution of intra-regional food trade to overall CARICOM food imports declining from 17.3% in 2000 to 12.7% in 2010. By 2011 this contribution rose to 14.1%, remaining basically flat up to 2016, when it was 14.9%. At the same time, infusion of modern technology in production remains low with significant underinvestment in research and development at national and regional levels, resulting in generally low levels of productivity. The enduring contribution however of the Jagdeo Initiative, according to Antoine (2009), is the concentrated focus it brought to the issues facing agricultural development. It also drew attention to the compelling need to establish an overarching policy for regional agriculture.

The next step in the movement towards the formulation of an overarching Agricultural Policy for the region occurred in 2010, when the Regional Food and Nutrition Security Policy and its accompanying Action Plan (RFNSP and RFNSAP) were formulated, in recognition of the need to address the broader dimensions of food security, particularly those related to health and education. The RFNSP was aimed at achieving the four main food and nutrition security objectives:

1. **Food Availability**—To promote the sustainable production, processing, preparation, commercialization and consumption of safe,

Constraints	Necessary Interventions
1. Limited financing and inadequate new investments	Establishment of a Regional Agricultural Modernisation Fund
2. Outdated and inefficient agriculture, health and food safety systems	Establishment of a Caribbean Agricultural Health and Food Safety Agency (CAHSFA)
3. Inadequate research and development	Definition and implementation of a regional R&D policy and Action Plan
4. Fragmented and unorganized private sector	Strengthening of private sector organisations and collaboration
5. Inefficient land and water distribution and management systems	Establishment of a system of incentives for improved land and water use
6. Deficient and uncoordinated risk management measures including praedial larceny	Development of integrated regional risk mitigation (natural disasters) and relief (including agricultural insurance)
7. Inadequate transportation system particularly for perishables	Determination of freight needs, upgrading of ports and consolidation of services
8. Weak and non-integrated information and intelligence systems	Integration and modernisation of industry and national information systems and services
9. Weak marketing systems, linkages and participation in growth markets	Strengthening of joint marketing opportunities and facilitation of access to EXIM-type financing
10. Lack of skilled human resources	Upgrading and integration of curriculum and training at all levels

Fig. 2.1 Key binding constraints to regional agricultural development

affordable, nutritious, high-quality Caribbean food commodities/ products.

2. **Food Access**—To ensure regular access of Caribbean households, especially the poor and vulnerable, to sufficient quantities of safe, affordable, quality food at all times, particularly in response to diverse socioeconomic and natural shocks.
3. **Food Utilization/Nutritional Adequacy**—To improve the nutritional status of the Caribbean population, particularly with respect to NCDs including diabetes, hypertension, overweight and obesity.
4. **Stability of Food Supply**—To improve the resilience of the region's national communities and households to natural and socio-economic crises

In October 2011, the CARICOM finally adopted the *Caribbean Community Agricultural Policy (CCAP)*. The document identified the Revised Treaty of Chaguaramas, the Jagdeo Initiative and the Liliendaal Declaration on Agriculture and Food Security, as the frameworks which set the political context of the policy. The CCAP is not a 'common policy' that binds all Member States, but rather seeks to "harmonize agricultural policies across the Member States and strengthen areas of comparative cost advantage" (CARICOM, 2011, p. 8). The CCAP was developed within the context of the erosion of preferential markets in the EU for traditional exports of sugar, rum, banana and rice; the increased liberalization of agricultural trade globally; the world food crisis of 2008/2009, which saw agricultural commodity and input prices spiralling out of control; and the reality of climate change, which impacts the region through prolonged droughts and frequent and intense hurricanes.

Against this background the vision of CCAP is to "sustain a broad-based and balanced development of the agricultural sector in order to ensure food security and economic growth in the agricultural sector and to protect the natural resource systems, improve rural livelihoods and build an internationally competitive agricultural sector through the promotion of economically viable enterprises, in order to achieve overall economic growth, reduce poverty and ensure fiscal stability and sustainability" (CARICOM, 2011, p. 18). The policy rests on five pillars viz:

I. Food and Nutrition Security

II. Production-Trade and Value Chains
III. Sustainable Development and Natural Resources
IV. Rural Modernization and Youth Programmes
V. Modern Agricultural knowledge and Information Systems.

The Policy identifies a critical role for private sector participation through investment in production and trade, with the public sector creating the enabling environment. The time horizon for the CCAP is 2011–2025.

In 2014, at the Regional Agricultural Planners' Forum it was agreed to collapse the Jagdeo Initiative binding constraints into four thematic areas for better alignment with the pillars of the CCAP. The areas were: Agricultural Health and Food Safety, Research and Human Resources Development, Climate Change and Natural Resource Management and Business Management.

The major shortcoming of the CCAP is the fact that it is not a 'common policy', but rather seeks to harmonize national policies. Within this context, the subsidiary principle which underpins the Policy, that is, pre-eminence of regional policies only when national policies are less advantageous to Member States, could seriously undermine its implementation. Antoine (2009) points to the slow pace, and even reluctance sometimes of Member States to transition from a national to a regional perspective. Agritrade (2012) identified the potential of distortions of competition in the absence of common policies. For example, companies in Member States which are recipients of heavy subsidies would have an unfair advantage in markets where competing companies are not in receipt of similar levels of support. The failure of Member States to comply with provisions in the Revised Treaty to advance intra-regional trade and enhance regional food security is both real and prevalent. Stanberry (2022) for instance highlights the frustration experienced by Belize, which has the capacity to supply in excess of 70% of the region's demand for refined sugar, but has been faced with the refusal of some Member Countries to apply the CET on extra-regional imports of refined sugar.

The onset of the COVID-19 pandemic in early 2020 ushered in new concerns for food security. Given the region's high dependence on imported foods and agricultural inputs, the disruption of supply chains constituted a major challenge. This challenge, although highlighting the region's vulnerability, simultaneously provided opportunities to refocus attention on increasing regional agricultural production to meet a greater share of region's demand for food. Against this background, the Heads of Government of CARICOM in February 2021 revisited the matter of food security and committed to reducing the region's large food import bill by 25% by 2025. To this end, the CARICOM Agri-Food Systems Strategy was developed to be implemented in the Member States. This Strategy, while recognizing the continued existence of the binding constraints identified in the Jagdoe Initiative, is centred essentially on the commercialization of the region's agricultural production, through large-scale private sector investment. The Strategy therefore emphasizes the critical role of "a supporting policy framework" to induce the injection of "large-scale private sector investments in the agri-business sector, productive activities and supporting infrastructure" (Ali, 2021). In this regard, the Strategy proposes a number of concrete policy initiatives to attract private sector investments, such as establishment of Special Economic Zones for providing fiscal incentives, and the development of new financial instruments to address production, infrastructure and crop insurance. The Strategy however is careful to balance the thrust for large-scale private sector investment with preserving a place for small farmers, to prevent their marginalization. The promotion of contract farming/buying arrangements in the Strategy is therefore important in this context. This is particularly important given the dominance of small farmers in the current agricultural landscape in the region.

In relation to production, special attention will be given to priority crops and products such as poultry, corn, soya, meat (Goat, Sheep, Beef), rice and niche vegetables which are highly imported products in the region. Attention will also be focused on, but not limited to the following areas:

- Increased Production and Productivity
- Market-Driven Production and Intelligence
- Cross-Border Production and Investments
- Climate Smart Agriculture
- Regional Food and Nutrition Security Status
- Coordination and Governance Mechanism
- Digitalization of the Sector
- De-risking and Financial Literacy of the Regional Agriculture Sector
- Sanitary and Phyto-Sanitary (SPS) and Trade Related Policies.

The '25 by 25' Initiative is certainly an improvement over the previous food security initiatives in the region, with its emphasis on private sector-led commercial production, as against public investments in production. Importantly also, the Strategy articulates critical enabling activities that governments must address to catalyse large-scale commercial production, such as risk management instruments, capital and transportation. Specific crops are identified and targets established. Even more critical, the regional private sector has bought into the vision. The CARICOM Private Sector Organization (CPSO), established in 2019 and adopted as an Associate Member of CARICOM in 2020, is fully behind the regional 25 by 2025 initiative. In fact, in 2020 the CPSO itself presented to CARICOM Heads a range of Investment Business Cases in support of the '25 by 25' Initiative in the areas of poultry meat and hatching eggs, animal feed, meat products, cassava, coconut products and vegetables. These cases were identified based on an analysis of the regional food import bill, with clear targets in terms of increase in production and savings along 'regional agricultural corridors' and value chains. The focus here, however, seems to have reverted to the commodity approach rather than a food systems approach, which is being promoted internationally.

A review of the executive and membership of the CPSO reveals an array of powerful business moguls across the region. The composition of the CPSO and their access to Heads and Ministers, through COTED, can make a qualitative difference to the advancement of the '25 by 25' Initiative. Notwithstanding the strong private sector endorsement of and involvement in the '25 by 2025' Initiative, like other regional initiatives, this one is dogged by implementation issues in relation to Member Countries failing to comply with the provisions of the Revised Treaty (see Box 2.1).

Box 2.1 SEPROD's Challenge in Supplying Region with Condensed Milk

SEPROD Group of Companies is a large food manufacturer in Jamaica, which started operations in 1940, producing coconut oil and soaps. Over time this company has grown, taking on dairy operations and manufacturing of dairy products, as well as animal feeds, detergents, bleach, biscuits and other snacks, flour and sugar. Importantly, its manufacturing of dairy products and sugar was linked backwards to agricultural activities of dairy operations producing raw milk and sugar cane production.

Recently, the company took a strategic decision to extend its reach regionally and increase its exports to cover 35% of its manufacturing base. Consistent with this objective, the company began to take a keen interest in CARICOM and deliberations at COTED, as it believes its domestic space is in fact not just Jamaica, but CARICOM. The company identified condensed milk as a product for which it could satisfy the regional demand. Accordingly, over a 4-year period, SEPROD invested some US$75 million in its dairy operations, attaining a capacity 6.5 times the region's demand for condensed milk. Regional demand for condensed milk stands at approximately 9000 metric tonnes, 90% of which was imported from outside the region.

Having attained the capacity to supply in excess of 75% of the region's demand for condensed milk, SEPROD applied for and succeeded in having COTED remove condensed milk from its List A to the List of Ineligibles at its Special Meeting on March 26, 2021. This meant that effectively Member States are obliged to impose a CET of 30%/55% on all condensed milk imported from outside the region, commencing January 1, 2022. Some seven Member States refused to impose the CET on extra-regional imports, effectively locking out SEPROD's exports from their markets. SEPROD therefore had to lodge complaints at the 54th and 55th Regular Meetings of COTED in April and November 2022, respectively. COTED has given the necessary directives for all countries to comply, and non-compliant countries have given timelines for compliance.

Whether COTED's directives will be heeded remains to be seen. SEPROD is willing however, to engage the Caribbean Court of Justice to enforce compliance. SEPROD's Executives believe that distributors in the non-compliant States are the forces behind the non-compliance. If this is true, it would demonstrate how powerful private interests can frustrate and even thwart the efforts of the region to increase its food security. The main lesson learned from this experience is that clear rules and strict compliance to said rules, which ensure predictability and investor confidence, are indispensable to the success of the region's food security initiatives.

There is a groundswell of support from the private sector, Heads of Government and regional agricultural institutions for the '25 by 25' Initiative. One regional agricultural specialist highly endorses the Initiative as necessary, but not sufficient. In addition to the show of support, governments of the region must now create the enabling environment for the growth and development of the agricultural sector, similar to the support given to tourism and manufacturing. All across the region, governments have legislated significant fiscal incentives for these two sectors. In the case of tourism, the governments directly fund marketing campaigns, and generally provide development capital. It is now agriculture's moment.

The success of the '25 by 25' Initiative will equally require a shift in the orientation of the regional private sector. The endorsement of the Initiative by CPSO and the efforts by SEPROD to expand capacity to serve the region's food needs, as highlighted in the case study, are steps in the right direction. However, the region's private sector is diverse, and not all private sector entities are oriented to support regional food security initiatives. There are still many private sector conglomerates with large, fully integrated distribution networks, covering supermarket chains, warehouses, shipping lines and logistics infrastructure, carefully and deliberately designed to move food out of North America for distribution in the Caribbean. In recent times, some of these companies have been acquiring supermarket chains in the USA to further bolster their position of supplier of foods from the United States, rather than investing in agricultural production in the region and collaborating with local farmers.

On the manufacturing side, there are multilateral companies based in the Caribbean, which own farms outside of the region to supply their raw material. When one examines the food import bill of the region, the importation of purees, raw nuts and fruit concentrate to feed these manufacturing entities is staggering. Some of the manufacturing entities even manufacture the finished products entirely outside of the region, and simply import same and use their existing local distribution networks to get these products into the retail chain. Again, governments have to re-examine the existing incentive structure and policy framework to re-orient these businesses to local/regional production to support regional food security initiatives. Admittedly, given the riskiness of agriculture in the region, as well as the sector's low productivity and hence lack of competitiveness, it is easier for such multilateral businesses to import and distribute food, as well as raw material for manufacturing. However, carefully designed policies can reverse this trend over time. The challenge is, given the undeniable influence of these large food distributors and manufacturers over government policies, born out of their funding of political campaigns, can this influence be reversed in the short run? And if so, how?

Regional Institutional Framework for Food Security

In order to support the successful implementation of the RFP and generally boost agricultural production and galvanize the region for a greater level of food security, CARICOM established an impressive array of institutions. Recognizing the primacy of research to drive increases in agricultural productivity, the Caribbean Agricultural Research and Development Institute (CARDI) was established in 1975. According to the CARICOM's website, the overall aim of CARDI "is to contribute to agricultural development by conducting research and by exposing farmers and other persons involved in agriculture to appropriate technology".

The Caribbean Food Corporation (CFC) was established in August 1976 with the objective of "production, processing, packing, storage, transportation, distribution and marketing of food", according to CARICOM. The focus of CFC was supposed to be on the development of crops that would be alternatives to sugar and other plantation export crops. This entity was therefore positioned as the major driver of the implementation of the RFP. The entity leveraged funds from external and regional development agencies such as United States Agency for International Development (USAID), the Caribbean Development Bank (CDB) and the European Union and in combination with its own equity, invested in identified projects.

Recognizing the criticality of a proper marketing infrastructure to boost agricultural production, improve food security and enhance intra-regional trade in food within the frame of the RFP; CFC in October 1981 incorporated the Caribbean Agricultural Trading Company Limited (CATCO), in Barbados. The CATCO was 51% owned by CFC, with the private sector across the region afforded an opportunity to buy shares in the company as follows: Jamaica, Trinidad and Tobago and Guyana—14% each, Barbados—5%, Belize—1% and LDCs—1%. It was agreed by the Board of CFC that CATCO would be managed under management contract by a suitably experienced regional organization skilled in agricultural trade. In terms of its modus operandi, CATCO essentially would enter into contracts with producers of specific crops across the Caribbean to purchase their produce for distribution across the region. In turn, CATCO would work closely with farmers to supply them with quality inputs to ensure that they attain superior yields and high-quality produce. The crops selected were those crops which were imported extra-regionally, so that the objective of import substitution could be achieved, without disrupting local farmers. Concomitantly, CATCO's role was to export non-traditional agricultural produce, particularly to the EU. To minimise disruption to existing distributors of inputs, these non-agricultural products would be incorporated in the model. The benefits of this arrangement were expected to be a reduction in the region's food import bill through selected import substitution, improved foreign exchange earnings through exports, expanded agricultural production principally through improved yields, better quality produce for consumers and a reduction in spoilage through improved post-harvest handling of produce.

As the focus of regional food security initiatives shifted from import substitution to building a modern, efficient, competitive and commercially driven agriculture, new regional institutions were created to deal with standards and agricultural health and food safety. Issues relating to food standards, labelling, packaging, plant health, animal health and food safety are absolutely critical for the region's full participation in international and intra-regional trade. Within the WTO, agreements have been established on sanitary and phytosanitary conditions to promote food safety. These same agreements and standards can also be used as non-trade barriers. The CARICOM Regional Organization for Standards and Quality (CSOSQ) was established in 2002 with a mandate to harmonize and circulate standards of Member States, thus promoting international and regional trade. The Caribbean Agricultural Health and Food Safety Agency (CAHFSA) was established in 2014 "to oversee and coordinate all actions relating to agricultural health and food safety and sanitary and phytosanitary measures along the entire production and marketing chain" (CARICOM, 2011, p. 35). In keeping with the Article 60 of the Revised Treaty of Chaguaramas, which speaks to the sustainable development and exploitation of the region's fishery resources, the Caribbean Regional Fisheries Mechanism (CRFM) was established in 2003. The mandate of the CRFM is to facilitate and promote the responsible use of the region's fisheries and other aquatic resources.

Other regional organizations to complete the institutional regime to support agriculture and food security in the region are the University of the West Indies (UWI), and the various Ministries of Foreign Trade across the region. Although the Caribbean Food and Nutrition Institute (CFNI), founded in 1967, predates CARICOM, it played a critical role in promoting proper nutrition in the region. In January 2013, CFNI was merged with the four other public health agencies in the Caribbean to form the Caribbean Public Health Agency (CARPHA), which is the regional organization dedicated to advancing the public health priorities of the region.

While CARDI's mandate is to focus on applied agricultural research, the UWI has a wide-ranging role in supporting food security by pulling together the disciplines of agriculture, biological sciences, engineering, economics, inter alia, in keeping with the multifaceted nature of the phenomenon of food security. The UWI also plays an important role, not only in research and development but also in building capacity in the region.

Given the region's susceptibility to weather-related disasters, being exacerbated by climate change, the support of the Caribbean Disaster Management Agency (CDEMA) and the Caribbean Institute of Meteorology and Hydrology (CIMH) is critical in coordinating support for the restoration of production after disasters, and in forecasting weather trends to allow for climate smart planning and climate proofing the agrifood sector.

Given the impact of globalization and the increasing liberalization of agricultural trade globally on the food security of the region, the Ministries of Foreign Trade must play a key role in participating in international trade negotiations to secure the interest of CARICOM member States. As small island developing states (SIDS), the region has heightened levels of vulnerability to the impacts of climate change, the unrestricted opening of its economy to imports and require longer adjustment periods to participate in open trade and even to take advantage of new opportunities for exports afforded by trade liberalization. This is particularly important given the region's loss of its preferential markets in the EU for banana and sugar (Thomas, 2006) and the devastating impact that this has had on livelihoods and food security at the community level (Stanberry, 2022). With the negotiations on an agreement on Agriculture in the WTO, and the developed world's reticence on the principle of differential treatment for small economies, the nations of the CARICOM need to be at the table. In this regard, the Office of Trade Negotiation (OTN) of CARICOM has a significant role to play in the food security of the region.

The region is indeed richly endowed with a plethora of institutions, designed to support the development of the agricultural sector and advance the cause of food security, and reflecting the vision of the leadership of CARICOM. Despite this wide array of institutions however, the region has not experienced the anticipated revolution in agriculture, with the food import bill more than doubling since 2000, and some 16% of the region's population undernourished. In fact, a former Executive Director of CARDI opined that "the institutions are floundering because of Member Countries' failure to pay their contribution". Wuddivira et al. (2017), point out that "... institutional settings are such that resources, equipment and funding are not strong enough for research and development in local agricultural commodity development in order to increase comparative advantage". The financial ill-health of a number of these institutions is particularly chronic, reflected in challenges to meet salaries and emoluments costs, and the level of salaries frozen for years. Funding for executing the core work programmes of some of these institutions is extremely limited, inhibiting them from efficiently and effectively carrying out their mandates. Former Executive Director of CARDI lamented that CARDI has now been converted to "a technical coordination institution, implementing projects sponsored by multi-lateral institutions". However, the objectives and programmes of these institutions do not always converge with the interests of donor agencies. The reality is Member Countries have fiscal challenges, as they are not experiencing the kinds of economic growth necessary to support such a wide array of institutions within CARICOM. In light of this reality, it might be worthwhile to consider a rationalization of these institutions. For instance, the feasibility of merging the institutions focused on standards and food health and safety (CROSQ and CAHSFA) should be explored. Similarly, CRFM and CARDI could be merged, or at minimum have some kind of shared services in the administrative areas.

These institutions, notwithstanding their financial struggles, remain critical to the development of regional agriculture, particularly in the smaller territories, where the Ministries of Agriculture might not necessarily have all the capacities necessary to effectively service the agricultural sector. In light of these realities, the former Executive Director of CARDI commended the funding model for EMBRAPA and INTA, the national research agencies of Brazil and Argentina respectively. In the case of EMBRAPA, the Brazilian Government, as a beneficiary of the United States' PL 480 Programme, used the surplus generated from that programme to train researchers at the graduate levels to build the capacity of EMBRAPA. INTA is being funded by a cess levied on all imports by the Government of Argentina. Such innovative approaches need to be employed by Member States of CARICOM to fund agricultural research. A special cess on imports of agricultural goods should be considered. Tourism and airport infrastructure are funded throughout the region by head tax on visitors. Other alternatives can be the use of the wind fall from debt forgiveness and debt swaps. The region's food security initiatives need strong institutions to support them.

National Institutional Frameworks for Food Security

The issue of food insecurity and the prevalence of malnutrition have been matters of concern in the English-speaking Caribbean even before independence. Jefferson (1972), for instance, points to a survey conducted in the 1950s showing high levels of malnutrition in the Jamaican population, which continued up to the early 1970s, and as much as 50% of cases of child mortality was attributed to malnutrition, as well as the high incidence of impaired growth. Indeed, in 1962, the year of attaining independence in Jamaica, the food import bill increased by 12% above the 1961 level of £14.5 million. It is not surprizing therefore that independent English-speaking countries, from the very onset of nationhood concentrated their energies on addressing the issues of food insecurity and malnutrition. Among the major initiatives undertaken in this regard was the creation of an appropriate institutional framework at the national level to expand domestic food crop and livestock production, as a means of diversifying the agricultural sector, which was hitherto dominated by the traditional export crops—sugar, banana, cocoa and coffee. Apart from the long neglect of the domestic food crop sector during the long periods of slavery and colonialism, national governments were equally concerned about the rising food import bill. Hence, the institutional framework being created at the dawn of independence was intended to deliver on the policy objective of import substitution. So critical has the issue of food security become, that in at least 2 countries—Barbados and St. Lucia, food security is highlighted in the Ministry's name.

Central to the new institutional framework was the modernization of Ministries of Agriculture to provide support to small-scale farmers operating in the domestic food crop arena, that is, engaged in the production of tubers, vegetables, fruits, spices and condiments, as well as protein from animal origin. This orientation is justified given the profile of the agricultural sector across the Caribbean—dominated by small-sized farms, situated on marginal land and operated largely by farmers who are aged and with limited formal education. Indeed, Dolly and Ennis (2017) show that based on the most recent available data, the percentage of farms comprising less than 10 hectares is 71% in Barbados, 97% in Dominica, 99% in St. Vincent and 96% in Trinidad and Tobago. In fact, a farm of 10 hectares in the Caribbean context is considered medium sized, especially in the smaller territories. If these data were on a more granular basis, it would be seen that large proportions of farmers are operating of farms even less than 1 hectare! For instance, based on data from Jamaica's 2007 Agricultural Census, 79% of all farms were less than 1 hectare, up from 69.4% in 1996. Over the same period, the number of farmers in the Census classified as 'landless', almost doubled from 14,980 to 28,070. Within the context of this reality, these small farmers, unaided, will be challenged to operate beyond the subsistence level, and their farming enterprise will be characterized by low productivity. Given this profile of the region's farmers, strong Ministries of Agriculture are required to provide technical support to farmers in the areas of technology transfer, marketing, food safety, soil conservation and water management, as well as capacity building in managing their farms as a business and for export readiness. Ministries of Agriculture must therefore have a strong focus on extension services and Extension services must go beyond the provision of production advice.

Countries, like Jamaica, Guyana and Trinidad and Tobago, have over time created an impressive array of institutions under their Ministries of Agriculture to execute these services, in the form of statutory corporations and government companies. Jamaica has such institutions as the Rural Agricultural Development Authority, the Jamaica Agricultural Commodities Regulatory Authority, the National Irrigation Commission, Agro Invest Corporation, the Jamaica Dairy Development Board, National Fisheries Authority, Banana Board, as well as strong divisions within the Ministry focusing on Veterinary services, research, plant protection, etc. In the case of Trinidad and Tobago there are the Agricultural Development Bank, Agricultural Society of Trinidad and Tobago, Cocoa Development Company of Trinidad and Tobago, National Agricultural Marketing and Development Corporation, Livestock and Livestock Products Board, etc. Guyana has the Guyana Livestock Development Agency, Guyana Marketing Corporation, Guyana Rice Development Board, National Agricultural Research Extension and Institute, National Drainage and

Irrigation Authority, etc. The other countries tend to have fewer statutory bodies, and most of the services to farmers are delivered by the Ministry. Given the small populations of the islands in the Eastern Caribbean, the Ministries of Agriculture are typically not outfitted with the wide array of specialists/departments required to adequately deliver services in research, extension, agricultural health and food safety, irrigation, marketing, etc. In these islands therefore, the presence and role of such multilateral partners as CARDI, IICA and FAO are critical to the growth and development of the agricultural sector. These partners closely collaborate with Ministries of Agriculture to support the priorities of Ministries in their respective areas of strength and focus.

One of the observed weaknesses in the operations of Ministries of Agriculture across the region is the overwhelming focus on dispensing benefits to farmers, rather than on developmental issues, that will help small farmers to increase productivity and operate on a more sustainable, efficient and profitable basis. Ministries tend to focus more on distributing seeds, fertilizers, chemicals, day-old chicks, etc., rather than building the capacity of farmers to increase their productivity through technology transfer, training in management of the farming enterprise, post-harvesting techniques and the building of clusters of farmers to achieve critical mass and economies of scale, which are advantageous in procurement of inputs, management of common infrastructure and marketing of goods. Ministries of Agriculture must also focus on empowering small-scale farmers with greater access to lands, through a renewed focus on land reforms, as well as access to credit through creative and innovative mechanisms.

The tendency of Ministries to focus on welfare issues has long been a feature of Caribbean agriculture. Jefferson (1972), for instance, bemoaned the failure to raise the productivity of small farmers in Jamaica between 1946 and 1968. Despite investment of some $56.4 million over the period in subsidies, loans and land settlement schemes, Jefferson (1972, p. 85) remarked that there was "no significant impact on overall production or in halting the widening gap between urban and rural area". With respect to the huge investment in land settlement schemes, Jefferson (1972, p. 85) further remarked that "the available evidence suggests that the output of small farms fell during 1955–1960". In fact, according to Jefferson (1972) between 1950 and 1968 food imports increased from J$9.8M to J$57.9M and correspondingly food import as a percentage of consumption increased from 16.2% to 32.2%.

Clientelism, the distribution of largesse and patronage are characteristic features of politics in the Caribbean, and hence the agricultural sector could not escape the infiltration of these practices. The limited availability of agricultural insurance in the Caribbean partially explains the pre-eminence of the welfare approach in agriculture. When small farmers have been rendered destitute in the Caribbean because of crop and livestock loss from natural disasters, the Ministry of Agriculture has to come to their rescue, because there is no recourse to insurance. Governments have therefore emerged as the insurer of last resort. Unfortunately, given the reality of climate change, with more frequent and intense adverse weather episodes, the doling out of seeds and fertilizer by Ministries is poised to remain a feature of the region's agriculture for the foreseeable future, unless the region can conceptualize and implement innovate crop insurance arrangements.

The welfare approach to supporting farmers is quick and provides a 'feel good' effect, but it is unsustainable and in the long run only condemns the small farmer to a life of perpetual subsistence existence. What is really required are programmes aimed at building the capacity of the farmers to operate in clusters to benefit from discounts in bulk purchasing of inputs, to receive extension service, given the general low numbers of Extension Officers; training in water and soil management, low cost irrigation techniques, records and business management, storage and post-harvest handling of produce to reduce waste and optimise the value of their farming efforts; and technology transfers aimed at increasing productivity and climate-proofing production.

Farmers' groups should also be encouraged to establish special Disaster Risk saving accounts which provide funds to its members for rapid recovery in the wake of disasters.

A new approach also needs to be taken in relation to land reforms, which focuses not only at placing lands in the lands of farmers, but land with appropriate infrastructure (roads, irrigation, etc.), access to farm equipment and the capacity to manage equipment pools, real access to credit and markets through expanded contract farming arrangements.

Contract farming between large processors and manufacturers and farmers must be bolstered by inputs and technical advisory services provided by buyers. Building the capacity of farmers to operate in the export market is also essential, particularly in agricultural health, food safety and certification. Ministries must also focus their programmes on business facilitation, provision of infrastructure of a public goods nature, which are critical to lifting productivity, such as good farm roads, irrigation systems, cold storage facilities, tractor services, laboratories for soil testing and product testing and development to ensure food safety, establishment of traceability systems, infrastructure for preservation of plant genetic resources and rapid multiplication facilities to produce planting material and for livestock (artificial insemination and embryo transfer services).

Quite apart from the identified weaknesses in the structure and programmes of Ministries of Agriculture across the regions, there exists as well a fundamental contradiction in the structure and architecture of governments in respect to the attainment of the goal of food security. While Ministries of Agriculture are busy promoting policies and programmes to enhance food security, other Ministries such as Commerce and Trade and Tourism often promote policies and programmes inhibiting the attainment of food security. The objective of Ministries of Commerce and Trade is to ensure that the country is supplied with a steady flow of food, regardless of the source of such food—local production or imports. So the Ministry of Agriculture may be busy promoting import substitution, while the Ministry of Trade and Commerce is busy seeking waivers of CET from CARICOM Secretariat to import from outside the region. It is also the case that Ministries of Tourism might be busy providing incentives to hotels to import food from overseas to feed tourists, based on the assumption that the American tourists want Texas beef on their plates in the hotels or American apples, grapes and an array of fruits from the temperate region. It is also the case that while Ministries of Education have been supporting school feeding programmes, little deliberate effort is being made to for the food for those programmes to be supplied by local farmers. Given the multi-faceted and multi-dimensional nature of food security, what governments need is, according to Dr. Chelston Braithwaite, (former Director General of IICA (2002–2010)), are 'Ministry of Foods'. Ministries of Food must incorporate all elements of the agriculture value chain spanning production, processing, marketing, distribution and consumption. An important element of this coordinated effort among the various players in the food sector is data and information to determine the demand and supply and to coordinate production planning and imports. In this regard, the Statistical Divisions of the Ministries as well as the Central Statistical Units are critical.

Conclusion

Through their long history of slavery and colonialism, Caribbean States have been structurally conditioned to be food insecure, through their orientation of producing a narrow band of commodities on a monoculture plantation basis for exports, while they import most of their food from their colonial masters. With the dawn of independence, Caribbean countries quickly set about to diversify their agriculture with emphasis on promoting domestic agricultural production to support food security and rural development. Accordingly, a wide array of national institutions were created to support domestic agriculture, at the centre of which lies modernized Ministries of Agriculture.

Given their small size and their inability to navigate the complex international trade area singly, Caribbean countries soon realize the imperative of regional integration to increase their survival in an increasing fierce and complex international arena, as well as to promote trade among themselves and development in the region. From the ashes of the failed West Indies Federation of 1958, CARICOM was formed in 1973 and the regional integration process was deepened in 2001 with the process of creating a single regional market and economy. Regional integration efforts from the very inception of CARICOM in 1973 embraced the ideal of increasing regional food security, by reducing food imports and building the capacity to expand regional food production and trade. These efforts have resulted in an impressive array of policies, institutions and programmes that support the expansion of regional food production, increase intra-regional trade in food and overall enhancement of regional food security.

The development of the regional institutional and policy framework for increased food production, trade and food security has however been slow and protracted. Worse, there has been a lack of consistency among member countries in terms of commitment to policies and rules supporting intra-regional trade in food and a chronic under-funding of critical regional institutions supporting agriculture and food security. The various policies and institutions designed to bolster the region's food security have been undermined by their very architects. What is urgently required is a revisiting of these institutions and policies with a view to their rationalization and a new vision of regional integration and a new commitment regionalism.

References

Agritrade. (2012). *The Caribbean Community Agricultural Policy: Challenges Ahead*. Special Report December 2012. CTA.

Ali, M. (2021). *Advancing The CARICOM Agri-Food Systems Agenda*. Proposa; by His Excellency Dr. Mohamed Irfaan Ali, President of the Cooperative Republic of Guyana.

Antoine, P. (2009). *Implementing a CSME Community Agricultural Policy: Issues, Options and Process*. IICA, Port of Spain, Trinidad and Tobago.

Beckford, G. (1972). *Persistent Poverty: Underdevelopment in Plantation Economies in the Third World*. Oxford University Press.

Best, L. (1968). Outlines of a Model of Pure Plantation Economy. *Social and Economic Studies, 17*(3), 283–326.

Bolland, O. (1981). Systems of Domination After Slavery: Control of Land and Labour in the British West Indies After 1838. *Comparative Studies in Society and History, 23*(4), 591–619.

CARICOM. (2002). *Revised Treaty of Chaguaramas Establishing the Caribbean Community Including the CARICOM Single Market & Economy*. CARICOM Secretariat.

CARICOM. (2011). *Caribbean Community Agricultural Policy*. Georgetown, Guyana. CARICOM Secretariat.

Dolly, D., & Ennis, G. (2017). *Characterization of Family Farms in the Caribbean: A Study of Guyana, Haiti, Jamaica, and St. Vincent and the Grenadines*. IICA, Port of Spain, Trinidad and Tobago.

Dutta, H., & Saikia, A. (2018). Food Security: A Review on Its Definition, Levels and Evolution. *Asian Journal of Multidimensional Research, 7*(7).

Gillespie, J. (1920). *The Influence of Overseas Expansion on England to 1700: Columbia University Studies in History, Economics, and Law* (Vol. 91). Columbia University Press.

Government of Jamaica. (1963). *Five Year Independence Development Plan 1963–1968: A Long Term Development Programme for Jamaica*. . Kingston, Jamaica.

Jefferson, O. (1972). *The Post-War Economic Development of Jamaica*. University of the West Indies.

Mintz, S. (1971). The Caribbean as a Socio-Cultural Area. In M. Horowitz (Ed.), *Peoples and Cultures of the Caribbean* (pp. 17–46). The Natural History Press.

Mintz, S. (1985). *Sweetness and Power: The Place of Sugar in Modern History*. Penguin Books.

Sherlock, P., & Bennett, H. (1998). *The Story of the Jamaican People*. Ian Randle Publishers.

Stanberry, D. (2022). *How Trade Liberalization Affects a Sugar-Dependent Community in Jamaica: Global Action, Local Impact*. Palgrave Macmillan.

Statistical Institute of Jamaica. (2007). *Census of Agriculture 2007*. Kingston, Jamaica.

Thomas, M. (2006). Jamaica and the Case in the WTO Against the European Communities Regime for the Importation, Sale and Distribution of Bananas (1992–2001). In R. Grynberg (Ed.), *WTO at the Margins: Small States and the Multilateral Trading System*. Cambridge University Press.

Thomas, R., & McCloskey, D. (1981). Overseas Trade and Empire, 1700–1860. In R. Floud & D. McCloskey (Eds.), *The Economic History of Britain Since 1700* (pp. 87–1020). Cambridge University Press.

Thompson, E. (1957). *The Plantation: A Bibliography.* Pan American Union.

Wagley, C. (1957). *Plantation America: A cultural sphere.* In V. Rubin (Ed.), Caribbeab studies - A symposium. Institute of Social and Economic Research, University College of the West Indies.

Williams, E. (1944). *Capitalism and Slavery.* University of North Carolina Press.

Wuddivira, M., Gannes, V., Meerdink, G., Dalrymple, N., & Henry, S. (2017, November). Challenges of Food and Nutrition Security in the Caribbean. In *Challenges and Opportunities for Food and Nutrition Security in the Americas: The View of the Academies of Sciences.* IANAS Regional Report.

CHAPTER 3

The State of Food Security in the Caribbean

In this chapter, we examine the state of food security across the Caribbean region, looking at food security trends over the past 15 or so years. The aim is to highlight the specificity and peculiarities of the Caribbean situation vis-à-vis the rest of the world, as well as to identify the factors that are responsible for the Caribbean situation.

The data are primarily taken from FAO's publications on the State of Food Insecurity, as well as some regional statistics published by agencies such as the CARICOM Secretariat, UNICEF and the Caribbean Development Bank, inter alia. The targets and indicators of hunger and food security are those adopted by the United Nations in the context of the Sustainable Development Goals (SDGs) since they provide a universal standard for assessing of progress towards eliminating hunger and food insecurity regionally and globally.

Undernourishment

Table 3.1 shows that the Caribbean region made significant gains in reducing undernourishment between 2005 and 2015, with the number of undernourished persons declining from 7.4 million to 6.1 million. The number remained relatively stable between 2016 and 2017 at 6.2 million,

D. Stanberry and L. Fletcher-Paul, *Food Security in the Caribbean*, Palgrave Studies in Agricultural Economics and Food Policy,
https://doi.org/10.1007/978-3-031-66055-9_3

Table 3.1 Number of undernourished persons (million) in the world by region between 2005 and 2021

Region	*Year*								
	2005	*2010*	*2015*	*2016*	*2017*	*2018*	*2019*	*2020*	*2021*
Caribbean	7.4	6.3	6.1	6.2	6.2	6.6	6.6	7.2	7.2
Latin America	44.3	32.8	29.8	36.3	34.5	35.9	36.7	45.1	49.3
Africa	189.9	171	187.4	198	203.5	216.8	227.5	262.8	278
Asia	552.5	381.5	356.4	336.2	320.8	323.1	339.9	398.2	424.5
World	805.5	601.3	588.6	585.1	573.3	590.6	618.4	721.7	769.9

but began to increase again in 2018 to 6.6 million, with a further increase in 2020 to just short of the levels of 2005 at 7.2 million.

Figure 3.1 indicates that the prevalence of undernourishment showed a similar trend as the number of undernourished, declining steadily from 18.4% to 14.2% between 2005 and 2015, increasing to 15.2% in 2018 and 2019, with a further increase to 16.4% in 2020 and 2021. This trend is consistent the with global figures which showed that between 2005 and 2010, substantial gains were made in addressing undernourishment, with the rates of undernourishment declining from 12.3% to 8.6% and remaining between 7.6 and 8.0% during the period 2015 to 2019. But thereafter, global prevalence rates increased slightly from 9.3 and 9.8%, respectively.

Compared with the rest of the world, undernourishment rates in the Caribbean were almost twice the world average, second only to the African region, which had a prevalence level of 20.7% in 2005 and 16.5% in 2010. Undernourishment rates in Latin America by comparison were generally less than half that of the Caribbean, ranging from a high of 8.6% in 2005 to a low of 5.8% in 2015.

The number of undernourished persons disaggregated by country shows where the hungry people are located in the Caribbean. Table 3.2 shows that the high levels of undernourishment in the Caribbean are found in Haiti whose population of 11.2 million (in 2019) accounts for 61% of the total population of the region and thus, heavily influences the data. Between 2004 and 2006 the prevalence of undernourishment in Haiti was 52.9%. By comparison, among the other CARICOM countries for which data are available, the prevalence of undernourishment was highest in Trinidad and Tobago with rates of 11.1% while the other

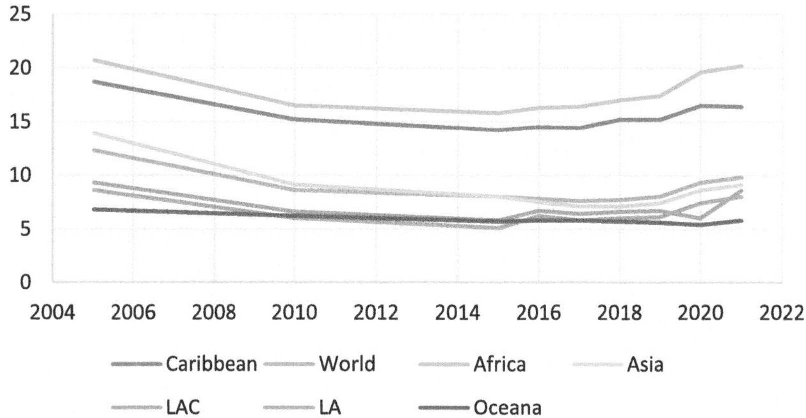

Fig. 3.1 Prevalence of undernourishment (%) in the Caribbean and the major regions of the world

countries ranged between 5.4 (Dominica) and 7.9% (St Vincent and the Grenadines).

Between 2019 and 2021, although there was a slight decline in Haiti to 47.2%, this level was still at least 6 times higher than the other CARICOM countries, which ranged between 3.4% in Barbados and 7.6% in St Vincent and the Grenadines.

Food Insecurity Based on the Food Insecurity Experience Scale (FIES)

The FIES, which was developed by the FAO, is one of the indicators used to measure progress toward achieving one of the Sustainable Development Goals (SDGs). Goal 2.1 seeks to achieve zero hunger and malnutrition by 2030. The FIES is used to:

- **assess** the population **prevalence of food insecurity** (for both SDG monitoring and national use)
- **identify vulnerable** populations
- **guide** and **monitor** the effects of food security **policies and programs**
- **identify risk factors and consequences** of food insecurity.

Table 3.2 Key indicators of food insecurity among Caribbean countries between 2004 to 2006 and 2019 to 2021

Country	*Prevalence of undernourishment in the total population (%)*		*Prevalence of severe food insecurity in the total population (%)*		*Prevalence of moderate or severe food insecurity in the total population (%)*	
	2004–2006	*2019–2021*	*2004–2006*	*2019–2021*	*2004–2006*	*2019–2021*
Barbados	6.1	3.4	n.a	7.4	n.a	31.1
Dominica	5.4	6.9	n.a	n.a	n.a	n.a
Grenada	n.a	n.a	n.a	7.5	n.a	22.3
Haiti	52.9	47.2	n.a	45.2	n.a	82.5
Jamaica	7.4	6.9	25.3	23.1	48.3	50.3
St Kitts and Nevis	n.a	n.a	8.1	6.4	21.1	26.9
St. Lucia	n.a	n.a	4.5	n.a	22.2	n.a
St Vincent and the Grenadines	7.9	7.6	n.a	10.3	n.a	33.3
Trinidad and Tobago	11.1	7.5	n.a	10.2	n.a	43.3

The FIES scale estimates the proportion of the population who suffer from moderate or severe constraints in their ability to get sufficient food over the period of one year. Moderate insecurity describes situations when individuals face uncertainties about their ability to obtain food and have been forced to reduce at times during the year, the quality and/or quantity of food they consume due to lack of money or other resources. Severe food insecurity refers to situations when individuals have run out of food, experienced hunger and, at the most extreme, have gone for days without eating, putting their health and well-being at serious risk.

Because of the dearth of relevant and reliable data for the Caribbean, it was not possible to estimate the FIES for all the countries of the region until 2019. Nevertheless, the data in Table 3.3 show that compared to the global averages and the averages for the other regions of the world, the Caribbean had the highest prevalence of severe food insecurity of 36.6% in 2020, which declined to 30.5% in 2021.

With respect to ***moderate*** food insecurity, all regions individually and collectively showed an increasing trend between 2014 and 2021. The highest levels of moderate food insecurity were found in the Caribbean at

Table 3.3 Prevalence of food insecurity at severe level only and moderate or severe level based on the Food Insecurity Experience Scale (2014–2021), in the Caribbean and selected regions of the world

Region	*Prevalence of severe food insecurity (%)*						*Prevalence of moderate food insecurity (%)*					
	2014	*2016*	*2018*	*2019*	*2020*	*2021*	*2014*	*2016*	*2018*	*2019*	*2020*	*2021*
World	7.7	7.8	9.0	9.3	10.9	11.7	21.2	22.7	25.0	25.4	29.5	29.3
Caribbean	n.a	n.a	n.a	n.a	36.6	30.5	n.a	n.a	n.a	n.a	68.4	64.0
Latin America	5.7	7.1	7.5	8.2	11.1	13.0	21.8	28.7	29.1	29.4	37.5	38.9
Asia	7.1	6.4	8.1	8.2	9.7	10.5	17.6	17.7	21.1	21.3	25.8	24.6
Africa	16.7	19.2	19.3	20.2	22.4	23.4	44.4	49.7	51.3	52.4	56.0	57.9
Oceania	2.5	3.3	3.7	3.8	2.6	4.5	11.4	11.9	13.1	13.6	12.0	13.0
North America and Europe	1.4	1.3	1.0	0.9	1.2	1.5	9.3	8.7	7.6	7.1	7.8	8.0

68.4 and 64.0%, respectively, in 2020 and 2021. Among the other regions of the world, only Africa had levels in excess of 50% from 2018 onwards.

Further disaggregation of the data by country shows that between 2019 and 2021, the high levels of severe undernourishment in the Caribbean were not only experienced in Haiti which had a level of 82.5%, but also in Jamaica (50.3%), Trinidad and Tobago (43.3%), St Vincent and the Grenadines (33.3%) and Barbados (31.1%) (Table 3.2).

In terms of the number of people experiencing ***severe levels*** of food insecurity in the Caribbean, the available data for 2020 and 2021 show a decline from 15.9 to 13. 3 million respectively between 2020 and 2021 (Table 3.4). Similarly for the number of persons either severely or moderately food insecure, there was a slight reduction from 29.8 to 28 million over the same period. These figures contrast with all other regions in the world which have generally shown an increasing number of severely or moderately and severely undernourished persons between 2014 and 2021.

The trend was somewhat different for the English-speaking Caribbean. According to the World Food Programme and CARICOM COVID-19 Food Security and Livelihoods study of 2021, the number of moderately food insecure people declined from 2.5 million during June 2020 to

Table 3.4 Number of people experiencing food insecurity at severe level only and at moderate or severe level, based on Food Insecurity Experience Scale (FIES) 2014–2021 in the Caribbean and selected regions of the world

	Number of severely food insecure people (millions)						*Number of severely or moderately food insecure people (millions)*					
	2014	*2016*	*2018*	*2019*	*2020*	*2021*	*2014*	*2016*	*2018*	*2019*	*2020*	*2021*
World	564.9	588.5	687.4	716.9	850.1	923.7	1543.9	1693.4	1905.4	1955.9	2297.8	2306.5
Caribbean	n.a	n.a	n.a	n.a	15.9	13.3	n.a	n.a	n.a	n.a	29.8	28
Latin America	32.9	41.9	45.2	49.4	67.8	80.1	125.4	168.6	174.1	178.1	228.6	239.7
Asia	310.4	284.8	368	376.8	451.6	489.1	773.5	794	960.1	980.4	1196.8	1151.4
Africa	192.1	232.7	246.8	264.2	300.5	322	512	602.8	654.1	685	750.9	794.7
Oceania	1	1.3	1.5	1.6	1.1	2	4.5	4.8	5.5	5.7	5.1	5.6
North America and Europe	15.2	14.1	10.7	10.3	13.2	17.2	102.1	96.4	84.2	79.6	86.7	89.1

February 2021, but the number of severely food insecure people increased by 57% to 482,000 in February 2021.

Stunting and Wasting

Two other indicators which are commonly used to determine the level of food insecurity in a country are the prevalence of stunting and wasting among children under the age of 5 years. Figure 3.2 shows that the prevalence of moderate and severe stunting in the Caribbean in 2000 and 2020 is among the lowest in the world, second only to Europe.

In all regions except Oceania, Figs. 3.2 and 3.3 show that the prevalence of moderate and severe stunting and wasting declined over the period 2000 and 2020. The reduction in the prevalence of wasting was more marked, with rates in all regions declining by more than 50%.

For the Caribbean, the reduction in stunting over the period was from 15.7 to 11.8% and for wasting it was from 2.8 to 0.8%, respectively. Further disaggregation of the data by country in Table 3.5 showed that among the Caribbean Islands, St Lucia had the lowest prevalence of stunting of 2.7 and 2.8% in 2012 and 2020, respectively, while Haiti far exceeded the other countries of the region with corresponding stunting

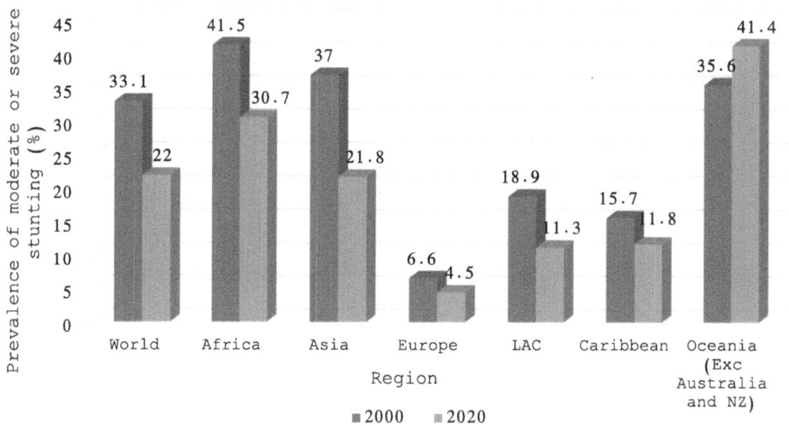

Fig. 3.2 Prevalence of moderate or severe stunting in children under 5 years in 2000 and 2020 by region

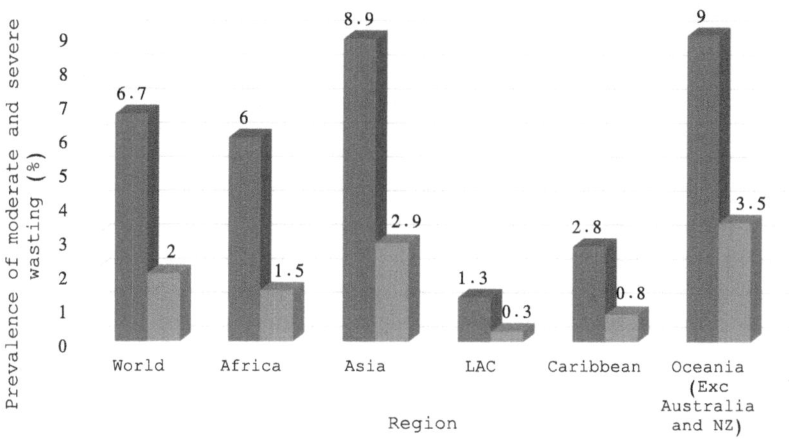

Fig. 3.3 Prevalence of moderate or severe wasting in children under 5 years in 2000 and 2020 by region

Table 3.5 Prevalence of stunting and wasting in children under the age of 5 years in the Caribbean 2012 and 2022

Country	*Prevalence of Stunting in Children (under 5 years of age) (%)*		*Prevalence of Wasting in Children (Under 5 years of age) (%)*
	2012	*2020*	*2020*
Barbados	7.6	6.6	n.a
Dominica	n.a	n.a	n.a
Grenada	n.a	n.a	n.a
Haiti	23.9	20.4	3.7
Jamaica	6.8	8.5	3.3
St Kitts and Nevis	n.a	n.a	8.1
St. Lucia	2.7	2.8	n.a
St Vincent and the Grenadines	n.a	n.a	n.a
Trinidad and Tobago	8.5	8.7	n.a

rates of 23.9 and 20.4% in 2012 and 2020. Jamaica showed a marked increase in stunting between 2012 and 2020 from 6.8% to 8.5%.

Overweight and Obesity

The Caribbean also faces a double burden of food insecurity in that in addition to undernourishment, there is also a problem of overnutrition resulting in overweight and obesity. This overweight and obesity has been linked to the high incidence of chronic non-communicable diseases such as diabetes, stroke, hypertension and some forms of cancer which are the leading cause of death in the region.

Figure 3.4 shows trend in the prevalence of moderate and severe overweight between 2000 and 2020 in all the regions of the world. The data indicate that the prevalence of overweight increased in all regions except Africa. In the case of the Caribbean the increase was from 5.8 to 6.6%.

A breakdown of the overweight data by country (Fig. 3.5) revealed that Barbados, Trinidad and Tobago and Cuba had the highest percentage of overweight children over the period of the study with rates over 9% in 2012 and 2020. Haiti had the lowest prevalence of overweight in children with rates of 7.8 and 7.6%, respectively. The prevalence of overweight

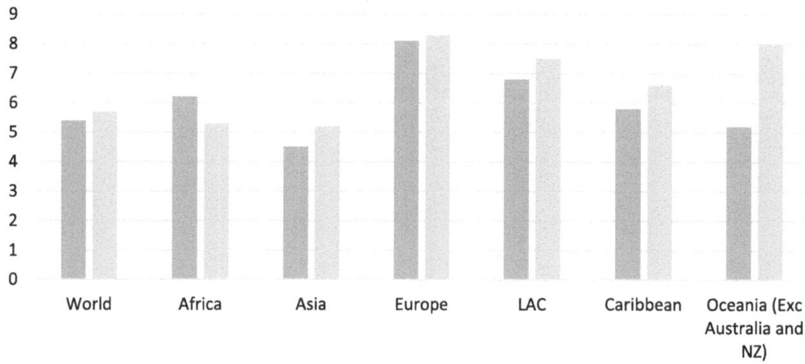

Fig. 3.4 Prevalence of overweight in 2000 and 2020 by region

children showed an increasing trend in Barbados, Cuba, St Lucia and Trinidad and Tobago between 2000 and 2020.

The prevalence of Obesity among adults 18 years and over (Fig. 3.6) increased in all countries between 2012 and 2020. The highest prevalence was observed in Dominica, with rates of 25.5 and 27.9% in 2012 and 2020, respectively, while the lowest rates were observed in Trinidad and Tobago with corresponding rates of 16.3 and 18.5%.

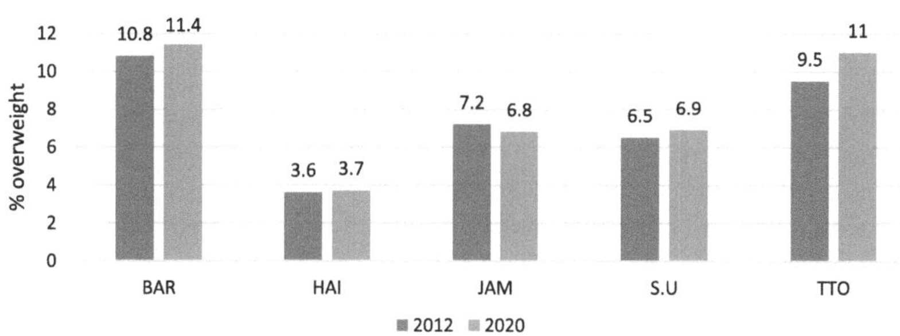

Fig. 3.5 Prevalence of overweight in children (under the age of 5 years in the Caribbean 2012 and 2020)

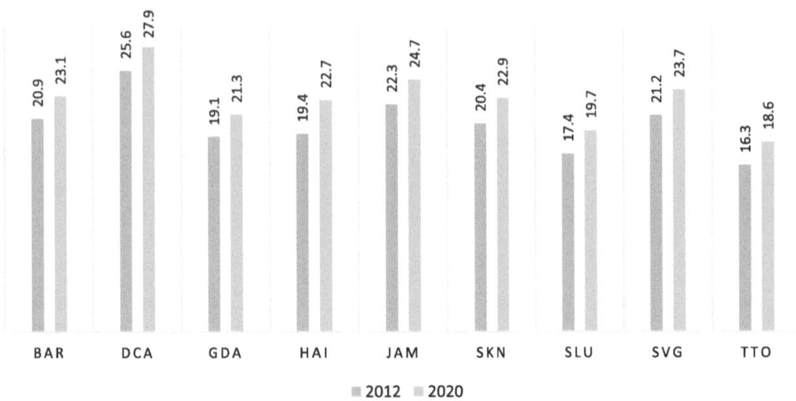

Fig. 3.6 Prevalence of obesity in adults (18 years and older)

Responsible Factors

The high levels of food insecurity and particularly severe and moderate undernourishment in the Caribbean are heavily influenced by food insecurity in Haiti, where high levels of poverty and unemployment affect access to food. Notwithstanding the high levels in Haiti, the other Caribbean islands have all seen an increasing trend in food insecurity since 2018. According to the CDB FAO study conducted in 2019, "There are multiple causal factors of food security and nutritional challenges in the CARICOM region, which are compounded by the scale of food imports and the related food import bill, vulnerability to natural disasters, and the high risk of fiscal crisis".

The main factors which have contributed to this rising trend are: (1) food access, primarily due high prices (especially for imported food items), unequal distribution and the lack of diversity of affordable food at certain periods of time, (ii) food availability, particularly of sufficient quantities of locally produced diversified food, (iii) food stability due to the frequent occurrence of natural disasters and the absence of appropriate resilience and risk mitigation strategies for food production systems especially at the household level and (iv) food utilization, due to nutritionally poor food choices and food consumption patterns, as a result of limited knowledge of poor attitudes and practices towards healthy diets. In addition, the preponderance of imported food which is high in calories, fat, sodium and sugar has also contributed to the current situation of food and nutrition insecurity.

The CDB/FAO (2019) report also cited the need for a more strategic, multidisciplinary and coordinated approach to addressing the challenges, as well as the dearth of reliable and appropriately disaggregated data among the contribution factors.

In the last two years, these challenges have been further exacerbated by the COVID-19 pandemic and the Ukraine crisis. The CARICOM/CDEMA/WFP/FAO livelihoods survey of 2022 showed that the pandemic has triggered a reduction in food availability, increased food prices as well as a reduction in disposable incomes, particularly among vulnerable groups. In some households, these factors have contributed to persons skipping meals or purchasing less healthy foods, to cope.

Ukraine and the Russian Federation, individually or together are ranked among the top three global exporters of wheat, barley, maize, rapeseed and rapeseed oil, sunflower seed and sunflower oil. The Russian Federation is also ranked as the world's top exporter of nitrogen fertilizers, the second leading supplier of potassium fertilizers and the third largest exporter of phosphorous fertilizers (FAO, 2022). The Ukraine crisis has, therefore, triggered in an increase in food and commodity prices resulting from higher fuel and transportation costs as well as disruptions in international supply chains. The supply and price of fertilizers have also been affected and this in turn is expected to cause a reduction in yields of some commodities. The price of commodities, such as wheat, corn and oil, is also predicted to increase since Ukraine and Russia are responsible for 25% of the world's wheat exports. This increase in wheat and corn prices has resulted in an increase in the price of bread and other wheat products.

According to ECLAC (2022), "The outlook for the region in 2022 is difficult. Firstly, the external context even before the war was one of slowing growth in economic activity and international trade, but it has been complicated further by the conflict, the persistence of COVID-19, and rises in energy and food prices. Secondly, situations at the domestic level are characterized by abrupt slowdowns in economic activity, rising inflation and sluggish and incomplete recoveries in labour markets, driving both poverty and inequality".

Conclusions

Over the past 15 years, the Caribbean region has experienced fluctuations in food security, with notable progress in reducing undernourishment until 2015, followed by a concerning increase thereafter. Despite efforts to address food insecurity, recent data show a reversal of gains, highlighting persistent challenges.

The lack of comprehensive and reliable data for the Caribbean region until 2019 hinders accurate estimation of food insecurity levels. This underscores the need for improved data collection and analysis methods to inform policy and intervention strategies effectively.

Despite data limitations, available figures highlight alarmingly high levels of food insecurity in the region. In 2020, the region exhibited the highest prevalence of severe food insecurity globally although there was a slight improvement in 2021. Moderate food insecurity rates also remained notably high, surpassing 50% in both years, indicating widespread vulnerability. While Haiti stands out with extreme levels of severe undernourishment, other countries such as Jamaica, Trinidad and Tobago, St Vincent and the Grenadines, and Barbados also experience substantial challenges.

Notwithstanding a marginal decline in the number of severely food insecure individuals from 2020 to 2021, the overall trend in the Caribbean contrasts with global patterns. While other regions witnessed an increase in food insecurity, the Caribbean showed a modest reduction, albeit remaining critically high.

With respect to stunting and wasting among children under 5 years old, the prevalence of moderate and severe stunting in the Caribbean in 2000 and 2020 ranks among the lowest globally, second only to Europe, indicating relatively better nutritional outcomes in the region. There has been a general reduction in stunting and wasting rates over the years. However, despite improvements, disparities persist among Caribbean countries, with notable variations in stunting prevalence, with Haiti exhibiting significantly higher rates compared to other countries.

In addition to problems of undernourishment, the region also grapples with a dual challenge of overnutrition, manifested in overweight and obesity. This poses significant health risks, contributing to the prevalence of chronic non-communicable diseases (NCDs) such as diabetes, stroke, hypertension and certain cancers, which are leading causes of death in the region. With respect to overweight and obesity there is a concerning trend of increasing prevalence of moderate and severe overweight across all regions of the world from 2000 to 2020, with the Caribbean experiencing a rise from 5.8% to 6.6%. This upward trajectory is particularly pronounced in countries like Barbados, Trinidad and Tobago, and St Lucia, where rates of overweight children surged over the study period.

The breakdown of overweight data by country highlights variations in prevalence rates within the Caribbean. Barbados and Trinidad and Tobago emerge as having the highest percentages of overweight children, while Haiti reports the lowest rates. Similarly, obesity among adults increased across all Caribbean countries between 2012 and 2020, with Dominica exhibiting the highest prevalence and Trinidad and Tobago the lowest.

Multiple factors contribute to food insecurity in the Caribbean, including limited access to affordable and diverse food, vulnerability to natural disasters, and poor food utilization practices. Import dependency and the nutritional quality of imported foods further compound the issue. Recent crises, such as the COVID-19 pandemic and the Ukraine crisis, have exacerbated food insecurity in the region. Disruptions in supply chains, increased food prices and economic challenges have also negatively affected food access and affordability.

The outlook for the region remains challenging, with economic slowdowns, rising inflation and persistent poverty and inequality exacerbating food insecurity. Sustainable solutions will necessitate concerted efforts at both regional and national levels to address systemic issues and build resilience against future crises.

References

CARICOM, CDEMA, WFP, FAO. (2022). *Caribbean Food Security and Livelihoods Survey Report for August 2022.*

ECLAC. (2022, June 6). *Repercussions in Latin America and the Caribbean of the War in Ukraine: How Should the Region Face This New Crisis?* Santiago. https://repositorio.cepal.org/server/api/core/bitstreams/8240d230-f012-47ca-9603-40d6f03a1d0f/content

FAO. (2022, March 25). *The Importance of Ukraine and the Russian Federation for Global Agricultural Markets and the Risks Associated with the Current Conflict*. Information Note. Rome. Update https://www.fao.org/3/cb9236en/cb9236en.pdf

FAO and CDB. (2019). *Study on the State of Agriculture in the Caribbean* (212 pp.). Rome. Licence: CC BY-NC-SA 3.0 IGO.

FAO, IFAD, PAHO, UNICEF and WFP. (2023). *Regional Overview of Food Security and Nutrition—Latin America and the Caribbean 2022: Towards Improving Affordability of Healthy Diets*. Santiago. https://doi.org/10.4060/cc3859en

CHAPTER 4

Food Availability in the Caribbean

Introduction

Food availability is the first concern of food security and the pillar which occupied the attention of the international community until the recent past when attention began to be focused on the critical pillars of access, utilization and stability. The fact is, food availability, while not a sufficient condition to ensure food security, is a necessary condition for access and utilization. Food availability is determined by production capacity, capacity to import food and access to food aid. The Caribbean region is comprised mainly of states categorized as middle income countries, based on per capita income. This level of per capita income reflects a state of development which is not consistent with the depth of poverty and economic deprivation which warrants food aid. The exception to this rule is of course Haiti, whose economic development has been undermined by obligations imposed by its erstwhile colonial master France—to pay for its independence which it attained in 1791. In addition, a poor record of governance over a protracted period of dictatorship and a series of natural disasters have also stymied the country's development. For the region therefore, food availability has been mainly a factor of domestic production and food imports.

The region's agricultural production has historically been oriented towards exports of commodities, notably sugar and banana, to satisfy the

D. Stanberry and L. Fletcher-Paul, *Food Security in the Caribbean*, Palgrave Studies in Agricultural Economics and Food Policy, https://doi.org/10.1007/978-3-031-66055-9_4

demand of their colonial masters for these exotic products. The production of these commodities typically commanded the largest share of the most fertile agricultural lands and was conducted on a large-scale plantation basis. The production of other food crops to satisfy domestic demand was typically relegated to a number of small-scaled farmers, operating on marginal lands and receiving little support from the State in terms of infrastructure, marketing, distribution and post-harvest facilities. The attainment of independence by these states has seen deliberate and concerted efforts to bolster domestic agriculture in support of food security through appropriate policies, institutions and funding. The emergence of a manufacturing sector, predominantly food processing, in newly independent Caribbean States, as well as the development of a vibrant tourism sector, have created enormous opportunities for the agriculture sector to provide raw material to the former and food to the latter.

However, obviously the region has not done enough to incentivise this linkage between agriculture and the manufacturing and tourism sectors. As a consequence of this failure, the Region's food import bill has been consistently increasing, moving from US$2.08 billion in 2000 to US$5.03 billion in 2018 (Ali, 2023). A significant portion of this import bill relates to importation of raw material for manufacturing and food for the hotel and hospitality industry. At the same time the Region's agriculture has not been responding to the opportunities for exports now made available with the substantial liberalization of agricultural trade under the WTO. While the region will not be able to compete on volume due to diseconomies of scale associated with size, the region has the potential to position itself in the export market with niche products, such as exotic fruits, spices and herbs, as well as value-added products such as juices, beverages, jellies, jams, seasonings mix and other products uniquely Caribbean and differentiated by distinct taste and quality. In this regard value-added products of coffee, cocoa, ginger and a range of spices have significant potential, because of their superior, independently validated taste profile. A critical aspect of food security involves maximizing export production to generate the resources required to be able to import those food products which are critically required.

This chapter will examine the production trends in agriculture in the region, the extent to which domestic production is satisfying food demand and the expanding role of imports in satisfying Caribbean's demand for food. It will also examine the extent to which a portion of food imports can be sustainably replaced by local production, and the policy, legislative, institutional framework and investment that will be required to bolster local production both for import replacement and exports.

Food Production Levels and Trends

Data on agricultural production across the English-speaking Caribbean, particularly domestic food crops are not readily available to do a comprehensive analysis of food production levels and trends. Aggregate data from the FAO (FAOSTAT), showing the value of gross agricultural production in current United States dollars, are available for Guyana, Jamaica, Suriname and Trinidad and Tobago over the period 1991 to 2020. These four countries, in addition to Belize, possess the greatest potential for agricultural production in relation to available arable lands. From Fig. 4.1, it can be seen that over the 29-year period there was a general increasing trend in the value of agricultural production, with the greatest expansion in Guyana and Suriname, and more modestly in Jamaica and Trinidad and Tobago.

Guyana

The growth in Guyana is particularly impressive, increasing multiple fold between 2012 and 2020, in comparison with the 1991 to 2011 period.

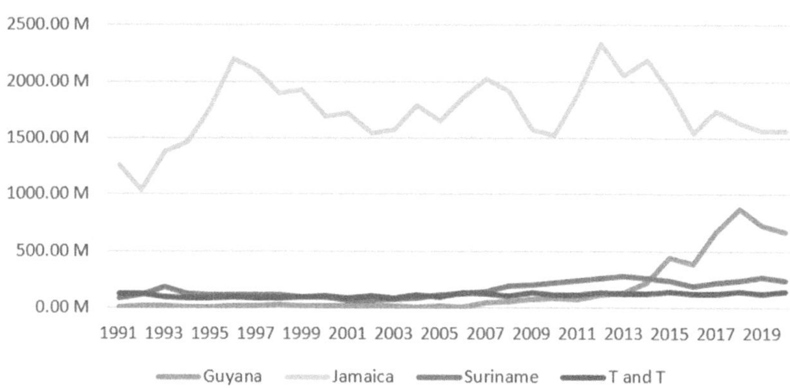

Fig. 4.1 Agriculture gross production, million USD (*Source* FAOSTAT)

Like the rest of ACP, Guyana suffered significant fallout in its sugar exports to the EU over the last 20 years due to erosion of its preferential treatment in that market, however, it has significantly increased it rice production and export. Rice production moved from 121,233 tonnes in 1960 to some 650,000 tonnes according to data from the Guyanese Ministry of Agriculture. More importantly, whilst growing this traditional crop, focus is also being placed on value-added production, that is, to increase the proportion of packaged rice to over 20% of total rice production (GOG, 2013). The country has also made significant strides in diversifying its agriculture through investment in marine and inland fisheries, livestock, corn and soya, as well as a range of non-traditional exports. The performance of agriculture in Guyana, as reflected in the spectacular growth in the value of gross production, reflects the priority accorded to this sector by the government, with agriculture receiving some 11% of the government's budgetary allocation in 2013, according to the Government's *National Strategy for Agriculture in Guyana: 2013–2020 (GOG,* 2013). This compares favourably with other countries' allocation to the sector, which for Antigua, Bahamas, Grenada, for example, was well below 2% over the period 2014–2020, according to data from the FAOSTAT.

This focus on agriculture has paid high dividends for Guyana, with agriculture employing 33% of the country's labour force, contributing 20% of GDP and 40% of total exports in 2013 (GOG, 2013). With the emergence of the petroleum industry in Guyana in recent years, the relative contribution of agriculture has diminished. However, the sector remains important to the Guyanese economy, contributing 13.5% to GDP in 2021 and employing 15% of the labour force in 2019 (Ali, 2023). Significantly, Guyana remains the most food secure of the CARICOM countries, with a positive food trade balance. The government is also leading the charge of reducing the Region's food import bill through the 25 by 25 Initiative and has been aggressively promoting private sector investments in the sector, while making substantial investment in public goods, including infrastructure. With only 2.1% of its total land area engaged in agricultural production (Ali, 2023), and abundant water resources, there exists enormous potential for increasing agricultural production in this country, and hence food availability, not only to Guyana, but to the rest of CARICOM. This is consistent with the vision of the National Strategy for Guyana to become the "bread basket of the Caribbean" (GOG, 2013, p. 14).

Suriname

The value of gross agricultural production in Suriname has been on an upward trajectory over the 29-year period 1991 to 2020. Up until 2004, there was some fluctuation in the value of gross agricultural production. However in 2004, the value of gross agricultural production took a sharp upward turn and has been on a general upward trajectory since. The average annual value of gross agricultural production between 2010 and 2020 was US$240,052,000, compared toUS$99,723,000 over the period 1991 to 2001, an increase of 241%. This substantial increase in the value of gross agricultural production in Suriname has been facilitated by an equally significant expansion in the percentage of agricultural lands under production, which is estimated to have increased from 0.2% in 1961 to 0.4% in 2013 (Wuddivira et al., 2017). With an estimated 1.5 million hectares of agricultural lands, Suriname has significant potential for expansion of agricultural production to further reduce its own food inadequacy, already on the lower range at 18.8% between 2011 and 2013, (Wuddivira et al.,2017), as well as to serve alongside Guyana as another 'bread basket' of the Caribbean. With some 85% of its agricultural lands on the Caribbean coast, Suriname's prospect for agricultural development will be constrained by water management issues and the sector is particularly challenged by coastal erosion and saline intrusion (Hayman, 2023). Notwithstanding these issues, enough land and water resources are available for significant expansion of production to satisfy the food demand of the rest of the Caribbean, especially in such products as rice, shrimp and other shell fish, aquaculture and banana.

Jamaica

The value of Jamaica's gross agricultural production in the 29 years FAOSTAT time series between 1991 and 2020 has been on a general upward trend, peaking in 2012, where the value of gross production was almost twice that of 1991. Since the peak of 2012, the value of gross agricultural production has been generally trending down, albeit above the 1991 value. The general downward trend after 2012 reflects the impact of the fallout in sugar exports to the EU. The EU unilaterally renounced the Sugar Protocol of the LOME Agreement, consequent on the successful challenge of the EU Sugar Regime in the WTO by Thailand, Brazil and Australia in 2003. Under the pressure of liberalization, the EU was forced to remove preferential treatment of sugar imports from ACP countries and open up its market to non-ACP sugar producers, which were generally more competitive. The loss of its preferential treatment in the EU market dealt a devastating blow to sugar production and export revenues in Jamaica. Data from Jamaica's Sugar Industry Authority show a steady decline in sugar production from 123,120.39 tonnes in the 2014/15 crop year to 43,946.86 tonnes in the 2019/20 crop year. Correspondingly, export revenue from sugar declined from US$65.3 million in 2014 to US$3.5 million according to data from the Sugar Industry Authority. At its peak Jamaica produced over 500,000 tonnes of sugar in 1965.

Jamaica's other major agricultural export crop—banana, experienced a similar decline as sugar over the last 15 years. In the case of banana, the loss of Jamaica's preferential access to the EU market due to liberalization of that market was further compounded by the impact of a series of hurricanes, which have all but destroyed the commercial production of banana for export. According to data from Jamaica's Ministry of Agriculture, overall banana production declined from 177,923 tonnes in 1996 to 64,731 in 2021, with export volume declining from 88,917 tonnes in 1996 to 17,473 tonnes in 2007, when Hurricane Dean dealt the final blow to banana exports in Jamaica. Export earnings from banana over the same period declined from US$44.1 million to US$9.2 million. In fact, every single traditional export crop in Jamaica has been in decline—sugar, banana, citrus, cocoa, coffee and pimento. Data from the *Economic and Social Survey, Jamaica* show that since 1996 export revenue from these traditional crops declined from US$89.3 million to US$18.1 million in 2021.

The performance of the value of Jamaica's gross agricultural production over the 29-year period 1991 to 2020 must also be examined within the context of the performance of the livestock sector. Supported by the pioneering work of Dr. T. P. Lecky, who developed tropical dairy and meat breeds of cattle (Jamaica Hope, Jamaica Red Poll and the Jamaica Black Poll) in Jamaica in the 1950s, data from the Statistical Institute indicate that in 1968, Jamaica's cattle population stood at 278,710 heads, which declined to 94,964 heads 2007, as measured by Agriculture Census for the respective periods (STATIN, 2007). By 2014, the Ministry of Agriculture data suggest that the cattle population further declined to 64,504. At the same time the population of cattle slaughtered declined 64,064 heads in 1997 to 29,046 heads in 2022. Concomitantly, milk production declined from 27.4 million litres in 1997 to 12.4 million litres in 2022.

The significant fall off in beef and milk production in Jamaica in the last 30 years relates to the lowering of import tariffs by the Jamaica Government in the early 1990s, ostensibly in pursuit of 'cheap food' for the poor, the impact of mad cow disease on consumers' demand for beef and the continued failure of the country to find local sustainable sources of animal feed. As a consequence of this declining local production of beef, the importation of beef products has ballooned, with significant volumes of prime cuts of beef imported for the tourism sector and beef trimmings and suet imported for the manufacture of patties, a major snack in Jamaica. With respect to milk, the lowering of tariffs on imported milk ushered in a flood of powdered milk into Jamaica from the United States and the EU, which reduced local milk production by two-thirds since 1992, and caused the exit of over 500 milk farmers from the business.

Although Jamaicans consume substantial volumes of goat meat and mutton, the production capacity has never been properly established to produce an appreciable portion of these meats locally, despite favourable conditions especially for goat production. Small ruminant production has been the focus of a number of projects by the Ministry of Agriculture and the CARDI, in terms of demonstrating housing for goats, local feeds, as well as rapid multiplication techniques. Despite these efforts, the number of heads of goats slaughtered in Jamaica from 1997 to 2022, based on data from the Ministry of Agriculture hovers around 45,000 heads per annum, satisfying less than 5% of local consumption. The performance of the small ruminant sector in Jamaica is consistent with the low-input and low-output system in the Caribbean and the low density of sheep and goats in the Region (Wuddivira, 2017).

The shining stars in the livestock sector in Jamaica are the pig and poultry sectors. Both sectors have experienced phenomenal growth, thanks to massive investments in these sectors by major commercial interests in a vertically integrated way. This includes the production of day-old chicks and superior genetic material and breeding techniques for pigs, production of animal feed, rearing of animal by farmers contracted to processors and provided with technical support and installation of modern processing facilities. The government has also played a significant role, particularly in the broiler industry, where import duties are set at well over 200%. The result of this coordinated approach to industry development has resulted in Jamaica being self-sufficient in poultry meat, eggs and fresh pork.

Pork production in Jamaica is somewhat cyclical, with occasional episodes of glut from time to time. Ministry of Agriculture data show pork production moving from 6.5 million kilograms from 104,157 heads of pigs slaughtered, peaking at 9.4 million kilograms from 158, 853 heads slaughtered, to 8.7 million kilograms from 129,505 heads slaughtered. Despite the decline in production in 2022 compared to peak production in 2005, productivity increased from 59 kilograms of pork per animal to 67 kilograms in 2022. This augurs well for the industry. The major challenge for this industry is to be able to export excess production to the rest of the region, given the periodic glut in the Jamaican market and the production capacity to export on a continuing basis. The further challenge is to move up the value chain with more processed products, since Jamaica's tourism industry still imports significant volumes of processed pork products.

Data from the Statistical Institute of Jamaica Agricultural Census of 1961 and 1968 show that in the poultry industry, the number of birds moved from 1,868,967 in 1961 to 3,727,168 birds in 1968. As a result of investments by two large private sector conglomerates and work with a contract farmer's model of production, Ministry of Agriculture data indicate that some 43,968,276 heads of birds were slaughtered in 1997 producing 59,310,211 kilograms of chicken meat, with a productivity of 1.35 kilograms per bird. By 2022, productivity rose to 1.65 kilograms per bird with some 84,876,934 birds slaughtered, producing 139,857,966 kilograms of meat. At the same time egg production moved from 129,538,324 eggs to 232,345,799 eggs. Thanks to this performance of the poultry industry, Jamaica is self-sufficient in both chicken meat and eggs. It is an accomplishment of strategic significance that a small developing country can be self-sufficient in a major source of protein. Additionally, 40% of the production of broiler birds is done by small and medium-sized farmers. It is noteworthy that under the 25 by 2025 Plan by CARICOM to reduce the Region's food import bill, broiler production is a major area of target. Despite this phenomenal success however, it is a matter of major concern that this industry, as well as the pig industry, rely almost exclusively on imported grains for animal feed. These imports constitute the largest chunk of the country's import bill (Stanberry, 2019). Also, despite Jamaica's self-sufficiency in eggs, there is still substantial importation of liquid eggs for the hotel sector, underscoring the need for this industry to move up the value chain, as it has the production capacity to produce the raw material for the production of liquid and powdered eggs.

In relation to the fisheries sector, data from the Ministry of Agriculture show a steady expansion in aquaculture production from 698 tonnes of fish (tilapia and basa) in 2014 to 1512 tonnes in 2018. At the same time, there was some fluctuation is marine fish capture (fin fish, conch, lobster and shrimp), moving from 11,256 tonnes in 2014, attaining a high level of 14,921 tonnes in 2017, with a sharp 27.1% decline in 2018 to 10,883 tonnes. The fluctuating fortunes of marine fish capture are directly related to increasing frequency of adverse weather-related events and increasingly smaller catches of near shore fishes because of overfishing and climate change. With respect to conch, poaching by foreign fishers continues to be an issue, compounded by Jamaica's inability to effectively monitor its vast territorial waters. Marine fishing however represents a huge potential for Jamaica to increase capture to enhance availability of a vital source of protein to the local population, as well as export earnings. The requisite investments need to made in appropriate vessels, safety equipment and training to exploit the rich pelagic resources in Jamaica's huge territorial waters and its Exclusive Economic Zone.

Given the sharp decline in the production of Jamaica's traditional export crops and the fact that these crops occupied some 46% of all arable lands in Jamaica (STATIN,2007); the huge fall off in beef and dairy production and the lacklustre performance of the fishing industry, it begs the question: What accounts for the increasing trend in the value of Jamaica's gross agricultural production over the period 1991 to 2020, as per the data from FAOSTAT? The answer lies in the domestic sector—as the traditional export crop subsector declined in the last 15 to 20 years, the domestic food crop subsector and non-traditional exports have been on the increase. Domestic food crops encompass a range of vegetables, fruits, condiments and spices, tubers and legumes, cultivated predominantly by over 200,000 small farmers, operating on small plots of land. Although these farmers barely operate above the subsistence level, when their production is aggregated, they provide sufficient vegetables, fruits, starches (yams, sweet potatoes, banana, breadfruit, dasheen, cacao, etc.), condiments, spices and legumes to satisfy the nation's demands in these food items. They therefore play a critical role in the state of Jamaica's food security.

The profile of these farmers, that is, operating on small plots of land (less than 1 hectare); semi-literate; average age above 50 years; without tenure to the lands they operate; without access to financing and insurance, dictate that the government provides substantial support to these farmers. This support is warranted not only from the perspective of the strategic importance of these farmers to food security, but from a social justice standpoint, in terms of righting the historic marginalization of this group of farmers through slavery and colonialism. It is a historic fact that efforts by the peasantry to establish independent livelihoods were systematically undermined by both sugar interests and the colonial authorities in the post-emancipation period in order to force them back to the plantation (Bolland, 1981; Hall, 1959). Support provided to farmers includes infrastructure (irrigation and farm roads), technical services (extension, marketing and training) and input and grants, particularly in the aftermath of natural disasters. Thanks to this support, Jamaica's small farmers moved the production of domestic food crops from some 400,109.5 tonnes of produce in 2008 to 846,508 tonnes in 2022, according to data from the Ministry of Agriculture. It is noteworthy that this subsector showed steady increases even during the COVID-19 years (2020–2022), reflecting the substantial stimulus package presented to the agricultural sector by the government during the pandemic. This increasing trend is consistent across all sub-groups within the domestic food crop sector, that is, legumes, vegetables, condiments, fruits, cereals and tubers. This consistently high level of domestic food crop production indicates that Jamaica possesses the capacity to produce in sufficient quantity the critical foods required to satisfy a significant share of the nutritional needs of its people for healthy growth and development. The major portion of Jamaica's food import bill relates to the importation of products of animal origin mostly for the hotels, cereal for animal feed, wheat and rice which locally grown tubers could substitute, as well as raw material (puree and concentrate) for further processing.

Non-traditional exports relate to all agricultural exports outside of the traditional sugar, banana, coffee, cocoa, citrus, coconut and pimento. These non-traditional exports comprise fruits, tubers, spices and herbs and vegetables, as well as a range of processed foods from raw material from domestic food crops. Export of fish (conch and lobster) would also fall in this category. Export of these items was significantly boosted under the Caribbean Basin Initiative of the early 1980s, through which a range of agricultural products gained tariff free access into the United States market. Exports to Canada were facilitated under CARIBCAN, a non-reciprocal trade agreement between Canada and CARICOM countries. Most of these products target the Jamaican diaspora in the United States, Canada and the United Kingdom.

Over the period 2009 to 2020, according to data from the Statistical Institute of Jamaica, the value of non-traditional exports has been moving on a generally increasing trajectory, rising from US$110.1 million to US$202.3 million, an increase of some 84%. Over the same period, the value of traditional export crops has been on a downward spiral, moving from US$114.1 million to US$28.4 million (see Fig. 4.2). In fact, in 2020 the value of yam exports at US$37.7 million eclipsed the value of all traditional exports! The major non-traditional exports by value were yams, ackee, baked products, sauces, fish (conch and lobster) and juices. Export of agricultural products plays a very critical role in enhancing food security, as the revenue generated supports the importation of those food items, which cannot be produced locally, but are critical for nutritional security. It is also important to note that these food exports are products in which the country is already self-sufficient, so that export will not impair local food security.

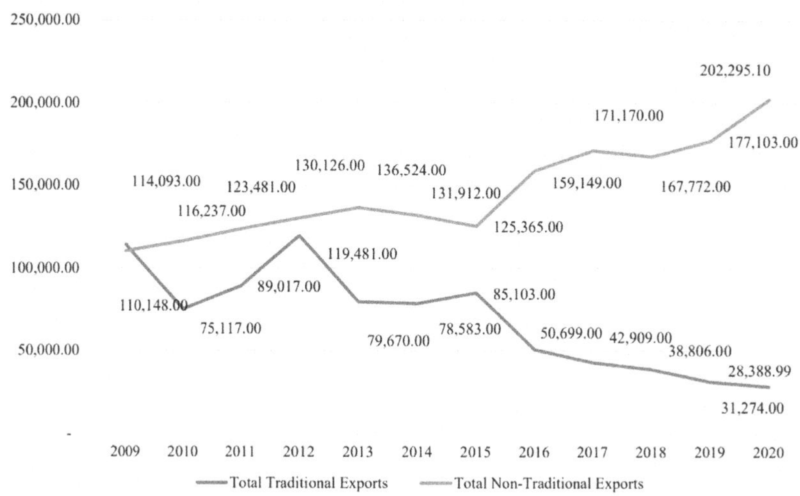

Fig. 4.2 Comparative export value (USD '000) between traditional and non-traditional crops, 2009–2020 (*Source* Statistical Institute of Jamaica [2021])

Trinidad and Tobago

Based on FAOSTAT data, between 1993 and 2005 the value of Trinidad and Tobago's gross agricultural production averaged around US$93 million per annum. Beginning in 2006 there was an upward trajectory in the movement of the value of gross agricultural production, reaching US$144.8 million in 2020. This growth however is not as impressive as Guyana's and Suriname's—countries with much smaller populations (804,567 and 612,985 in 2021, respectively), compared to 1,525,663 in Trinidad and Tobago in 2021 (Ali, 2023). Per capita agricultural output therefore is comparatively small in Trinidad and Tobago. Because of the dominance of oil and natural gas in the Trinidad economy, agriculture has always played a relatively minor role in this country. This is reflected in the mere 1% contribution of agriculture to Trinidad and Tobago's GDP, and only 18,951 farmers operating in the sector (Ali, 2023). Notwithstanding the comparatively modest growth in the value of agricultural output, it is commendable that most of this growth coincided with the period over which Trinidad exited from sugar production and export, due to the erosion of its preferential access to the EU market in the wake of the liberalization of that market.

Like most of the other English-speaking Caribbean countries, the production of tradition export crops dominated the agricultural landscape. These crops include sugar, cocoa, coffee, citrus and coconut. However, these crops have been on the decline, with sugar production ceasing in 2007. As producer of one of 8 fine flavoured cocoa in the world, Trinidad and has recently been investing heavily in the cocoa industry to improve varieties and increase value-added production particularly by small farmers.

Poultry has emerged as important subsector compensating for the overall decline in traditional export crops, followed by vegetables and root crops. The over-reliance on oil and gas and the softening of prices of these products internationally over recent years have impacted economic growth in Trinidad and Tobago between 2016 and 2021. The government has therefore sought to bolster economic growth through diversification. A very comprehensive range of incentives is available for inducement of investments in the agricultural sector, as well as to support existing farmers. The seriousness of the intent of the government to support the agricultural sector is reflected in the increase of the capital budget allocation to the Ministry of Agriculture, Lands and Fisheries in 2022/2023 to TT$160.6 million (3.5% of the capital budget), up fromTT$72.3 million in the 2021/2022 financial year, in addition to a TT$50.1 million allocation from the Infrastructure Development Fund, according to data from the Budget Guide of the Parliament of Trinidad and Tobago.

Notwithstanding the modest performance of the agricultural sector, Trinidad and Tobago has used its abundant oil and natural gas resources to its advantage in establishing a vibrant food manufacturing industry, based on imported agricultural raw material. In fact, because of the competitive advantage afforded by access to cheap oil, many food processing companies have relocated operations from Jamaica to Trinidad. Trinidad and Tobago has therefore emerged at the food manufacturing centre of the English-speaking Caribbean. The food, beverages and tobacco subsector of the manufacturing sector continues to grow, with its contribution to Trinidad and Tobago's GDP moving from 3.3% in 2019 to 5.2% in 2022. This position has enabled Trinidad and Tobago to have a very healthy balance of trade with the rest of CARICOM, which in 2022 stood at TT$4.6 billion for trade in non-petroleum related goods (Government of Trinidad and Tobago, 2023).

The vibrancy of the food processing and manufacturing sector of Trinidad and Tobago has not compensated for the limited role of the country's agricultural production in enhancing Trinidad's food security. Trinidad and Tobago remains highly dependent on food imports to satisfy local food demand, estimated to be at the level of 85% of local food consumption (Ali, 2023). According to the United States Department of Agriculture's International Trade Administration, US agricultural exports to Trinidad in 2021 stood at US$368 million, rendering Trinidad and Tobago the second-largest market for US agricultural exports to the English-speaking Caribbean. Trinidad and Tobago sources 40% of its food imports from the United States.

Other English-Speaking Caribbean Countries

The paucity of data does not allow for an in-depth analysis of the agricultural production levels and trends, for the remaining English-speaking Caribbean countries, as was done for Guyana, Suriname, Jamaica and Trinidad and Tobago. Of the remaining countries, Belize has the most substantial agricultural sector, with this sector accounting for 7.7% of GDP in 2021 and a positive food trade balance of approximately Bz$200 million, according to data from the Statistical Institute of Belize. Significantly, despite the loss of concessional market access to the EU sugar and banana market, which affected so many ACP countries, Belize seems to have restructured its sugar industry, with exports standing at 154.65 thousand tonnes in 2022 and banana exports at 187.85 thousand tonnes, based on data from the Statistical Institute of Belize. In fact, Stanberry (2022, p. 262) noted the significant investments made in the sugar industry of Belize since the reform of the EU sugar regime. An indicator of the state of food production in Belize can be gleaned from the more than doubling of the percentage of agricultural lands under cultivation, moving from 3.46% in 1961 to 7.54% in 2020, according to FAOSTAT. Concomitantly, Belize's prevalence of food inadequacy declined from 15.4% in the 1990–1992 period to 11.6% in the 2011–2013 period (Wuddivira et al., 2017). With only 7.54% of its agricultural lands in use, Belize, like Guyana and Suriname, has the potential to produce much more food, for itself and the rest of the region.

Barbados and St. Kitts and Nevis were major sugar exporters before the collapse of the highly concessionary EU market in early 2000s. Sugar cane occupied the major portion of cultivated lands on these islands, evidenced by the significant reduction in the percentage of cultivated land in total agricultural land. For Barbados, this share dropped from 44.19% in 1961 to 23.26% in 2020. The corresponding figures for St. Kitts and Nevis are 57.14% and 23.08% (FAOSTAT). Outside of sugar, these two islands are engaged in domestic production of fruits, vegetable, root tubers and livestock. However, production levels have not been satisfying the bulk of local consumption, with food imports accounting for 87% of consumption in Barbados in 2011 (up from 72% in 1995), and 95% in St. Kitts in 2011, up from 74% in 1995 (Wuddivira et al., 2017). For these two islands, the question arises as to whether the lands taken out of sugar production are still available for the production of other crops in order to reduce dependency on imported foods? Given Barbados' high dependence on food imports and the relative scarcity of agricultural land in that country, the initiative of Barbados for cross-border investments in Guyana and Suriname is commendable.

Dominica, St. Lucia, St. Vincent and the Grenadines and Grenada were major banana producers and exporters to the EU, until that market eliminated preferential terms of trade to ACP countries in the face of pressures from Latin American banana interests for liberalization. The loss of preferential access to the EU banana market has caused a significant downsizing of the banana industries in these countries, with a consequential reduction of their agricultural acreage. Of these countries, Dominica is probably the most dependent on agriculture (particularly banana production), which contributed over 30% to GDP before the decline of the banana industry. The decline in banana production has been precipitous, moving from 37,000 tonnes in 2000 to 11, 371 tonnes in 2014, with corresponding declines in exports from 3523 tonnes in 2010 to 539 tonnes in 2017 (Central Statistics Office, 2020). Consequently, between 2009 and 2017, agriculture's contribution to GDP declined from approximately 12% to 8.4% in 2017. This 28.8% decline in agriculture's GDP resulted from the impact of Hurricane Maria in 2016 (Central Statistics Office, 2020). The agricultural sector however rebounded, with its contribution to GDP climbing to 17% in 2021 (World Bank, 2023). Despite the sharp decline in banana production, crops such as plantain, coconut and citrus (grapefruit, oranges and lime) have more or less remained stable, while mango, yams and dasheen have seen steady increases over the same period (Central Statistics Office, 2020).

The improvement in agricultural production despite the downturn in banana production is confirmed by FAOSTAT data, which show that Dominica is one of the few countries in the region where the percentage of arable lands has been increasing, moving from 22.67% in 1961 to 33.33% in 2020. It is also the case that the incidence of food inadequacy declined from 9.5% in 1990/1992 to 5.2% in 2011/2013 (Wuddiviria et al., 2017). Notwithstanding this favourable position, Dominica still depends on imports to satisfy 55% of its local consumption in 2011 (Wuddiviria et al., 2017). The island remains highly vulnerable to climate change and natural disasters, which constitute major threats to enhancing its food security. It is against this background that the Government of Dominica has set a policy objective of becoming the world's first climate resilient island.

With respect to St. Lucia, St. Vincent and the Grenadines and Grenada, data from FAOSTAT show the percentage of cultivated area declining from 64.71% in 1961 to 23.53% in 2020 for Grenada; from 27.87% in 1961 to 16.3% for St. Lucia and from 25.64% to 17.95% in St. Vincent and the Grenadines. Correspondingly, in all of these countries' dependence on imported food to satisfy local consumption have increased from 53% in 1995 to 83% in 2011 for St. Lucia; 65% in 1995 to 81% in 2011 for Grenada and from 54% in 1995 to 68% in 2011 for St. Vincent and the Grenadines (Wuddiviria et al., 2017).

Antigua and Barbuda and the Bahamas represent two countries characterized by a relatively small agricultural sector, contributing approximately 2.2% and 0.5% to GDP, respectively, in 2021 (World Bank, 2023). Services (tourism and financial services) are the major contributor to GDP. These countries also have the distinction of their agriculture never been dominated by plantation export crops, such as sugar and banana. In Antigua and Barbuda, the lion's share of agricultural output comes from the fisheries sub-sector, with the fisheries sector contributing 1.12% to GDP in 2021, compared with 0.84% from agriculture (crops) and livestock, according to official statistics from the Government of Antigua and Barbuda. This sector is dominated by artisanal fishers, although in recent years the industry has been modernized (CARICOM, 2020). Vegetables, fruits, coconuts and livestock produced principally for domestic consumption, complete the agricultural sector (CARDI, 2018). Notwithstanding, the relatively minor role of agriculture in the Economy of Antigua and Barbuda, the sector has been growing, with the value of agricultural output increasing from EC$15.85 million in 1977 to EC$23.50million (constant 2006 prices) (Government of Antigua and Barbuda, 2023). This growth in output has been supported by an increase in the percentage of lands under production, moving from 15.91% in 1972 to 20.45% in 2020, according to data from FAOSTAT. Despite the growth in the value of agricultural output, food imports grew from US$99.2 million in 2012 to US$119.3 million in 2021, based on data from the CARICOM Secretariat. Food security therefore remains a critical issue in Antigua that will remain a challenge as long as its tourism sector continues to grow. Susceptibility to hurricanes and lack of adequate water resources will continue to be a threat to increasing food production. The government has been promoting investments in the sector both for export and import replacement. The areas identified are pineapples and sea-island cotton for export, and production of poultry, fruits and vegetables for import substitution (Caribbean Agribusiness, 2020).

The value of gross agricultural output at constant prices in 2018 in the Bahamas was B$98.1 million, which although up from the B$88.3 million recorded in 2017, was B$14.55 million below the 2012 level of B$115 million. Agricultural GDP in 2018 was a mere 0.9% of the GDP of the Bahamas (Bahamas National Statistical Institute, 2023). Clearly agriculture plays a minor role in the Economy of the Bahamas. Vegetables, root tubers and fruits are grown for domestic consumption. There is a fairly well-developed poultry and conch industry. Bahamas also exports citrus. With such a small agricultural sector, which itself has been in relative decline, the Bahamas relies heavily on importation of food, driven largely by its burgeoning tourism sector, estimated at over 5 million visitors per annum. According to data from the United States Department of Commerce, some 90% of domestic consumption is satisfied by imported food, most of which comes from the United States. Bahamian hotels and resorts purchase over 60% of their food and beverage from the United States. The Government of the Bahamas has in recent years been placing some emphasis on the agricultural sector in an effort to increase its food security. In 2014 it established the Bahamas Agriculture and Marine Institute to promote agricultural education and training, research and extension and outreach. With only 1.4% of its lands engaged in agriculture, according to FAOSTAT, Bahamas has available lands, plus the incentive of a large food import bill to expand agricultural production. It is however challenged by insufficient water resources, the hazards of weather and labour shortages.

Food Imports, Net Food Trade and Prospects for Sustainable Import Replacement

From the analysis for food production trends in the English-speaking Caribbean in the previous section, it can be seen that while the value of gross agricultural production has been on an increasing trajectory in Guyana, Suriname, Jamaica, Belize, and to a lesser extent in Dominica and Antigua and Barbuda, the Region as a whole is not producing sufficient food to satisfy a critical mass of its food consumption. While no country theoretically possesses all the agro-climatic conditions to be able to produce 100% of the food it consumes; and while the principle of comparative advantage in trade dictates that countries import where it is more cost effective to do so, the Caribbean region is way off the mark of optimizing its food production to enhance its own food security. Given the increase in conflicts that tend to disrupt supply chains and the growing tendency of net food exporting countries to impose restrictions on exports in times of crises, it is incumbent on small developing countries, such as those in the Caribbean, to strategically produce a critical mass of the food it consumes, lack of comparative advantage notwithstanding. In fact, comparative advantage is not a static concept. The efficiency of food production in the Caribbean can be considerably enhanced if the requisite investments are made in critical infrastructure and technology. Many comparatively small countries such as Costa Rica and Israel have demonstrated that such investments can make a difference to the efficiency of their agricultural production. The Caribbean also has unique products, the production of which need to be scaled up and positioned as niche in the export markets, where they can survive and flourish not on the basis of price, but the distinctness and superiority of their flavour. These products include coffee, cocoa, a range of spices and herbs, cannabis, sauces, jams, jellies, etc. The vast resources of the Caribbean Sea are also largely unexploited, due to lack of investment.

Based on data from the CARICOM Secretariat, the Region's food import bill (minus Haiti), stood at US$4.1 billion in 2021, moving from US$3.4 billion in 2016, after being stable at about US$3.5 billion between 2012 and 2015 (see Table 4.1). In 2021, the first full calendar year after the onset of the COVID-19 pandemic, despite the challenges of logistics and supply chain disruptions occasioned by widespread lockdowns worldwide, the food import bill increased by a significant 19% compared to 2020, the largest increase over the 2012–2021 period. It is quite possible that such a large increase is reflective of the price movement of imported foods, rather than the quantum of food imported. The FAO Food Price Index moved from 98.1 in 2020 to 125.7 in 2021 (FAO, 2024). This 27.6 point movement represents the sharpest movement in the index since 2005, including during the world food crisis of 2007/2008.

It can be seen from Table 4.1 that over the 2012–2021 period the structure of the region's food import bill remained fairly stable in terms of the share of individual countries. Jamaica and Trinidad are responsible for approximately 50% of the Region's food import bill, followed by the Bahamas, Barbados and Guyana. The huge share of Jamaica and Trinidad reflects their large population, the large tourism sector in Jamaica and the massive importation of agricultural raw material to sustain the buoyant manufacturing sector in Trinidad. Jamaica also has a well-developed poultry and pig industry, for which it imports large quantities of grains for the manufacturing of animal feed. With over 5 million tourists per annum and an agricultural sector that contributes a mere 1% to GDP, it is not surprising that Bahamas is the third-highest importer of food in the region. With a population of just over 400,000 in 2021, the Bahamas on a per capita basis is a bigger importer of foods than Jamaica and Trinidad, that is, US$1574 versus US$397 and US$576.4 for Jamaica and Trinidad and Tobago, respectively. Barbados at a per capita food import bill of

Table 4.1 Value of food imports by CARICOM countries, 2012–2021

Caricom Countries	*2012*		*2013*		*2014*		*2015*		*2016*	
	(US$'Mn)	*%*	*(US$'Mn)*	*%*	*(US$'Mn)*	*%*	*(US$'Mn)*	*%*	*(US$'Mn)*	*%*
CARICOM	*3527*	*100*	*3523*	*100*	*3624*	*100*	*3505*	*100*	*3369*	*100*
The Bahamas	483.7	13.7	466.5	13.2	512.0	14.0	507.9	14.5	489.6	14.5
Barbados	259.9	7.4	269.2	7.6	275.9	7.8	272.2	7.8	267.2	7.9
Guyana	213.9	6.1	211.7	6.0	203.2	5.5	201.7	5.8	199.1	5.9
Jamaica	957.8	27.2	961.2	27.3	918.5	25.3	839.9	24.0	839.5	24.9
Suriname	198.1	5.6	193.5	5.5	188.4	5.2	197.9	5.6	194.4	4.4
Trinidad and Tobago	835.3	23.7	850.0	24.1	913.4	25.2	880.8	25.1	814.2	24.1
Belize	96.2	2.7	101.0	2.9	132.5	3.6	123.2	3.5	123.1	3.7
Antigua and Barbuda	99.2	2.8	95.5	2.7	97.8	2.7	97.1	2.8	93.6	2.8
Dominica	40.0	1.1	38.7	1.1	47.1	1.3	44.8	1.3	42.3	1.3
Grenada	73.7	2.1	73.5	2.1	69.1	1.9	73.8	2.1	75.0	2.2
Montserrat	5.3	0.1	5.2	0.1	5.0	0.1	5.7	0.2	5.1	0.2
St. Kitts & Nevis	50.0	1.4	46.4	1.3	47.2	1.3	51.0	1.5	69.9	2.1
Saint Lucia	132.1	3.7	134.0	3.8	134.6	3.7	130.7	3.7	125.2	3.7
St. Vincent & the Grenadines	81.9	2.3	76.9	2.2	79.2	2.2	78.5	2.2	75.5	2.2

(continued)

Table 4.1 (continued)

Caricom Countries	*2017*		*2018*		*2019*		*2020*		*2021*	
	(US$'Mn)	*%*	*(US$'Mn)*	*%*	*(US$'Mn)*	*%*	*(US$'Mn)*	*%*	*(US$'Mn)*	*%*
CARICOM	*3457*	*100*	*3532*	*100*	*3772*	*100*	*3406*	*100*	*4058*	*100*
The Bahamas	533.1	15.4	505.7	14.3	587.9	15.6	389.8	11.4	460.8	15.8
Barbados	278.8	8.1	285.2	8.1	293.6	7.8	281.2	8.3	303.1	7.5
Guyana	200.3	5.8	208.7	5.9	174.9	4.6	241.8	7.1	285.9	7.0
Jamaica	841.1	24.3	901.1	25.5	1024.1	27.2	930.9	27.3	1121.8	27.6
Suriname	157.2	4.5	148.8	4.2	189.8	5.0	157.4	4.6	155.6	3.8
Trinidad and Tobago	824.8	23.9	833.6	23.6	834.0	22.1	788.5	23.2	879.6	21.7
Belize	116.5	3.4	115.4	3.3	120.9	3.2	118.5	3.5	128.6	3.2
Antigua and Barbuda	113.0	3.3	120.0	3.4	117.1	3.1	106.6	3.1	119.3	2.9
Dominica	33.0	1.0	37.1	1.1	42.7	1.1	37.5	1.1	37.3	1.0
Grenada	77.1	2.2	85.0	2.4	95.2	2.5	89.2	2.4	93.2	2.3
Montserrat	5.0	0.1	5.6	0.2	5.6	0.1	5.8	0.2	5.9	0.1
St. Kitts & Nevis	66.4	1.9	71.0	2.0	67.9	1.8	65.0	1.9	60.8	1.5
Saint Lucia	133.2	3.9	137.5	3.9	140.0	3.7	122.3	3.6	137.6	3.4
St. Vincent & the Grenadines	77.6	2.2	77.3	2.2	78.5	2.1	77.5	2.3	88.9	2.2

Source CARICOM Secretariat

US$1078 is also faring worse than Jamaica and Trinidad and Tobago. In absolute terms the food import bill in the Bahamas, Jamaica, Trinidad and Tobago, Barbados, Grenada, St. Kitts and Nevis is trending upwards, while in Dominica, Suriname and Guyana (with the exception of 2020 and 2021), the value of food imports has been on a downward trajectory. For Belize, Antigua and Barbuda, St. Lucia and St. Vincent and the Grenadines, although there are slight fluctuations annually over the 2012–2021 period, the food import bill can be characterized as stable.

Obviously, it is highly desirable that the region increases its agricultural production to increase exports and replace that portion of its food imports that can be sustainably replaced in an effort to enhance food security, save and earn foreign exchange, increase GDP and support rural development. It is therefore important to carefully examine the region's agricultural trade data to identify the possibilities for sustainable import replacement and increased exports. Table 4.2 shows groups of agricultural items exported and imported by CARICOM Member States over the period 2016–2018, along with balance of trade for each group of food items. It can be seen that products of animal origin (beef parts, dairy products, live animal including live birds for the poultry industry, honey, goat meat, pork cuts, fresh, frozen and processed fish) accounted for some 26.2% of the Region's food import bill in 2018. This speaks to the state of the livestock industry in the Region, in terms of production and productivity.

Only the poultry and pork industry are making an appreciable contribution to the region's food security, and even in these industries a significant portion of their inputs are imported—fertilized eggs and day old chicks for the poultry industry, and almost all the grains (corn and soya) for animal feed. It is not surprising therefore that the category "residue and waste from the food industry and prepared animal fodder" valued US$208.1 million or 5.5% of the food import bill in 2018. Also, a portion of the US$300 million expended in 2018 on the importation of cereals, relate to the importation of corn and soya bean for the manufacturing of animal feed. Therefore, well over 30% of the Region's food import bill relates to the livestock sector. Only a minute portion of the meat from goat and sheep consumed in the Region is produced locally. Although the region has vast marine spaces, a significant quantum of exotic fish is imported for the tourism sector, as well as processed fish (canned fish and salted fish, herring and mackerel) for the local populace. Notwithstanding significant poultry production, the inferior parts of

Table 4.2 CARICOM apicultural trade balance, 2016–2018

Products	*2016*			*2017*			*2018*		
	Export	*Import*	*Balance*	*Export*	*Import*	*Balance*	*Export*	*Import*	*Balance*
Live animals	3.6	7.3	−3.7	4.4	5.7	−1.3	3.7	7.4	−3.7
Meat and edible meat and offals	5.7	265.4	−259.7	5.4	286	−280.6	5.4	300.8	−295.5
Fish and crustaceans, molluscs and other aquatic Invertebrates	105	121.8	−16.8	169.4	30.6	38.8	170	143.3	26.7
Dairy produce; birds' eggs; natural honey; edible products of animal origin	13.1	300.7	−287.6	13	325.1	−312	12.9	360.8	−347.9
Other products of animal origin	0.3	1.9	−1.6	0.3	1.9	−1.7	0.3	1.9	−1.6
Live trees and other plants; bulbs, roots and the like; cut flowers and ornamental foliage	0.2	6.8	−6.6	0.2	6.7	−6.5	0.2	6.6	−6.4
Edible vegetables and certain roots and tubers	50.8	150.3	−99.9	53.5	155.1	−101.7	52.2	150.3	−98.1
Edible fruit and nuts; peels of citrus fruit or melons	69	81.2	−12.2	80.3	83.2	−2.9	78	88.8	−10.8
Coffee, tea, mat, and spices	49.8	37.8	12	44.1	37.6	6.5	37.3	38.9	−1.6
Cereals	184.7	297.4	−112.7	206.7	288.6	−82	153.2	300.2	−147.1
Products of the milling industry; malt; starches; inulin; wheat gluten	35.4	93	−57.6	29.3	90.5	−61.2	27	87.9	−61
Oil seeds and oleaginous fruits; miscellaneous grains, seeds and fruit; industrial or medicinal plants; straw and fodder	3.3	45.6	−42.3	3.4	50.8	−47.4	2.8	57.4	−54.6
Lac; gums, resins and other vegetable saps and extracts	0.1	3.7	−3.7	0.1	3.2	−3.1	0.1	4.1	−4
Vegetable plaiting material; other vegetable products	0.1	0.2	−0.1	0.1	0.1	0	0.1	0.2	0

Products	*2016*			*2017*			*2018*		
	Export	*Import*	*Balance*	*Export*	*Import*	*Balance*	*Export*	*Import*	*Balance*
Animal or vegetable fats and oils and their cleavages products; prepared edible fats; animal or vegetable waxes	24.5	146.5	−122	25.6	189	−63.4	25.3	186.4	−161.1
Preparations of meat, of fish or of crustaceans, molluscs or other aquatic invertibrates	12.4	167.1	−154.7	13.1	171.2	−158.1	11.8	180.4	−168.6
Sugar and sugar confectionery	178.9	173.2	5.7	175.8	183.6	−7.7	165.2	166.4	−1.2
Cocoa and cocoa preparations	16.6	45.4	−28.8	23.1	48.5	−25.4	19.5	49.9	−30.4
Preparations of cereals, flour, starch or milk; pastrycooks' products	114.6	286.5	−171.9	117.8	293	−175.2	123.5	300.3	−176.3
Preparations of vegetables, fruit, nuts or other parts of plants	117.6	240.9	−123.3	103.1	238.4	−135.3	105.3	243.2	−137.9
Miscellaneous edible preparations	79	369.9	−290.9	85.7	364.5	−278.8	83.5	417.4	−334
Beverages, spirits and vinegar	334.3	403.3	−69.1	344.8	396.5	−51.8	361.2	392.8	−31.6
Residues and waste from the food industries; prepared animal fodder	30.7	205.7	−175	24.3	183.1	−158.8	22.7	208.1	−185.4
Tobacco and manufactured tobacco substitutes	47	105.5	105.5	49.3	90.3	90.3	36.8	98.1	98.1
Total for CARICOM	1479	3557	−1916	1573	3623	−1919	1499	3792	−2134

Source CARICOM Secretariat

the chicken (back and neck) as well as processed chicken (sausages and burgers) are imported both for direct consumption locally, as well as for the burgeoning fast food industry. Bacon, ham and processed pork are also imported, despite significant production of fresh pork in the region.

A further examination of the food import bill reveals a huge importation of cereals—relating to wheat for production of flour, rice paddy/finished branded rice, cornmeal and a range of finished products from cereals. In 2018 the value of these imported food products was some US$600.5 million or some 16% of the region's food import bill. The high consumption of wheat products relates to the adoption of an alien taste in the region, where wheat is not produced, and where there is an abundance of healthier starch substitutes, such as yams, sweet potato, cassava, breadfruit, dasheen, cacoa (eddoes), which not only can be consumed in their primary form, but can also be processed into flour. Rice is produced in the region in Guyana and Suriname.

Also substantial in terms of the value of imports are beverages and spirits which account for approximately US$400 million or 10.5% of the region's food import bill. Undoubtedly a sizable portion of this is destined for the very vibrant restaurant and hotel sector. Closely related to this is the large volume of fruit concentrate and puree imported for the manufacturing of drinks and juices. This sits within the category 'preparations of vegetables, fruit, nuts or other parts of plants'. The two other significant categories of food imports are 'miscellaneous edible preparation' (US$417 million in 2018 or 11% of the import bill), which aggregates a plethora of finished (processed) products, including snacks; as well as vegetable and animal oils (US$186.4 million or 5% of the food import bill). Imports of food products from plant origin are generally lower than imports of products of animal origin. Fresh vegetables are not imported in large volumes, perhaps related to high tariff rates on these items in the Caribbean.

An examination of the region's food import bill by country, based on data from the CARICOM Secretariat by country (see Fig. 4.3), shows basically a similar structure of imports with products of animal origin toping the categories of imports, followed by cereal and cereal preparations and miscellaneous edibles and preparations. Barbados, Antigua and Barbuda, St. Kitts and Nevis and Trinidad and Tobago however import a large share of vegetables and fruits, compared to the rest of the region. Jamaica in relative and absolute terms imports more animal fodder than the rest of CARICOM, underlining its highly developed poultry and pork industries.

In relation to exports, the region's major exports by category are spirits and beverages (24% of exports in 2018), fish and fish products (11.3%), sugar (11%), cereals (10.2%), preparation of cereals, flour, starch or milk, pastrycooks' products (8.3%) and preparations of vegetables, fruit, nuts or other parts of plant (7%). Although sugar production and exports have declined significantly over the last 15 years, the rum industry remains vibrant. The region also manufactures beers, juices and drinks, even if in many instances from imported raw material. It is therefore not surprising that spirits and beverages top the region's food exports. The export of fish and fish products relates mostly to the export of fish from Guyana, lobster and conch from Jamaica and shrimps and pawns from Belize. Despite the downsizing of the region's sugar industry, Belize still maintains a fairly vibrant sugar industry, and most of the export of sugar from the region now comes out of Belize. The export of cereals is dominated by exports of rice from Guyana and Suriname. The export of different products from cereals and baked products represent finished products mainly to the Caribbean diaspora in the United States, Canada and the

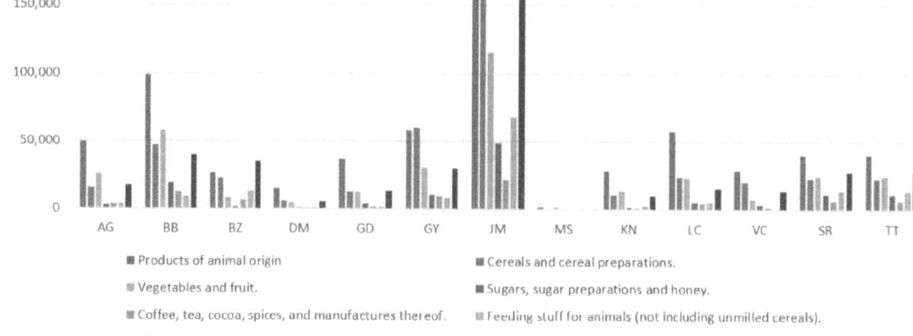

Fig. 4.3 Agricultural imports by products and country, 2018 (US$'000)

United Kingdom, coming mainly out of Jamaica and the manufacturing powerhouse of Trinidad and Tobago.

Based on the examination of the region's trade balance in food, it is clear that the region is highly dependent on imported food. From Table 4.2 it can be seen that of the 24 categories of agricultural products, over the three year period 2016–2018, a positive trade balance has only been attained for fish and crustaceans in 2018, coffee and teas in 2016 and 2017 and sugar in 2016. The overall food trade balance has been worsening over the period 2016 to 2018, moving from a deficit of US$1916 million to a deficit of US$2134 million. Looking on the trade balance on a country to country basis, only Guyana and Belize are in a net food exporting position and are in fact the least dependent on imports of food (Trotman et al., 2009).

Clearly the level of importation of foods in the region is not sustainable from a fiscal perspective, as well as within the context of the risk to the Caribbean's food security posed by increasing conflicts that disrupt the supply chain and the increasing frequency of export bans and other restrictions by net food exporting countries in times of crises. It is out of this realization that in 2020 the region adopted the "25 by 25" Initiative, championed by Guyanese President and CARICOM's Lead Head on agriculture Dr. Mohamed Irfaan Ali, essentially to reduce the region's food import bill by 25 by 25. The proposal has the backing of the CARICOM Private Sector Organization. The plan identifies opportunities for import replacement based on examination of the structure of the region's food import bill. The Initiative is premised on commercialization of the region's agricultural production with the private sector making substantial investment in the value chains surrounding poultry meat and hatching eggs, corn and rice for production of animal feed, meat (beef, pork and mutton), niche vegetables, cassava and coconut products (Ali, 2023). These targeted areas for investment are consistent with categories of food items comprising the bulk of the food import bill.

Although the '25 by 25' Initiative rests on commercialization and private sector investment, it envisions a critical role for the public sector in relation to investment in infrastructure (roads, irrigation) and research and development, creating a conducive policy environment, an incentive framework and de-risking of the sector. There is also a critical role identified for the CARICOM Secretariat as a regional institution in reforming the CET and the management of waivers and suspension of rules of origin to provide greater protection to regional production and trade.

The Secretariat also has a role in overhauling of critical institutions such as CAHFSA to deal with sanitary and phyto-sanitary issues; and CARDI to provide planting material, technology transfer and technical support to production endeavours. Critical also to the success of the initiative is the resolution of the transportation and logistics challenges of moving goods across the region, as well as digitization of markets to increase transparency of market information and acceleration of e-commerce to speed up transactions. Contract farming between large investors and small farmers is also encouraged to ensure that small holders have a stake in this new commercialized agriculture.

The tripartite partnership among government, private sector and farmers at the country level to realize the objectives of the '25 by 25' Initiative is crucial as demonstrated by efforts in Jamaica at import substitution (see Box 4.1). The '25 by 25' has also correctly identified the areas in the food import bill that must be targeted for local production in order to have desired impact, as well as the support required by the government. It is therefore critical to examine the capacity of the State to make these critical investments and create the policy environment. The major deficiency of the "25 by 25" Initiative is its lack of emphasis on nutritional security, focusing largely on expansion of food production.

Box 4.1 Irish Potato Production for Import Substitution in Jamaica

In the aftermath of the global food crisis of 2007/2008, the Government of Jamaica turned its attention to increasing production of critical staple crops, the consumption of which was being mainly satisfied by imports. The inspiration for this was the sharp rise in commodity prices attendant on the crisis and the consequential rise in the food import bill. In 2008 Jamaica's food import bill increased sharply to US$885 million up from US$731 million (21%). Although the food import bill fell to US$802 million in 2009, it was still 10% higher than the 2007 level. In 2010 therefore the Government initiated an import substitution programme involving irish potato.

Irish potato was selected because in 2009 local production of 8,707,998 tonnes was only satisfying approximately 50% of overall consumption of table irish potato. Also, Jamaica possesses the agro-climatic conditions to produce more irish potatoes. The production of this crop was engaged by small farmers operating in most instances on less than 1 hectare of land. Given this reality, it was imperative that Government throw its full support behind this initiative. Farmers were identified in the main potato growing areas and partially provided with such inputs as quality seeds, chemicals, fertilizer, land preparation support, training and extension. The farmers had to provide equity of some 50% of the cost of production. In this regard, the Ministry facilitated loans from the People's Cooperative Banks, secured by the distributors of irish potatoes, who provided secure contracts to the farmers for their expected output of irish potato. These distributors were in fact the major importers of irish potatoes, who were persuaded by the Government to reduce their level of imports and buy local irish potatoes from the farmers participating in the programme. They committed to buy all the irish potatoes produced by the farmers under the programme, store said irish potatoes and release to the market after the reaping season. After reaping the distributors ceased importation until all the local production in storage was exhausted. The results of the programme are shown in Table 4.3.

Table 4.3 Irish potato production and imports, Jamaica, 2008–2013

Year	*Gross production (t)*	*Imports (t)*	*Total availability (t)*	*% Local supply of total*
2008	4,928,994	10,586,575	15,515,569	32%
2009	8,707,998	8,319,255	17,027,253	51%
2010	11,221,998	5,408,715	16,630,731	67%
2011	15,334,000	4,658,866	19,992,866	77%
2012	15,395,800	3,912,798	19,308,598	79%
2013	17,421,000	2,241,923	19,662,923	87%

Source Ministry of Agriculture, Fisheries and Mining

The attainment of 87% self-sufficiency in table irish potatoes in Jamaica was a significant feat, saving foreign exchange, improving farmers' income, and boosting rural development and food security. The programme is still operational, with adjustments in the level of Government's monetary input from time to time and the level of imports based on disruption of local production due to adverse weather conditions. RADA reported that in the period 2016 to February 2020, the Ministry of Agriculture mobilized 14,000 farmers on 3551 hectares to produce some 43,433 tonnes of irish potatoes, expending some $558 million in support. Overall, irish potato production continues to flourish in Jamaica, from the 8,707,998 tonnes in 2009 to 18,669,000 in 2022 (PIOJ, 2023).

Systemic Factors Impacting Food Production

The overarching strategy of the '25 by 25' Initiative surrounds the commercialization of agricultural production in the region led by private sector investments (Ali, 2023). Commercialization implies the transformation of the largely subsistence nature of agriculture in the region, being dominated by a myriad of small holders, typically semi-literate, operating on small marginal plots, without access to technology, finance, insurance and transparent market information. These farmers also have to contend with the absence of adequate infrastructure—such as good farm roads, irrigation, drainage, post-harvest facilities. In Jamaica, 79% of the farmers were operating on less than 1 hectare of land, and together they own only 15% of farm lands in 2007 (STATIN, 2007). This picture is replicated across all the Region—in 1989 in Barbados 95% of holdings were under 1 hectare, comprising only 10% of all farm lands (Government of Barbados, 1992); in 1995 in Dominica 74% of holdings were under 1 hectare, representing 24% of all farm lands (Ministry of Agriculture & Central Statistics Office, 1995); in Trinidad and Tobago in 2004, 35% of all holdings were under 1 hectare, representing 3.3% of all farm lands (Ministry of Planning & Development, 2014); in 1986 in St. Vincent and the Grenadines 39% of all holdings were less than 1 hectare, accounting for 1% of all farm lands (Ministry of Agriculture, Industry and Labour, 1989); and for St. Lucia in 2007, 83% of all holdings were less than 1 hectare and comprising 32% of all farm lands (Ministry of Agriculture, Forestry and Fisheries, 2007). With such a large proportion of farmers operating on small acreages, they can barely produce a surplus beyond the consumption needs of their families and cannot in their current state be relied upon to engage in large-scale commercial production.

The widespread scenario of a substantial number of small holders in the sector is a direct product of the region's legacy of slavery and colonialism, when large acreages of land devoted to export agriculture were concentrated in the hands of a few. Despite the wave of independence in the region since 1962, this historically skewed distribution of lands has not been corrected, notwithstanding a plethora of land reform initiatives. This is a fundamental structural problem militating against commercialization of agriculture, which must be addressed, if existing small farmers must participate in this commercialization thrust embedded in the '25 by 25' Initiative. Given the modest utilization of available agricultural lands, especially in the larger territories of Guyana, Suriname, Belize, the

Bahamas, and to a lesser extent Jamaica and the other islands, deliberate efforts will have to be made by governments to address this situation. This is particularly important since the '25 by 25' Initiative envisions a critical role for existing small holders in the sector, working in a contractual relationship with the private sector, whose investments are being courted. Concomitant with providing more lands to farmers is the need for great efforts to cluster farmers and strengthen farmer organizations to partner to engage contract farming, better market their products and engage good farming practices.

Jamaica has had a very long and successful tradition of small farmers working with large private sector producers in the broiler industry on a contractual basis. In this relationship, the private sector players provide critical inputs and technical assistance to farmers to meet their product standards, while farmers provide the initial capital for the construction of bird houses, as well as labour and other working capital. The contract between the private sector players and the farmers plays a key role in the farmers accessing financing capital and gives the private player the security and assurance to provide critical inputs upfront, secure in the knowledge that 100% of the farmers output will be delivered to them. This model, with adjustments, can be replicated in other production areas and in other countries. There is also no shortage of capital in the region to inhibit the region's private sector from investing in the agricultural ventures outlined in the '25 by 25' proposal. The critical question is the government's willingness and capacity to create the enabling environment such as installing infrastructure of a public goods nature, creating the requisite incentive and policy regime to support local production and discourage imports, de-risk the sector and increase funding for research and development, extension and the building out of a modern agricultural health and food safety architecture, which are all critical elements of successful commercial agricultural production.

The '25 by 25' Initiative will require significant acreage of new lands going into production. The greatest impact in terms of reducing the import bill is to produce a critical portion of the animal feed and grains for animal feed imported from outside the region, as well as to expand livestock production—particularly beef, goat meat and milk. This is logical as these products represent the largest portion of the food import bill. This target is realistic, as up to the 1980s many countries in the region were producing a much larger percentage of the volumes of these products they consumed. These activities however, by their nature, are very land-intensive. A major role for governments will therefore be to make lands available for these ventures, as governments remain the major owners of lands across the region. Belize, Guyana and Suriname, which in 2020 were only engaging 7.54%, 6.31% and 0.54% of their agricultural lands according to data from FAOSTAT, are best poised to engage these production activities. Fortuitously also, these three countries are also the most endowed with water resources. Other territories such as Jamaica, Trinidad and Tobago, St. Kitts and Nevis and Barbados would also have some lands available which were formerly engaged in sugar production, given the reduction of sugar production in these islands. However they would not have the comparative advantage of Guyana, Belize and Suriname with more abundant water. Jamaica, Barbados, Trinidad and Tobago and St. Kitts and Nevis could therefore engage orchard production to produce fruits to substitute the huge volume of concentrates and purees being imported into the region by juice manufacturers. In the case of Barbados, Antigua and Barbuda, Trinidad and Tobago and St. Kitts and Nevis, production of fruits and vegetables need to be expanded, since they import a higher level of vegetables and fruits compared to the rest of CARICOM (see Fig. 4.3). Given relative scarcity of land in Barbados, Antigua and Barbuda and St. Kitts and Nevis, as well as lack of abundant water resources, intensive systems should be used to produce vegetables, such as hydroponics and greenhouse.

While land distribution to small holders and availability of land for expanded production are structural issues which need to be addressed in order to facilitate the envisioned commercialization and expansion of production, these matters are easily resolved, as governments are huge land owners. Availability of lands however, is necessary but not sufficient. For efficient and sustainable production, agricultural lands must be outfitted with the critical infrastructure of irrigation, drainage (where necessary) and roads. The absence of these infrastructure represents one of the critical structural issues inhibiting expanded production, rendering production uncompetitive and reinforcing the predominance of small holders in the agricultural landscape. For high yielding and sustainable production, irrigation is non-negotiable, particularly with the almost yearly cycle of droughts, precipitated by climate change. Rain-fed agriculture, as practised by thousands of small holders cannot give the kind of productivity and reliability of production, which are critical conditions for profitable, sustainable production.

Installation of irrigation systems is however a capital-intensive endeavour and is clearly a public good, warranting investment by the State. The record of CARICOM States in investing in critical infrastructure is wanting. According to FAOSTATS data on 'Agriculture net capital stock', which measures investment in physical investment in agriculture, only the Bahamas, Belize, Guyana and Suriname, of the 12 countries for which data is available, show any appreciable increase in the agricultural investment over the period 1995 to 2021 (see Fig. 4.4).

Specifically in relation to irrigation, the countries with the largest areas of irrigated lands are Guyana, Haiti, Suriname, Jamaica and Trinidad and Tobago, although in relative terms the irrigated areas represent a minute fraction of total irrigable lands, and contrasts sharply with other Caribbean neighbours such as Cuba, Dominican Republic and Venezuela (FAO and CDB, 2019). In fact, irrigation schemes in the English-speaking typically serve traditional plantation crops and many were constructed in the colonial era (see Box 4.2 with history of irrigation investment in Jamaica).

Box 4.2 History of Investment in Irrigation in Jamaica

The history of irrigation expansion in Jamaica is inextricably linked with the history of the sugar industry, which dominated Jamaica's agricultural landscape until the 2000s when sugar production sharply declined. Up to independence in 1962, irrigation systems exclusively served sugar cane

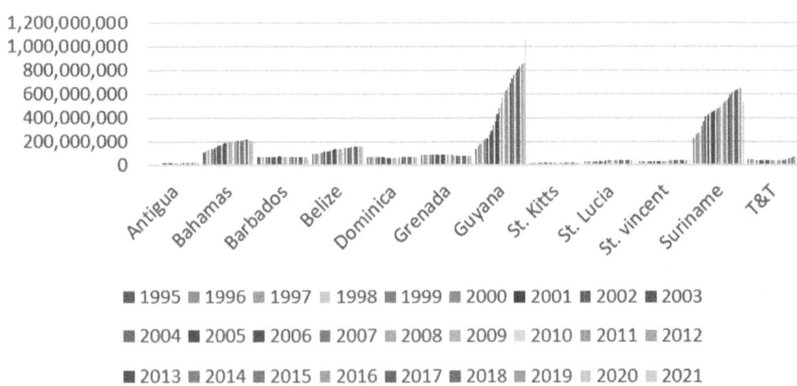

Fig. 4.4 Agriculture net capital stock, constant 1995 USD (*Source* FAOSTAT)

production. While cane was grown under rain fed conditions in Western, Eastern and the hilly interior of Jamaica, irrigation had to be employed on the vast alluvial plains of South Central Jamaica, spanning the parishes of Clarendon and St. Catherine. These plains had the most fertile soils in Jamaica, flat and amenable to mechanization, and therefore ideal for large scale commercial sugarcane production. The Rio Cobre Irrigation System was commissioned in 1876 to irrigate sugar cane in the Caymanas, Bernard Lodge and Inswood areas of St. Catherine. Cane growing west of these areas was supported by the St. Dorothy's Irrigation System, established in 1956. On the Clarendon side, the Mid-Clarendon Irrigation System was opened in 1950 to support cane growing on the western side of the parish, while on the eastern side the West Indies Sugar Company established a series of wells to support cane growing in the Monymusk area, where they had a factory.

It was only after independence that attention began to be focused on the irrigation needs of small farmers outside of the cane growing areas. A small system was established in Hounslow in a section of the highly productive South St. Elizabeth in 1968, followed by an even smaller system in Braco, Trelawny on the Jamaican North Coast in 1983, and a system in St. Thomas at Yallahs in 1993.

In 1998 the Government decided to take a comprehensive look at irrigation needs across the entire island. This inspired the formulation of the National Irrigation Development Plan (NIDP), which proposed some 51 irrigation projects across the Island at a then cost of US$106 million. In the 25 years since the formulation of this Master Plan, only six of those projects have been completed covering just over 2000 hectares of land, according to data from the National Irrigation Commission, involving rehabilitation and expansion of two existing system (Yallahs and Hounslow) and construction of four new systems—Beacon/Little Park in St. Elizabeth, Seven Rivers in St. James, New Forest/Duff House in Manchester/St. Elizabeth and Colbeck in St. Catherine. Two systems are now under construction in Clarendon and St. Catherine. These investments bring the irrigation coverage in Jamaica to only 6%.

The investment in irrigation has been made through multilateral loans. The pace of implementation of the NIDP must be accelerated if the transformation of the sector is to happen. Equally, attention has to be paid to the increased use of renewable energy to power these systems, to reduce the cost of the service to farmers, as well as the nation's carbon footprint. Greater technical support is also required by farmers in water management and greater use of water saving on-farm equipment, such as drip systems.

One of the critical structural issues facing the agriculture sector in the region is the failure of policymakers to embrace a value chain approach to agricultural development. The focus of government programmes in the past has been disproportionately on providing inputs to farmers and land distribution schemes, often without infrastructure (Jefferson, 1972). A more sustainable approach however ought to embrace every facet of the chain from 'farm to fork', that is, from pre-production to primary production, post-harvest management, value addition and marketing. While there are investments in each of these segments, efforts have been disjointed. For instance, while investments have been made in cocoa seedling production, distribution of seeds to farmers, systems for collection and consolidation from small farmers and facilities for drying and processing cocoa, little attention has been paid to value addition until in the recent past in Trinidad and Tobago and Jamaica. The region has been content in selling the raw product as commodity. Hence, Table 4.2 shows a continuing negative trade balance for cocoa products and preparations.

If the "25 by 25" Initiative is to succeed, then each of the identified areas for expansion of production must be the subject of an industry development programme. The entire value chain has to be examined to determine what are the weakest links in the chain, which will require investments to resolve, and who must make those investments? For example, to rebuild the region's livestock industry, which is the subject of the largest portion of food imports, does the region have sufficient heifers to expand the beef and dairy industry? Are there sufficient local feed stocks? Does the region possess the capacity to rapidly expand local grass varieties for pastures? How large is the capacity for rapid multiplication of local breeds in relation to artificial insemination, embryo transfer, etc.? Given the low numbers and productivity of goats and cattle is there need to import more productive breeds and adopt them to local conditions? To what extent food safety infrastructure will have to be enhanced, that is, modern abattoirs and traceability systems installed? What is the processing capacity for milk and dairy products? In what areas should public investment be directed and what areas are suitable for private investment?

One of the critical bottlenecks for expanded production of almost any crop or livestock enterprise is the availability of clean planting material and animals. The region has not been investing sufficiently in preserving its plant and animal genetic resources for food production. Hence, it has become dependent on importation for planting material for most crops and live animals and semen for livestock production. CARDI has been doing a mammoth job in terms of seed production in specific crops such as hot pepper, cassava and some legumes, as well as proliferating rapid multiplication techniques for small ruminants. Diseases have ravaged a number of the region's crops and work needs to be done in cleaning a number varieties of sweet potato, cassava, yams, ginger, coconuts, citrus and other crops. CARDI has also been involved in work on improving germplasm for a number of crops including forage legumes, root crops, vegetable crops, fruit crops, cereals and ornamentals. However, the most developed plant breeding programmes in the region relate to traditional export crops, particularly sugar cane and banana. A sustainable supply of good quality seeds and planting material therefore remains a challenge (Mitchell & Ahmad, 2003). The productivity of a number of local breeds of animals has been reduced because of a lack of improvement of these breeds. Research and Development Departments of Ministries must direct urgent attention to this area, in partnership with development partners and the private sector. No industry can be built or expanded in the agricultural sector without a sustainable source of good planting material and breeds of animals.

Other critical infrastructure required for expanded production for import substitution and export expansion are post-harvest facilities for storage, grading, sorting and processing of primary production, as well as a robust agricultural health and food safety infrastructure to facilitate testing, traceability and labelling. Even given relatively low levels of production, the region is losing as high as an estimated 30–40% of its production of fresh fruits and vegetables to post-harvest losses. Regional food exports have to meet stringent food quality standards and traceability must be assured. Local consumers are also deserving of safe foods, that is, both food produced locally and imported. The huge tourism industry in the region as well as the plethora of foreign-based fast food franchises in the region are similarly demanding food certified to be of a particular standard. Modern commercial agriculture therefore needs this kind of infrastructure to survive. Even intra-regional trade in food is being stymied by issues related to sanitary and phyto-sanitary considerations. The long struggle to get Jamaican patties into Trinidad and honey from Grenada into Trinidad and Tobago are cases in point. At the national level therefore, countries have to invest more in these facilities, as well as training of primary producers and workers in post-harvest facilities in Good Agriculture Practices and Good Manufacturing Practices.

At the regional level, institutions like CAHFSA and CROS-Q must be strengthened to provide training and technical support at the local level.

Apart from the structural impediments to regional agricultural expansion mentioned above, which are mainly physical in nature, at both the regional and country level, there are critical policy issues that need to be resolved to facilitate the expansion of agriculture in the region. The entire incentive regime at the country level needs to be revisited. In the nascent post-independence period the development of the manufacturing and tourism sectors were catalysed through a comprehensive set of well thought-out incentives. Many of these incentives were the subject of legislation and range from tax holidays, waiver of duties on importation of inputs, accelerated depreciation, etc. In fact some of these incentives worked against the agricultural sector. For example, waiver of duties on agricultural raw material undermined local production of said raw material. Within the context of the new thrust of expanding agricultural production for food security and exports, a comprehensive slew of incentives must now be contemplated to attract and sustain the private sector investments envisioned, including strengthening the linkages between agriculture and tourism (see Box 4.3 for Jamaica's experience in linking agriculture and tourism). The new wave of incentives now being rolled out in some countries relates to the Business Processing Outsourcing industry. Many countries have enacted Special Economic Zone legislation. To what extent are these tailored to facilitate agricultural production as opposed to factory and processing activities?

Box 4.3 The Tourism Linkage Programme, Jamaica

The Government of Jamaica through its *Master Plan for Tourism* and the *Vision 2030 National Development Plan* identified the development and strengthening of sustainable linkages between tourism and the productive sectors of agriculture and manufacturing as a strategic objective for economic growth. In keeping with this objective, in June 2013 by Cabinet decision the Tourism Linkage Programme was established in the Ministry of Tourism and Entertainment to promote and foster increased consumption of local agricultural and manufactured good within the tourism industry.

In 2015 the Ministry commissioned a demand study to estimate the demand for agricultural products in the tourism industry, ascertain the source of supply of these products, expenditure on agricultural goods, the level of leakage of revenue from the sector through the importation of agricultural goods and the receptivity of interests in the tourism sector to substitute local supplies for imports. The study shows that the estimated demand for agricultural goods was $19.4 billion, 75% of which represents poultry, meats and seafood and fruits. (Ministry of Tourism and Entertainment, 2015). It was estimated that between $1.6 billion and $5 billion of this expenditure was leaked through importation. There was therefore enormous opportunities for import substitution and cantaloupe, iceberg lettuce, irish potatoes, red jumbo onions, rice and sweet corn were identified as prime candidates for import substitution. The study also indicates high level of receptivity of tourism interests to source more agricultural produce locally. There were however some key constraints the agricultural sector had to overcome in order to seize this opportunity. The constraints include the inability of local farmers to produce the quantum and quality of produce demanded by the tourism sector on a consistent basis due to their size and the tendency of local farmers not to honour contractual obligations and sell to the highest bidder.

In the face of the structural challenges of size militating against the capacity of local farmers to supply the tourism sector consistently, the Ministry of Agriculture rolled out an Agro Park Programme. Under this programme, the Ministry organised farmers in clusters on designated lands outfitted with irrigation, roads, post-harvest facilities, as well as provided farmers with technical support and facilitated contracts with buyers in the hotel and restaurant sector, as well as loans from the People's Cooperative Blank. The Tourism Linkage Programme itself evolved into the Tourism Linkages Network, under which the Ministry of Tourism established the Agri-Linkages Exchange (ALEX), an online marketing platform connecting agricultural producers with buyers in the tourism sector. The Ministry of Tourism also supported the production of strawberries for supplying the tourism sector, as well an annual Coffee Festival to promote the sale and consumption of Blue Mountain Coffee by tourists and locals. These initiatives have paid good dividends to the agricultural sector directly and the Jamaican economy generally. Data from the Ministry of Tourism show that there are currently 1200 farmers registered on the ALEX platform and between September 2018 and August 2023 agricultural produce to the value of approximately $1.1 billion sold to hotels and restaurants on this platform.

Possibilities still abound for Jamaican farmers to harvest wealth from the tourism sector. A follow up 2019 Demand study show that with the addition of 32 new hotels since the 2015 study, demand for agricultural produce in the sector doubled to $39.6 billion, with estimated leakage of $6.5 billion through imports (Ministry of Tourism, 2019). With well over 4 million tourists visiting the island and growing, and with over 31,000 hotel rooms and growing, properly organised, Jamaican farmers can grow and supply more of the food imported by the sector, particularly products of animal origin, which comprise 75% of food imported into the tourism sector.

On the regional side, the chronic under funding of regional institutions such as CARDI, CAHFSA and CRFM must be resolved if agricultural sector is to flourish and expand. In many of the smaller OECS countries, CARDI is in fact larger than Ministries' research capacity. The implementation deficit in respect to the management of CET is a critical issue. Private sector will not expand production, if having attained the capacity to supply regional demand with these products, they face resistance from individual countries in applying the CET to extra regional competing imports. The CARICOM Secretariat must be more judicious with the suspension of CET and waiving of rules of origin, which are counterproductive to regional production and trade. There is also the need for a faster and more predictable mechanism to resolve issues relating to non-trade barriers and the region must come together to find innovative means of resolving the chronic intra-regional transport problem to facilitate the movement of goods and people.

Conclusion

While agricultural production is on an upward trajectory in countries such as Guyana, Suriname, Belize, and to a lesser extent Jamaica and Trinidad and Tobago, the Region's production is simply not making a sufficient contribution to its food security. It is however commendable that the Region's agriculture survived the onslaught of trade liberalization in its main export market in the EU for sugar and banana, by increasing production of domestic food crop and non-traditional export. However the growth in these subsectors have not been able to arrest the growing imports of food. Dependence on food imports is high, satisfying more than 50% of local consumption, and as high as over 90% in countries such as the Bahamas and Barbados.

The structure of the Region's food import bill shows a predominance of food of animal origin, animal feed and grains for the manufacturing of animal feed, to support the Region's poultry and pork industries. Cereals—rice and wheat, as well as processed cereal products, is the next largest category of imports, reflecting the Caribbean's acquired taste for a foreign staple, even when the region is producing enough and better carbohydrate (yams, bananas, breadfruit, dasheen, sweet potatoes), to satisfy its dietary need for this category of food. The region also imports large quantities of fruit concentrate and puree for the manufacturing of juices. These imported products provide opportunities for import substitution. The region similarly needs to scale up production of niche products for exports, such as herbs, spices, cocoa, coffee and ginger, for which it has a distinctive advantage in relation to taste and quality. These products in their value-added form now have access to a number of markets, such as the EU, under the Economic Partnership Agreement with CARIFORUM.

However, in order to sustainably replace an appreciable portion of the identified imported foods, as well as ramp up exports, the region must address a number of structural impediments to production and trade, in order to increase the competiveness of production, attract private sector investment, and transform small holders' production from subsistence to profitable production. Critical imperatives in this regard include land reforms; investment in physical infrastructure such as irrigation, drainage, roads, post-harvest facilities and traceability systems; investment in research and development, extension and technology transfer, marketing and training; and governments creating the policy and regulatory framework to incentivise production, de-risk the sector and promote linkages between agriculture and the tourism and manufacturing sectors. At the regional level, regional institutions should be bolstered and properly funded to support expanded agricultural production through the increasing the capacity for the production and supply of clean planting material, preserving germplasm, assisting firms and countries navigate technical issues in trade, particularly phytosanitary issues, and judiciously managing CET regime.

Attention to expanded agricultural production is imperative in the face of increased conflicts across the world, disrupting supply chains and the increased vulnerability of the region to export restrictions by net food exporting countries in times of crises. Fiscally also the levels of food imports to the region is not sustainable. Every effort must therefore be made to support the "25 by 25" Initiative.

References

Ali, M. (2023, February). *From Crisis to Opportunity. An Innovative Approach to Food Security in the Region*. CARICOM.

Bahamas National Statistical Institute. (2023). *Economic Accounts*.

Bolland, O. (1981). Systems of Domination After Slavery: Control of Land and Labour in the British West Indies After 1838. *Comparative Studies in Society and History, 23*(4), 591–619.

Caribbean Agribusiness. (2020). *Profile of Antigua and Barbuda*. CARICOM Secretariat, Georgetown.

Caribbean Agricultural Research and Development Institute. (2018). *Building a Productive and Resilient Regional Agriculture Sector. CARDI Strategic Plan 2018–2022.*

Central Statistics Office of Dominica. (2020). *2018 National Accounts Statistics.*

FAO. (2024). *World Food Situation*. fao.org/worldfoodsituation/foodpricesindex/en/

FAO and CDB. (2019). *Study on the State of Agriculture in the Caribbean* (212pp.). Rome. Licence:CCBY-NC-SA,3.0 IGO.

Government of Barbados. (1992). *1989 Agricultural Census*. Bridgetown.

Government of Guyana.(2013). *National Strategy for Agriculture in Guyana: 2013- 2020*. Georgetown.

Government of Trinidad and Tobago. (2023). *Review of the Economy 2023*. finance.gov.tt/wp-content/uploads/2023/10/ROE-2023-WEB.pdf

Hall, D. (1959). *Free Jamaica 1838–1865: An Economic History*. Yale University Press.

Hayman, A. (2023). *Building Climate Resilient Agriculture in Caribbean Countries: Suriname*. IICA.

Jefferson, O. (1972). *The Post-War Development of Jamaica*. The Gresham Press, England.

Ministry of Agriculture and Central Statistics Office. (1995). *1995 Dominica Agricultural Census. Final Results*. Roseau, Dominica.

Ministry of Agriculture, Forestry and Fisheries. (2007). *2007 St. Lucia Census of Agriculture. Final Report*. Castries, St. Lucia.

Ministry of Agriculture, Industry and Labour. (1989). *1985–86 Agricultural for St. Vincent and the Grenadines*. Kingtown.

Ministry of Planning and Development. (2014). *2004 Agricultural Census*. Port of Spain, Trinidad and Tobago.

Ministry of Tourism. (2019). Tourism Demand Study. Kingston.

Ministry of Tourism and Entertainment. (2015). *Tourism Demand Study.* Kingston.

Mitchel, S., & Ahmad, M. (2003, February). Agricultural Biotechnology in the Caribbean. *AgBiotechNet 2003,* Vol. 5, ABN 106.

Parliament of the Republic of Trinidad and Tobago. (2022). *Budget Guide 2023. Ministry of Agriculture, Land and Fisheries.* https://www.ttparliament.org/budget-guide-2023-ministry-of-agricuture-land-and-fisheries

Planning Institute of Jamaica. (2021). *Economic and Social Survey, Jamaica.* Kingston.

Planning Institute of Jamaica. (2023). *Social and Economic Survey, Jamaica.* Kingston.

Stanberry, D. (2019, December 22). *Deciphering the Food Import Bill (Part 1).* Sunday Gleaner.

Stanberry, D. (2022). *How Trade Liberalization Affects a Sugar—Dependent Community in Jamaica: Global Action, Local Impact.* Palgrave Macmillan.

Statistical Institute of Jamaica. (2007). *Census of Agriculture.* Kingston.

Trotman, A., Gordon, R., Hutchinson, S., Singh, R., & McRae-Smith, D. (2009). Policy Responses to GEC Impacts on Food Availability and Affordability in the Caribbean Community. *Environmental Science and Policy, 12,* 529–541.

World Bank. (2023). *Agriculture, Forestry and Fisheries, Value Added 8% of GDP Dominica.* https://data.worldbank.org/indicator/NV.AGR.TOTL.25?Locations=DM

Wuddivira, M. et al. (2017). *Challenges of Food and Nutrition Security in the Caribbean.* In Challenges and Opportunities For Food and Nutrition Security in the Americas: The View of the Academies of Sciences.

CHAPTER 5

Food Access in the Caribbean

Access to food refers to an individual's ability to acquire adequate resources to obtain sufficient, good quality, appropriate food for a nutritious diet. These resources may be physical or they may be economic in nature to ensure that the food is within easy reach and affordable. Lowitt et al. (2016) found that of the four dimensions of Food Security, food access has received the least attention from both regional and national actors.

This chapter will, therefore, explore the two main aspects of food access—physical and economic access, with the aim of highlighting the challenges faced by Caribbean countries as well as the policies and programmes being implemented to address the challenges. *Case studies will also be presented to show best practices and success stories where selected countries or the region as a whole have overcome these challenges.* The policy gaps which still need to be addressed will also be highlighted.

> The SDG targets of relevance to Food Access are:
>
> **2.1** By 2030, end hunger and ensure access by all people, in particular the poor and people in vulnerable situations, including infants, to safe, nutritious and sufficient food all year round.

D. Stanberry and L. Fletcher-Paul, *Food Security in the Caribbean*, Palgrave Studies in Agricultural Economics and Food Policy,
https://doi.org/10.1007/978-3-031-66055-9_5

2.A Increase investment, including through enhanced international cooperation, in rural infrastructure, agricultural research and extension services, technology development and plant and livestock gene banks in order to enhance agricultural productive capacity in developing countries, in particular least developed countries.
2.B Correct and prevent trade restrictions and distortions in world agricultural markets, including through the parallel elimination of all forms of agricultural export subsidies and all export measures with equivalent effect, in accordance with the mandate of the Doha Development Round.
2.C Adopt measures to ensure the proper functioning of food commodity markets and their derivatives and facilitate timely access to market information, including on food reserves, in order to help limit extreme food price volatility.

Physical Access

Physical Access refers to, inter alia, the roads, markets and marketing infrastructure which provide farmers with the means to sell their produce and earn an income from the sale of the produce. For households, physical access represents the places where consumers purchase healthy nutritious food, such as the community markets, supermarkets and food vendors.

At the national level, the network of roads that link farmers and consumers to markets, especially in rural areas, as well as the ability to access factors of production such as land and labour are key considerations of physical access. At the regional and international levels, issues such as trade, transportation and market access are important concerns. Other factors which affect physical access include war, civil strife, inadequate logistics for food distribution, disruptions due to climatic events and market imperfections.

Economic Access

Economic access refers to the ability of households to purchase or afford food. According to the FAO's State of Food Insecurity Report 2022, "Currently, almost 3.1 billion people in the world cannot afford even the cheapest healthy diet even though this diet is essential to good health and well-being".

Key considerations for estimating economic access include employment and poverty levels, income, inflation rates and food prices. Social and political factors which affect the ability of vulnerable groups such as women, youth, indigenous peoples and migrants to acquire food are therefore, major considerations of economic access.

The FAO in its publication on the Future of Food and Agriculture—Drivers and Triggers for Transformation (2022) has identified rural and urban poverty, food prices and widespread and deep rooted inequalities as the main drivers affecting food access and livelihoods. They posit that by addressing these drivers, it may be possible to shape the future of agrifood systems.

Measurement of Food Access

Because of its many dimensions, food access is determined as a function of several factors—rural road networks, incomes, consumption, poverty levels, food prices, inflation and more recently food affordability, to name a few. In the Caribbean, where there is a dearth of reliable and timely data, the development of reliable indicators of food access has proved to be a daunting task.

With respect to physical access, the rural road network in continental Caribbean countries such as Guyana, Suriname and Belize and the larger islands such as Jamaica and Trinidad and Tobago may be a considered to account for transporting food produced in remote, rural interior communities to the urban centres. Even in the smaller countries of the Lesser Antilles, the condition of the rural roads may also affect physical access. The presence of markets in rural communities may also be an important indicator of physical access, particularly by persons living in those communities.

At the national and regional levels, poverty indices are a good indicator of economic access. National Reports on Living Standards are therefore, a good source of information on poverty levels in the Caribbean. However, in many Caribbean countries, the most recent poverty assessments were conducted in the early 2000s. Belize, Jamaica and St Lucia are notable exceptions. The Statistical Institute of Belize conducted a Poverty Study in 2018/19, which was published in 2021. In the case of Jamaica and St Lucia, National Reports on Living Standards in those two countries were conducted in 2019 and 2018, respectively.

Unemployment data may also be used as an indicator of economic access. Data on unemployment are published by agencies such as the International Labour Organization and the World Bank annually and they are also disaggregated by gender and age.

At the household level, data on the amount of money spent on food and other necessities, food consumed and market value over specified periods of time are gathered from household income and expenditure surveys. Food consumption tables are then used to convert food expenditure and consumption to energy intake. For some indices, questions are also asked about coping strategies for managing food shortages.

The FAO and CDB Study of the State of Agriculture in the Caribbean (2019) measured Food Access by the depth of the food deficit i.e.—how many calories are needed to help the undernourished escape from their current status, all things being equal.

More recently, the FAO in its Regional Overview of Food Security and Nutrition in Latin America and the Caribbean, 2022, used the cost and affordability of a healthy diet as indicators of food access. They further developed an index of food affordability which identifies "the least-cost healthy diet available at each given time and place that meets recommendations from food-based dietary guidelines (FBDGs)". To develop the indicators, they analysed three reference diets (FAO et al., 2020)—an energy-sufficient diet that provides adequate daily calories relative to energy needs; a nutrient-adequate diet that provides not only adequate calories but also adequate amounts of essential nutrients in a balanced mix of carbohydrates, protein, fat, essential vitamins and minerals, with macronutrient intakes within the Acceptable Macronutrient Distribution Range (AMDR) set by the Institute of Medicine (IOM); and a healthy diet that provides adequate calories and nutrients but also includes more diversified foods from several different food groups, as recommended by food-based dietary guidelines (FBDGs).

The cost of a healthy diet is defined as the cost of the least expensive locally available foods to meet energy requirements of 2330 kcal/day as well as nutrient requirements established by national FBDGs. Affordability was measured by the percentage and the number of people unable to afford the cost of a healthy diet, the cost is compared with country-specific income distributions. A healthy diet is considered unaffordable when its cost exceeds 52% of the income in a country.

Status of Food Access in the Caribbean

Poverty

According to the UN Sustainable Development Goals Report of 2023, just prior to the COVID-19 pandemic, globally extreme poverty levels fell from 10.8% in 2015 to 8.5% in 2019 (Fig. 5.1). However, with the advent of the pandemic in 2020, extreme poverty levels rose to 9.3%, with the number of persons living in extreme poverty reaching 724 million, some 90 million more than the pre-pandemic projection. In 2021, the extreme poverty rate post pandemic fell to 8.8%, but recovery rates varied among countries. Forty-one percent of low-income countries experienced higher poverty rates compared with the previous year while only 13% of upper-middle income countries experienced an increase in rates. It is predicted that if current trends continue, approximately 575 million people or 7% of the global population will still be living in extreme poverty by 2030, the majority in sub-Sahara Africa. Moreover, the UN further predicts that only one third of countries globally will halve their national poverty rates by 2030 from 2015.

At the regional level, the United Nations Economic Commission for Latin America and the Caribbean (ECLAC) in its Social Panorama of

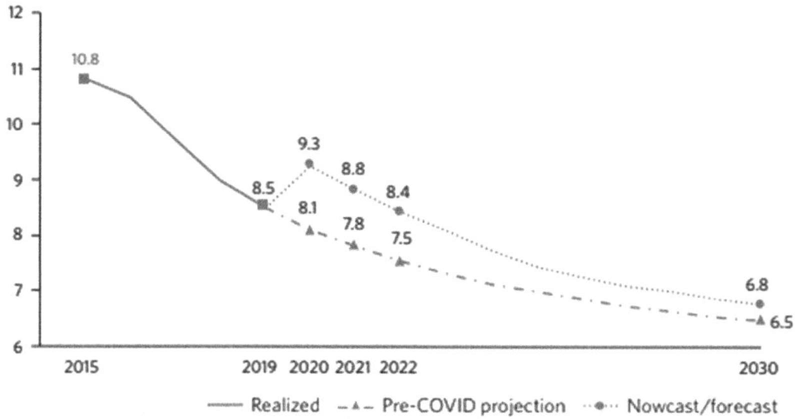

Fig. 5.1 Proportion of the world's population living below $2.15/day, 2015–2019 realized and 2020–2030 forecast and projected (percentage) (*Source* Sustainable Development Goals Report for 2023)

Latin America and the Caribbean 2022 report, indicated that while there was a slight decline in poverty and extreme poverty rates recorded in Latin America and the Caribbean in 2021, the levels remain above pre-pandemic levels in 2022. However, the report focused mainly on Latin America as data from most Caribbean countries are not available.

At the National level, the data on poverty levels in selected CARICOM countries are presented in Fig. 5.2. The data reveal that Haiti, with its ongoing problems of political instability, violence and insecurity, continues to be the country with the highest poverty rates in the region and indeed, is among the poorest in the world. The World Bank in 2021, estimated a poverty rate of 87.6% with 30.3% of the population living below the extreme poverty line. The data further indicate that Jamaica has the lowest poverty rate in the region with a rate of 11.0% in 2019—a decline from 12.4% in 2018.

While poverty rates measure the proportion of the population living below a certain income threshold, indigence rates specifically focus on the proportion living in extreme poverty, experiencing severe deprivation in basic necessities such as food, clean water, sanitation and shelter. In the Caribbean, after Haiti, Belize had one of the highest indigence rates in the region (9.2%). Notwithstanding its low poverty rate, Antigua and Barbuda had the third highest rate of indigence among all the islands at 4.5%. St Kitts and Nevis, St Lucia and Trinidad and Tobago had indigence rates under 2%.

In Jamaica, extreme poverty is measured by the Food Poverty Rate rather than the indigence rate. Persons living in Food Poverty cannot afford the necessary food to live a healthy life and are forced to forgo food to afford non-food essentials. The Voluntary National Assessment (2022) for SDG 1—Zero Poverty for Jamaica reported that the food poverty rate of 4.0% in 2019.

The data for Belize and Jamaica also indicate differences in poverty rates between the urban and rural areas. In Belize, the poverty rate in the rural areas increased from 55% in 2009 to 59% in 2018, while there was a bigger increase in urban areas from 28% in 2009 to 43% in 2018 (Statistical Institute of Belize Poverty Study, 2020). In the case of Jamaica, poverty levels were lowest between 2017 and 2019 in the Greater Kingston Metropolitan Area and other Urban Centres compared with the rural areas (Fig. 5.3) (Jamaica Survey of Living Conditions, 2022). A similar difference was found for food poverty, in the GKMA and other Urban Centres in 2018 and 2019. In 2018, the rates were 2.9,

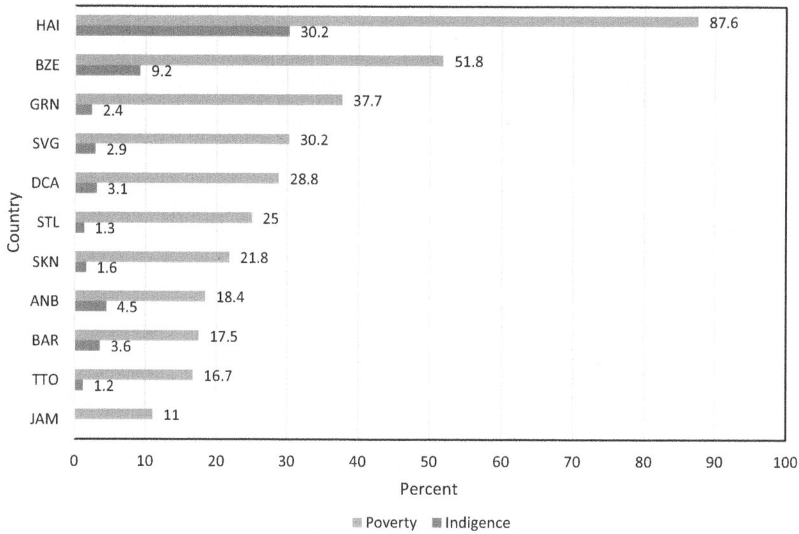

Fig. 5.2 Poverty and indigence rates in selected CARICOM countries (*Source* OECS Commission/United Nations Children's Fund, Child Poverty in the Eastern Caribbean Area, Final Report, OECS Commission/UNICEF, Castries, Saint Lucia, 2017, 1–15; Kairi Consultants Limited, Saint Lucia National Report of Living Conditions, 2016, Kairi Consultants Limited, Tunapuna, Trinidad and Tobago, 2018; Inter-American Development Bank, Barbados Survey of Living Conditions, 2016–2017, IDB, New York, NY, USA, 2017; Kairi Consultants Limited, Analysis of the Trinidad and Tobago Survey of Living Conditions, 2005, Kairi Consultants Limited, Tunapuna, Trinidad and Tobago, 2007; Planning Institute of Jamaica, Voluntary National Review, 2022)

3.9 and 3.7% for GKMA, Other Urban centres and Rural Areas, respectively while in 2019 it was 0.4% and 3.5% respectively, compared with 6.7% in the rural areas. However, in 2017, food poverty rates were fairly similar in the GKMA (5.5%) and rural areas (5.6%) and higher than in other Urban Centres (4.8%). The trend over the years shows a significant decline in poverty and food poverty rates in the GKMA and the other Urban areas while in the rural areas, poverty levels declined between 2017 and 2018 but increased in 2019. These results show the need for targeted poverty reduction and social protection in the rural areas of both Belize and Jamaica.

	Poverty			Food Poverty		
	2017r	2018	2019	2017r	2018	2019
Region						
Greater Kingston Metropolitan Area (GKMA)	17.7	9.2	4.7	5.5	2.9	0.4
Other Urban Centres (OUC)	19.8	12.0	13.4	4.8	3.9	3.5
Rural Areas	20.2	15.0	14.2	5.6	3.7	6.7
Jamaica	**19.3**	**12.6**	**11.0**	**5.4**	**3.5**	**4.0**

r - Revised
Per cent estimates are weighted
Discrepancies may be due to rounding.
Source: Compiled by PIOJ with data supplied by STATIN

Fig. 5.3 Prevalence of poverty by region in Jamaica 2017–2019

In both countries, households with larger families had higher poverty rates. In Belize poverty and indigence rates where highest in households with 7 or more persons (79% and 20%, respectively). The corresponding rates in one-member households were 37 and 7%. Differences were also apparent among ethnic groups in Belize. Poverty rates were highest among the Mayans at 77% in 2018 and lowest in the creoles (47%) (Statistical Institute of Belize Poverty Analysis, 2018).

In Jamaica, the gap in poverty rates of female- and male-headed households reduced between 2017 and 2019 (Fig. 5.4). In 2017, there was a 7.1 percentage point difference between the two genders and by 2019 there was a negligible difference of 0.2%. In the case of Belize, the data for 2018 showed that there was very little difference in poverty rates between the sexes with poverty rates in male and female household at 52 and 51%, respectively (Statistical Institute of Belize Poverty Analysis, 2018).

Further disaggregation of the data by age groups shows that the poverty rates were highest among children and adolescents in all islands, with poverty levels in these two groups exceeding 30% in all countries except Antigua and Barbuda and Jamaica (Fig. 5.5). Grenada had the highest rates of childhood and adolescent poverty at 50.9 and 47.9%, respectively. Grenada, St Vincent and the Grenadines and Trinidad and

	2017	2018	2019
Sex of Household Head			
Male	15.7	11.0	11.1
Female	22.8	14.4	10.9

Fig. 5.4 Prevalence of poverty by sex in Jamaica (%) 2017–2019 (*Source* Jamaica Survey of Living Conditions [2022])

Tobago had the highest adult poverty rates in the region at 30.2, 30.2 and 30%, respectively.

The OECS/UNICEF report on Child Poverty in the Eastern Caribbean (2017) found that households with four or more children had poverty rates averaging 80% higher than the overall child poverty rate. In contrast, households with one or two children had poverty rates below or close to the adult and overall poverty rates. In seven out of the nine countries for which data was available, these large households accounted for over 40% (rising to almost 60%) of all poor children.

The advent of COVID-19 in 2020 resulted in an increase in poverty rates in all countries. The disruption of supply chains exacerbated by the conflict in Ukraine has also contributed to the increased poverty rates.

At the household level, the FAO and CDB Study of the State of Agriculture in the Caribbean (2019) measured Food Access by the depth of the food deficit, i.e.—how many calories are needed to help the undernourished escape from their current status, all things being equal.

The study was conducted using data from 19 countries in the region. The countries were divided into three main groups—(i) small island states comprising 13 islands with populations less than 400,000 (Bahamas, Barbados, the islands of the Organization of Eastern Caribbean States as well as the British Overseas Territories of Anguilla, British Virgin Islands Turks and Caicos Islands and the Cayman Islands); (ii) the large island states with populations ranging between 1.4 and 10.8 million (Jamaica, Haiti and Trinidad and Tobago) and (iii) continental states with population sizes between 350,000 and 800,000 (Belize, Guyana and Suriname). The study revealed that food access was of concern in all 19 countries, with the large island states having higher food deficits than the smaller islands and continental states (Fig. 5.6). Furthermore, the study found

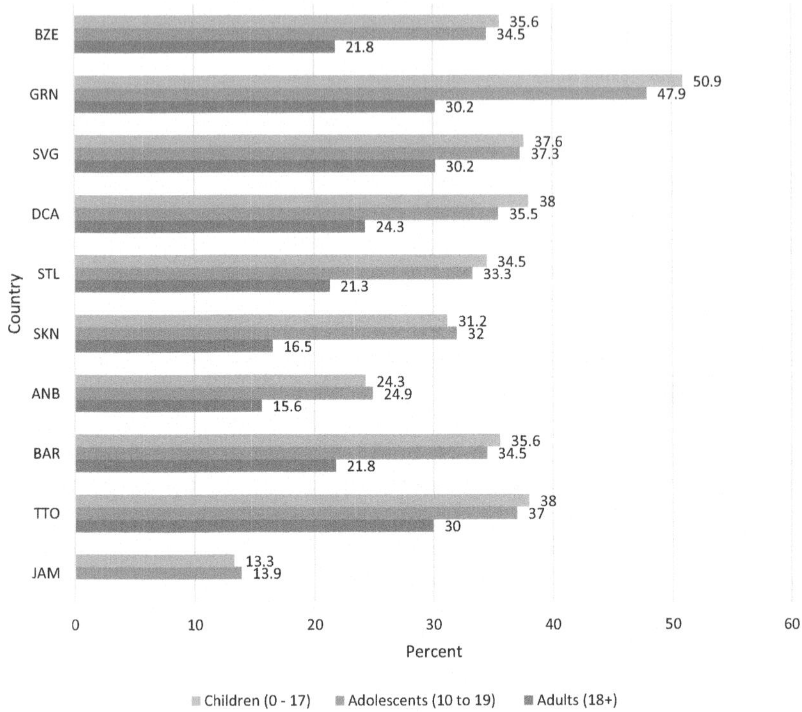

Fig. 5.5 Poverty rates for children, adolescents and adults in selected CARICOM Countries (%) (*Note* Data not available for poverty rates in Adults (18+) in Jamaica. *Source* OECS Commission/United Nations Children's Fund, Child Poverty in the Eastern Caribbean Area, Final Report, OECS Commission/ UNICEF, Castries, Saint Lucia, 2017, 1–15; Kairi Consultants Limited, Saint Lucia National Report of Living Conditions, 2016, Kairi Consultants Limited, Tunapuna, Trinidad and Tobago, 2018; Inter-American Development Bank, Barbados Survey of Living Conditions, 2016–2017, IDB, New York, NY, USA, 2017; Kairi Consultants Limited, Analysis of the Trinidad and Tobago Survey of Living Conditions, 2005, Kairi Consultants Limited, Tunapuna, Trinidad and Tobago, 2007; Planning Institute of Jamaica, Voluntary National Review, 2022)

that food access is strongly related to poverty. Consequently, the countries with a large proportion of their population living below the poverty line have low food access. It can therefore, be deduced that households

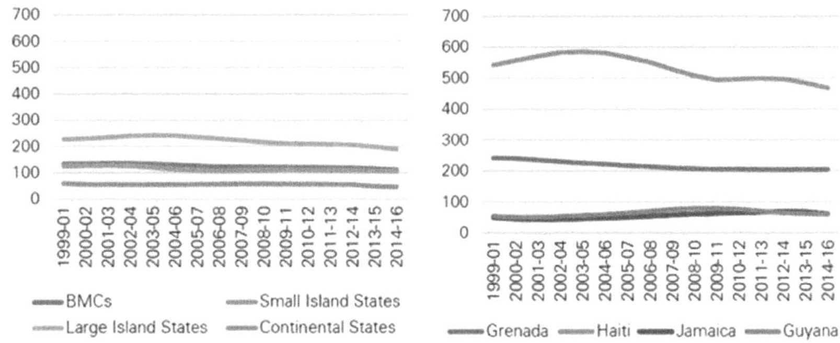

Fig. 5.6 Depth of the food deficit (*Source* Adapted from FAOSTAT data)

in Haiti, Belize, Grenada and St Vincent and the Grenadines, which had poverty rates in excess of 30% would have problems to access food.

Unemployment

Unemployment rates were only available for some countries. Figure 5.7 shows the unemployment rates for selected Caribbean countries for the period 2019 to 2021, as estimated by the ILO. The data indicate that among all the countries, in all three years for which the data are presented, St Vincent and the Grenadines had the highest unemployment levels with rates over 35%, while the larger island states of Trinidad and Tobago, Jamaica and the continental country of Belize had the lowest rates, with unemployment levels below 14%. Even though the larger islands have lower unemployment rates, the proportion of the population below the poverty line is still high. This disparity may be due to several reasons including, (i) low quality jobs which may not pay well or offer stable employment, (ii) economic inequality since low unemployment rates do not necessarily reflect equal distribution of wealth so persons at the bottom of the economic ladder struggle to find well-paying jobs; (iii) high cost of living relative to wages which make it difficult for persons to make ends meet. This in turn leads to a significant portion of the population living below the poverty line; (iv) structural unemployment—certain demographic groups or regions within the countries may experience higher levels of unemployment because of factors such as lack of skills, or education or even geographic barriers. This is evident in the case of Belize with the poverty levels are higher among the Mayan population; and (v) inadequate social safety nets to support those who are unable to find work or have low-paying jobs. This can exacerbate poverty levels, particularly for vulnerable populations such as the elderly, disabled or single-parent households.

Unemployment rates increased in all countries in 2020 with the advent of COVID-19 and the attendant shutdowns, the closure of the tourism industry and loss of jobs. However, in 2021, with the exception of St Lucia and Haiti, employment levels in all countries declined.

Disaggregation of the data by gender showed that in all countries except Barbados in 2019 and 2020, unemployment levels among women

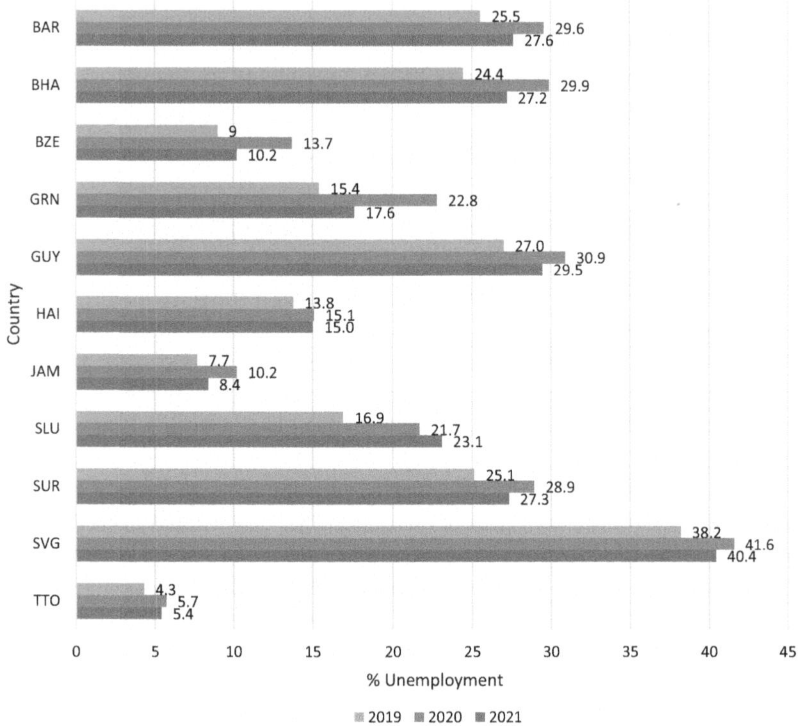

Fig. 5.7 Unemployment rates among selected Caribbean countries for the period 2019 to 2021 (*Source* ILO Database)

exceeded those of man. The biggest disparity was in Belize (5.9% male unemployment vs 13.3% in females) and Jamaica (5.8% for males vs 9.9% for females, respectively) (Figs. 5.8, 5.9, and 5.10).

More worrisome are the data disaggregated by age. Youth unemployment levels ranged from 10.7 (TTO) to 33.1% (SLU) in 2019; from 13.5 to 46.1% in 2020 and from 14.1 to 49.2% in 2021 in the two countries respectively (Fig. 5.11). In most countries, youth unemployment was at least twice that of the national average.

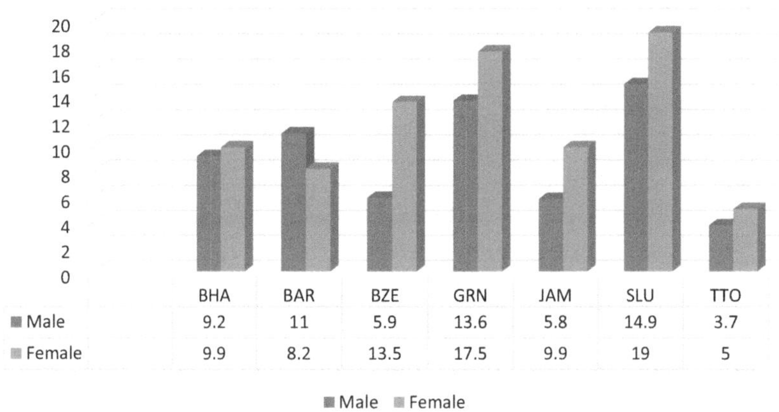

Fig. 5.8 % unemployment disaggregated by gender in selected CARICOM countries (2019)

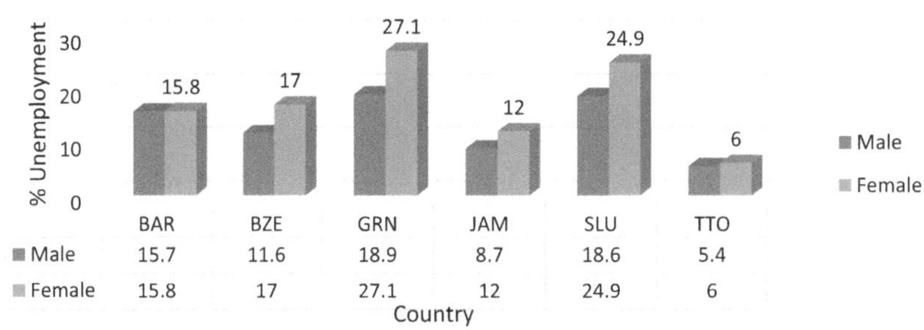

Fig. 5.9 % Unemployment disaggregated by gender in selected CARICOM countries (2020)

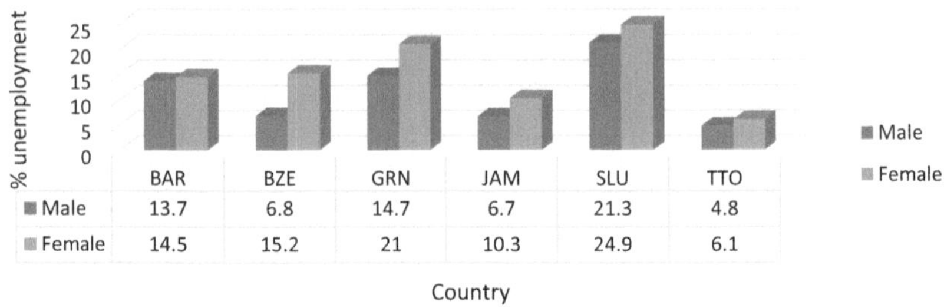

	BAR	BZE	GRN	JAM	SLU	TTO
Male	13.7	6.8	14.7	6.7	21.3	4.8
Female	14.5	15.2	21	10.3	24.9	6.1

Fig. 5.10 % Unemployment disaggregated by gender in selected CARICOM countries (2021)

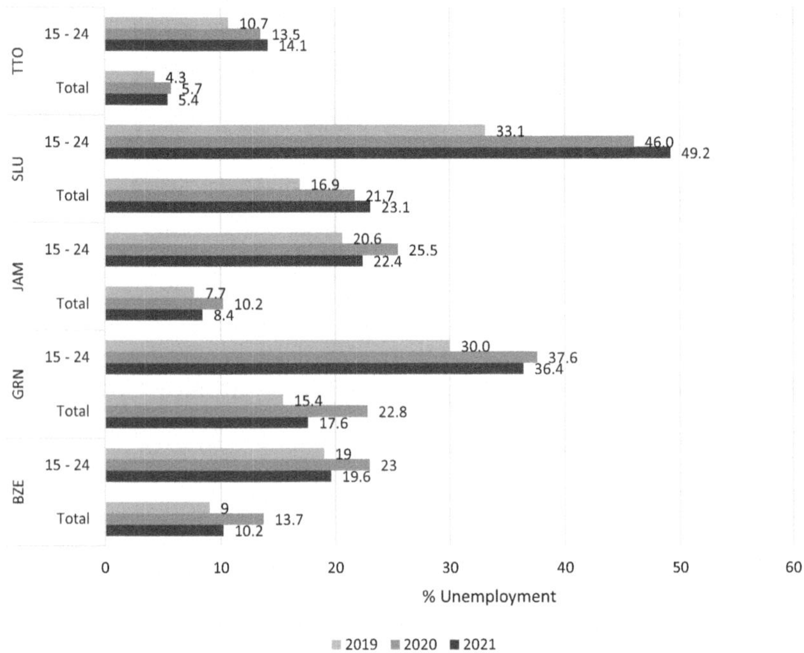

Fig. 5.11 Total and youth unemployment in selected CARICOM countries between 2019 and 2021 (*Source* ILO Database)

These results are consistent with the findings of a study conducted by UNICEF in 2020, on youth unemployment in Barbados and 9 OECS countries. The data from that study were based on a survey of databases received from National Statistical Offices in the respective countries as well as information from published reports over the period. All the data collected for that study were collected after the 2008 financial crisis and in several cases predate Hurricanes Irma and Maria, which affected the subregion in 2017 as well as the impact of COVID-19 pandemic. The study found that average youth[1] unemployment for the subregion was 26%, ranging between 2% (SKN) and 30% (SLU) of the total youth population of 103,000.

Food Cost and Affordability

Figure 5.12 which is taken from the FAO Review of Food Security and Nutrition in Latin America and the Caribbean in 2023 shows that the average cost of a healthy diet in the world is USD 3.54. Of all the regions of the world, the cost of a healthy diet was highest in Latin America and the Caribbean at USD 3.89. Moreover, it was found that the Caribbean had the highest cost of a healthy diet among all the regions of Latin America and the Caribbean, and by extension, the world at USD 4.23 (Fig. 5.13).

When the data are disaggregated at the country level for the Caribbean, the highest cost of a healthy diet ranged from USD 2.14 in Belize to USD 6.68 in Jamaica (Fig. 5.14). The World Bank estimates between 80 and 90% of all food consumed in the region comes from abroad, and only three Caribbean countries (Guyana, Belize and Haiti) produce more than 50% of their own food. It is interesting to note that of these three countries, only Belize had the lowest cost of a healthy diet, while Guyana and Haiti were among the countries with the highest cost of healthy food at USD 4.89 and USD 4.49, respectively. It begs the question about the source of the foods which constitute the healthy diet in these countries. Are they imported or locally produced and if locally produced are they more costly than their imported counterparts and hence less affordable?

With respect to affordability of healthy diets, the data represented in Fig. 5.15. The FAO study found that 52% of the population of the

[1] Defined as persons between the ages of 15 to 24.

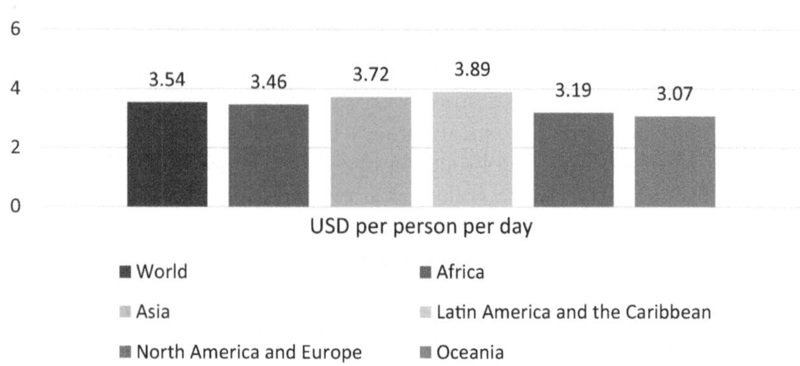

Fig. 5.12 Average cost in USD per person per day (purchasing power parity) of a healthy diet in the world and its regions in 2020

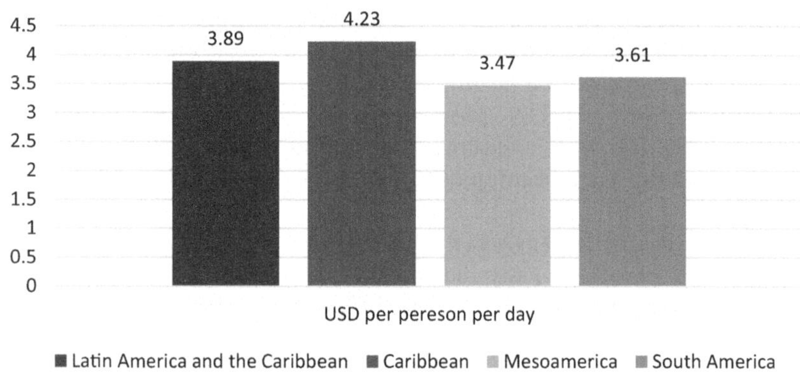

Fig. 5.13 Average cost in USD per person per day (purchasing power parity) of a healthy diet in the Latin America and the Caribbean by subregion in 2020 (*Source* FAO, IFAD, UNICEF, WFP and WHO, 2022. *The State of Food Security and Nutrition in the World 2022, Repurposing food and agricultural policies to make healthy diets more affordable*. Rome, FAO. https//doi.org/10.4060)

Caribbean is unable to afford a healthy diet. This compares with 22.5% for Latin America and the Caribbean and 42% globally. Among the countries of the Caribbean, 85.9% of the population of Haiti could not afford a healthy diet in 2020. Likewise in Jamaica and Suriname 66.2% and 58.8% of the population respectively could not afford a healthy diet. Among the

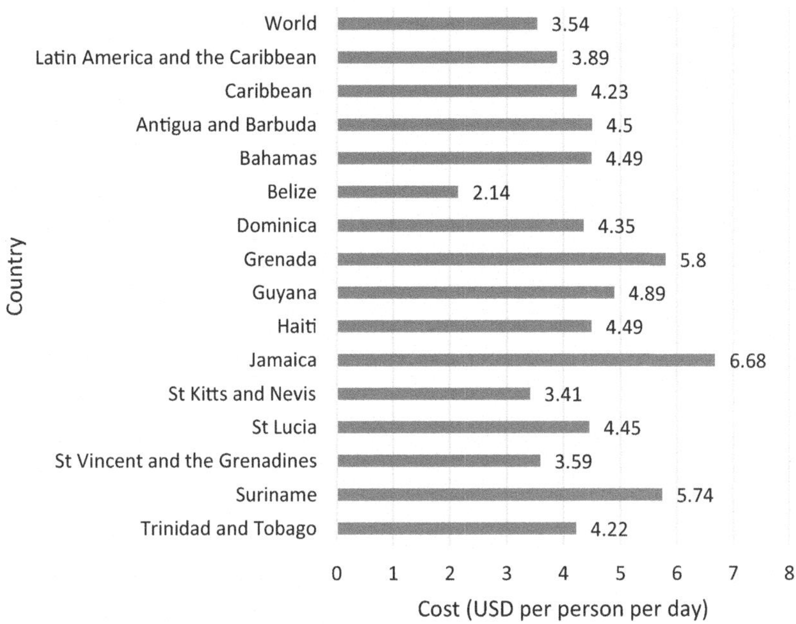

Fig. 5.14 Cost of healthy diets in the Caribbean, countries, the world and Latin America and Caribbean region (*Note* Cost and affordability data are not available for Barbados. *Source* FAO, IFAD, UNICEF, WFP and WHO. 2022. *The State of Food Security and Nutrition in the World 2022. Repurposing food and agricultural policies to make healthy diets more affordable*. Rome, FAO. https://doi.org/10.4060)

countries which produce more than 50% of their food, 43% of the population in Guyana and 36.4% of the population of Belize could not afford a healthy diet. By contrast, in Trinidad and Tobago 11.6% of the population and St Lucia 20.6% of the population could not afford a healthy diet even though the cost of the healthy diets were among the highest in the region at USD 4.22 and USD 4.45, respectively.

The results for Belize, St Lucia and Trinidad and Tobago are particularly interesting. In the case of Belize, despite having the lowest cost for a healthy diet (USD 2.14), 36% (more than one in three persons) could not afford a healthy diet in 2020. This is probably due to the high levels of poverty in that country. In 2018, prior to the COVID-19 pandemic,

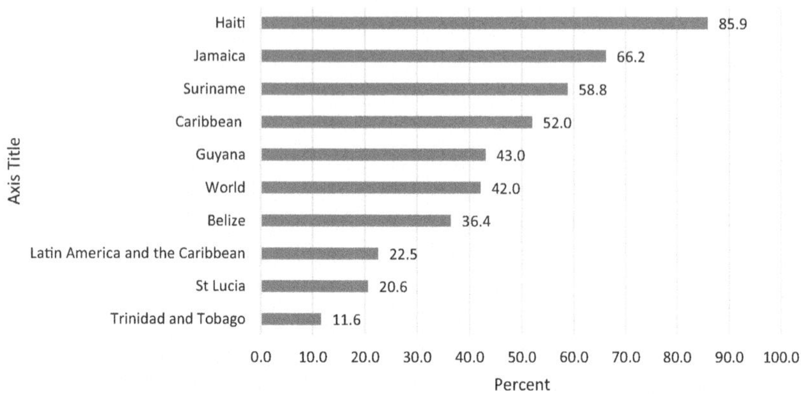

Fig. 5.15 Percentage of population which could not afford a healthy diet in 2020

according to the Poverty Survey conducted by the Statistical Institute of Belize (2018), the poverty rate of Belize stood at 52%,[2] up from 41% in 2009. Among the poor, 9% was classified as indigent or critically poor, compared with 16% in 2009. In addition, 11.5% of the population was classified as not poor but at risk of falling into poverty if they experienced any type of economic/exogenous shock or natural disaster. With the advent of the pandemic, that group was undoubtedly put further at risk. The 2018 Belize Poverty study further found that 59% of the population lived in rural areas and comprised small farmers and agricultural workers who lived in rural areas. However, there was also a significant increase in the poverty levels in urban areas from 28% in 2009 to 43% in 2018. The high unaffordability of the healthy diet despite its low cost suggests perhaps, that the healthy foods are not accessible by the rural communities, either because of cost or availability. Further research is, therefore, needed to determine the source of healthy, nutritious foods by persons living in both rural and urban areas in Belize.

In an effort to improve their access to healthy, nutritious food, particularly to poor and vulnerable communities, the government of Belize has some social protection programmes, which are aimed at alleviating poverty and promoting social cohesion and resilience. One

[2] http://sib.org.bz/wp-content/uploads/PovertyStudy2018.pdf.

such programme is the Boost Programme which is a cash transfer programme for families in need. The programme provides from BZ$44.00 (US$22.00) per month per beneficiary, up to a maximum of BZ$492 depending on the number of children in the home, their ages and educational status. These cash transfers are mainly used to pay for school supplies or food. The Food Pantry programmes also provide food to needy families. During the COVID-19 pandemic, through the Food Assistance Programme, the Ministry of Human Development, Social Transformation and Poverty Alleviation supported needy families and persons in quarantine by providing food baskets comprising basic food items including fruits and vegetables.

By contrast, Trinidad and Tobago, despite being among the Caribbean countries with the highest cost of healthy food, had the lowest percentage of people who could not afford a healthy diet. This may be due to the country's low unemployment figures in the region (less than 6%), which suggests that a larger proportion of the population had sufficient incomes to purchase the healthy food.

On the other hand, in St Lucia, which had relatively high poverty rates (25%) and unemployment rates (ranging between 16.9 and 23% from 2019 to 2021) only 20% of the population could not afford healthy diets. A review of the remittances to the OECS countries in Figs. 5.16 and 5.17 shows that between 2019 and 2020, St Lucia had the highest increase in remittances compared with the other islands (30.5%). This increase may have contributed to increased incomes and hence, persons being able to afford food during the COVID-19 pandemic. The World Bank also reported that it supported emergency transfers and short-term social protection measures to St Lucia as well as Bahamas, Barbados, Dominica, Grenada, Jamaica and St Vincent and the Grenadines during this time. This support would also have contributed to increased affordability and hence access to food for these countries during the early stages of the pandemic.

These findings suggest that policies to improve food access in the region must be aimed at poverty reduction, income generation particularly in rural communities and efforts also need to be made to make local healthy foods more affordable, particularly for the poor and vulnerable. Nutrition education is also needed to ensure that the foods produced and consumed particularly by poor families in rural areas are healthy and nutritious. In this regard, School Feeding Programmes play an important role, this topic is dealt with in greater detail in Chapter 6 on Food Utilization.

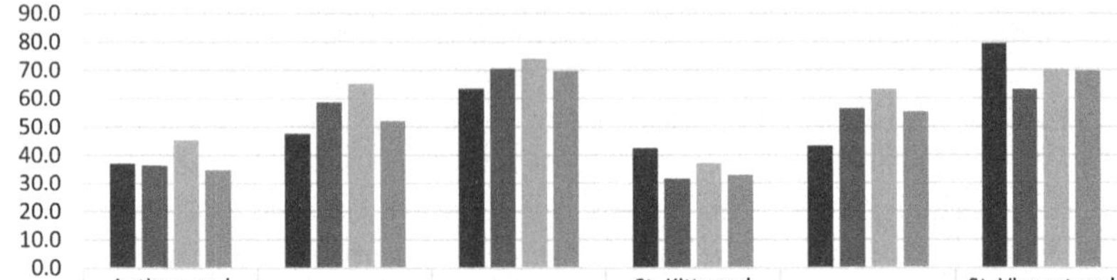

	Antigua and Barbuda	Dominica	Grenada	St. Kitts and Nevis	St. Lucia	St. Vincent and the Grenadines
2019	36.9	47.5	63.4	42.3	43.2	79.3
2020	36.2	58.5	70.4	31.6	56.4	63.0
2021	45.3	65.1	74.0	37.1	63.3	70.1
2022	34.6	52.0	69.4	33.0	55.2	69.6

■ 2019 ■ 2020 ■ 2021 ■ 2022

Fig. 5.16 Remittance inflows to selected Eastern Caribbean States (USD million) between 2019 and 2022

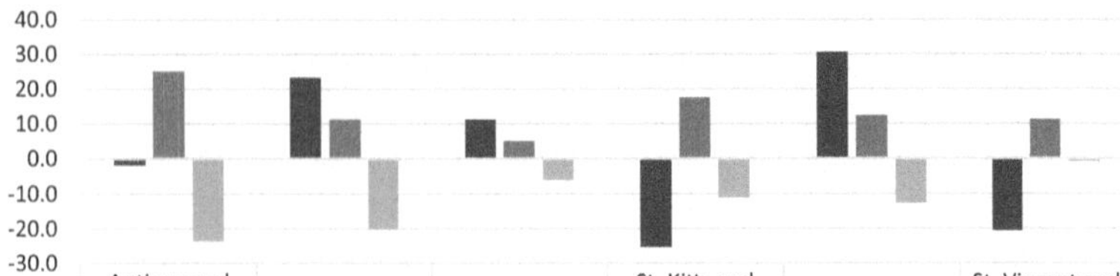

	Antigua and Barbuda	Dominica	Grenada	St. Kitts and Nevis	St. Lucia	St. Vincent and the Grenadines
2019 - 20	-1.8	23.2	11.2	-25.4	30.5	-20.6
2020 - 21	25.0	11.2	5.0	17.4	12.2	11.2
2021 - 22	-23.6	-20.1	-6.1	-11.1	-12.8	-0.7

■ 2019 - 20 ■ 2020 - 21 ■ 2021 - 22

Fig. 5.17 Percentage increase in remittances between 2019 and 2022 in the OECS

New and Emerging Issues That Affect Access

In 2020, the COVID-19 pandemic resulted in border closures and the suspension of global travel. This, in turn, caused the tourism industry—the mainstay of the economy of many Caribbean countries—to come to a standstill. *The Caribbean Tourism Organization reported that among Caribbean member states, the number of tourist arrivals in 2020 fell from 32 million in 2019 to just 11 million in 2020—a decline of 65.5 percent.*

Consequently, unemployment levels increased as persons employed in the tourism industry and other ancillary industries lost their jobs and livelihoods. In addition, supply chains for food and agricultural inputs were disrupted.

The war in Ukraine also presented and continues to present some challenges for food security in the Caribbean. Specifically, it has caused a disruption of supply chains for staples such as corn and wheat as well as agricultural inputs such as fertilizers. It has also resulted in increased fuel costs and it has sparked a global financial crisis with its attendant repercussions of protectionism, food price hikes and food shortages. All these challenges have in turn affected food access as the traditional markets for some foods have been disrupted, food prices have increased and consequently food has become less affordable.

The Caribbean Food Security and Livelihoods Survey Report for August 2022 confirmed that global food prices have increased since the start of the Ukraine conflict and this has caused local food prices to increase. Between March and August 2022, on average, food inflation rose by 10.2% across the 20 Caribbean countries surveyed. Moreover, high energy prices have exacerbated the food price crisis. The vast majority of respondents (97%) reported higher than normal food prices. Ninety-one percent (91%) of respondents reported that the main reason for limited market access was the lack of financial means. When asked what were their main worries, 48% of respondents indicated their inability to meet food needs as their main concern, followed by meeting essential needs (48%) and unemployment (36%). It was the first time in the five surveys conducted over two years that inability to meet food needs was mentioned as the number one concern.

Migration is also another emerging issue which has affected food access. Political unrests and upheavals in countries such as Venezuela, Colombia and Syria have prompted the migration of refugees and asylum seekers to the Caribbean in search of a better life. Between 2019 and 2021, the number of Venezuelans who were registered under the Government of Trinidad and Tobago's Venezuelan Registration Exercise increased from 16,523 to 35,300. (Migration Data Portal (IOM 2019 and Migration Data Portal.)

In addition, there has also been a significant amount of intraregional migration, caused not only by political unrests, but also by natural disasters such as earthquakes as in the case of Haiti, as well as from climate-related crises such as hurricanes. Hurricanes Irma and Maria prompted the migration of persons from Dominica to nearby Caribbean islands in 2016. UNDESA reported that the number of intraregional migrants from other Caribbean countries has almost doubled over the last 30 years, increasing from 437,177 in 1990 to 859,403 in 2020 (IOM, 2023). The majority of these regional migrants (63% or 567,956), are Haitian, and of these 87.4% live in the Dominican Republic. Other countries where Haitians have sought refuge include the Bahamas and Guyana.

Migration presents social challenges such as increased unemployment and poverty, lack of access to proper health and education to name a few. In addition, there is an increased demand for food as well as an increase in the number of persons who do not have access to food as the migrants are among the most vulnerable groups in the countries.

Despite the challenges posed by these emerging issues, migration presents tremendous opportunities for the Caribbean for increased availability of labour, expertise and new technologies in agricultural production (as has been shown in the case of the Venezuelan migrant workers in Trinidad and Tobago). These must, therefore, be harnessed among the strategies to address the problems of food access in the region.

Conclusions

Prior to the COVID-19 pandemic, global extreme poverty levels were declining, but with the onset of the pandemic, there was a rise in extreme poverty rates worldwide. Despite a post-pandemic recovery, extreme poverty rates are still higher than pre-pandemic levels, with projections indicating that a significant number of people will remain in extreme poverty by 2030. The COVID-19 pandemic and disruptions in supply chains, exacerbated by external conflicts, have contributed to increased poverty rates globally.

Latin America and the Caribbean experienced a slight decline in poverty rates post-pandemic, but levels remained higher than pre-pandemic. Haiti stands out as one of the poorest countries globally, with high poverty rates exacerbated by political instability, violence and insecurity.

Poverty rates vary significantly among CARICOM countries, with Jamaica having one of the lowest poverty rates in the region and Haiti facing the highest poverty rate. Urban areas generally have lower poverty rates compared to rural areas, but there are variations among countries.

Larger households tend to have higher poverty rates, with poverty rates being highest among households with seven or more members. Differences in poverty rates based on gender are diminishing in some countries, indicating progress in gender equality.

Children and adolescents have disproportionately high poverty rates across all islands, highlighting the vulnerability of this demographic group.

Food access is strongly related to poverty, with countries with higher poverty rates experiencing lower food access.

St Vincent and the Grenadines consistently had the highest unemployment rates among the selected Caribbean countries, exceeding 35%, while Trinidad and Tobago, Jamaica and Belize had the lowest rates, below 14%.

The onset of the COVID-19 pandemic led to increased unemployment rates across all countries in 2020, primarily due to shutdowns and job losses in the tourism industry. However, in 2021, employment levels declined further in most countries, except for St Lucia and Haiti.

In most countries, unemployment rates were higher among women compared to men, except for Barbados in 2019 and 2020. The largest disparity between male and female unemployment rates was observed in Belize and Jamaica.

Youth unemployment rates were significantly higher than the national average in most countries, ranging from 10.7% to 33.1% in 2019 and increasing in subsequent years.

The Caribbean region has the highest cost of a healthy diet among all regions and indeed, the world, with the cost ranging from USD 2.14 in Belize to USD 6.68 in Jamaica. However, despite the relatively low cost of a healthy diet in Belize, a significant portion of the population (36%) could not afford it, indicating accessibility issues. Affordability of healthy diets varied across countries, with higher percentages of the population unable to afford them in countries like Haiti, Jamaica and Suriname.

These conclusions underline the complex interplay of economic, social and political factors influencing poverty levels at the global, regional and national levels. They also emphasize the need for comprehensive strategies and targeted interventions to address the various dimensions of food access—poverty, unemployment, vulnerabilities among specific demographic groups factors, food affordability and other factors, all of which affect food insecurity in the Caribbean.

References

CARICOM, CDEMA, WFP, FAP. (2022). *Caribbean Food Security and Livelihoods Survey Report for August 2022.*

FAO. (2022). *The Future of Food and Agriculture—Drivers and Triggers for Transformation* (The Future of Food and Agriculture, No. 3). Rome. https://doi.org/10.4060/cc0959en

FAO and CDB. (2019). *Study on the State of Agriculture in the Caribbean* (212 pp.). Rome. Licence: CC BY-NC-SA 3.0 IGO.

FAO, IFAD, PAHO, UNICEF and WFP. (2023). *Regional Overview of Food Security and Nutrition—Latin America and the Caribbean 2022: Towards Improving Affordability of Healthy Diets.* Santiago. https://doi.org/10.4060/cc3859en

FAO, IFAD, UNICEF, WFP and WHO. (2020). *The State of Food Security and Nutrition in the World 2020. Transforming Food Systems for Affordable Healthy Diets*. Rome, FAO.

FAO, IFAD, UNICEF, WFP and WHO. (2022). *The State of Food Security and Nutrition in the World 2022. Repurposing Food and Agricultural Policies to Make Healthy Diets More Affordable.* Rome, FAO. https://doi.org/10.4060/cc0639en

International Organization for Migration. (2023). *Data Report: Trends in Caribbean Migration and Mobility.* San Jose, Costa Rica. https://rosanjose.iom.int/sites/g/files/tmzbdl1446/files/documents/2023-07/data-report-trends-in-caribbean-migration-and-mobility.pdf

Jamaica Survey of Living Conditions. (2022). Planning Institute of Jamaica.

Lowitt, K., Saint, V. A., Keddy, C. S. M., et al. (2016). Challenges and Opportunities for More Integrated Regional Food Security Policy in the Caribbean Community. *Regional Studies, Regional Science, 3*, 368–378. https://doi.org/10.1080/21681376.2016.1209983

OECS Commission and UNICEF. (2017). *Child Poverty in the Eastern Caribbean Area* (Final Report). OECS Commission and UNICEF. Statistical Institute of Belize Conducted a Poverty Study in 2018/19.

Statistical Institute of Belize Poverty Analysis. (2018). https://sib.org.bz/statistics/poverty-statistics/

Statistical Institute of Belize Poverty Study. (2020). *Multidimensional Poverty in Belize, 2021.* https://sib.org.bz/statistics/poverty-statistics/

The UN Sustainable Development Goals Report of 2023, Special Edition Towards a Rescue Plan for People and Planet.

United Nations Economic Commission for Latin America and the Caribbean (ECLAC) in Its Social Panorama of Latin America and the Caribbean 2022 Report.

Voluntary National Review Report: Implementation of the 2030 Agenda and the Sustainable Development Goals 2022/Planning Institute of Jamaica. https://hlpf.un.org/sites/default/files/vnrs/2022/VNR%202022%20Jamaica%20Report.pdf

CHAPTER 6

Food Utilization in the Caribbean

Food Utilization refers to the way the body uses the various nutrients in food. The nutritional status of individuals is determined by their consumption of sufficient energy and nutrients. This in turn is determined by the type, quantity and nutritional content of food they consume, the diversity of their diet and the intra-household distribution of food. In addition, the way the food is prepared is important to ensure that the food consumed is free from contaminants and food-borne diseases. Thus, food consumption, nutrition and food safety are all essential elements of Food Utilization.

This chapter will explore the two aspects of food utilization in the Caribbean—consumption and food safety. Specifically, the growing trends in overweight and obesity in the region which have been caused by a shift in consumption patterns from traditional domestically grown food to an explosion of highly processed food, facilitated largely by imports. The shift in consumption is correlated with the increasing incidence of non-communicable diseases (NCDs) in the region and its toll, not only on the health of consumers, but also on the healthcare system as a whole. Global and regional Initiatives to combat this problem will be examined, as well as national actions to deal with this challenge. An analysis will also be done of the factors that continue to impact diets and consumption patterns in the Caribbean, particularly consumer behaviour.

D. Stanberry and L. Fletcher-Paul, *Food Security in the Caribbean*, Palgrave Studies in Agricultural Economics and Food Policy, https://doi.org/10.1007/978-3-031-66055-9_6

The analysis will include the prospects of reversing or curtailing the influence of the foreign media and foreign based fast food chains. Initiatives to increase consumer awareness by ramping up public education campaigns in support of consumption of local foods (such as the "Eat What You Grow" campaign in Jamaica) as well as the growth, development and impact of school feeding programmes as a means of improving the consumption of healthy food in the Caribbean will be discussed.

The section on food safety will examine growing trends and the threats to food safety such as poor sanitation, international trade, fake foods and antimicrobial resistance.

SDG targets of relevance to Food Utilization is as follows:
Food utilization is considered under SDG 3—Ensure healthy lives and promote well-being for all at all ages. Specifically Targets 3.3, 3.4 and 3.9 are relevant to nutrition and food safety. These targets are as follows:

Target 3.3: By 2030, end the epidemics of AIDS, tuberculosis, malaria and neglected tropical diseases and combat hepatitis, **water-borne diseases** and other communicable diseases.

Target 3.4: By 2030, reduce by one third premature mortality from non-communicable diseases through prevention and treatment and promote mental health and well-being.

Target 3.9: By 2030, substantially reduce the number of deaths and illnesses from hazardous chemicals and air, water and soil pollution and contamination.

Measurement of Food Utilization

At the national level, Food Utilization is measured by unhealthy food regimes which in turn are reflected in the prevalence of overweight and obesity in the countries. The prevalence of overweight and obesity is determined by the Body Mass Index (BMI) which the World Health Organization defines as "a simple index of weight-for-height". Individuals with a BMI of under 18.5 kg/m^2 are considered underweight, persons with BMI between 25.0 and 30.0 kg/m^2 are classified as overweight while persons whose BMI is greater than 30.0 kg/m^2 are obese. The prevalence of obesity is, therefore, the proportion of the adult population whose BMI is greater than 30 kg/m^2.

- BMI under 18.5 = underweight
- BMI 18.5 to <25 = healthy
- BMI 25 to <30 = overweight
- BMI 30 to <35 = obese (class 1)
- BMI 35 to <40 = obese (class 2)
- BMI 40 or higher = obese (class 3—morbid)

Household surveys are commonly used to determine the diversity and nutrient content of the diet at the household level. However, Manikas et al. (2023) have indicated that the main weakness of the dietary diversity measures is that they do not account for the quantity and quality and hence the nutritional value of the diet consumed.

Food safety is commonly measured by the occurrence and severity of foodborne illnesses, injuries and deaths. Because of the sensitive nature of this information, many countries are reluctant to reveal such statistics. However, for the purposes of measurement of achievement of the relevant SDG targets, the FAO (2021) has developed Food Safety indicators. Whereas other food security and nutrition indicators are represented in numbers to be achieved, food safety indicators are methodologies and approaches that countries could use to serve their particular purpose for food safety. In addition to assisting countries to determine their progress in achieving the SDG targets, the indicators also help to assess capacity development needs and identify food safety priorities.

Prevalence of Overweight and Obesity in the Caribbean

In Chapter 2 we showed that undernourishment is an important aspect of food security in the Caribbean, particularly in the case of Haiti, where there is a high prevalence of stunting and wasting. However, the Caribbean also faces the double burden of overweight and obesity.

The prevalence of obesity in adults increased in all countries over the period 2000 to 2016 (Fig. 6.1). The highest levels of obesity were evident in the Bahamas, which increased from 23.9 to 31.6%, while Trinidad and Tobago had the lowest prevalence of obesity with corresponding levels of 10.6 to 18.6% over the period of study.

Obesity was more prevalent in women (Fig. 6.2). The Bahamas had the highest prevalence of obesity among females (38.1%) while Antigua

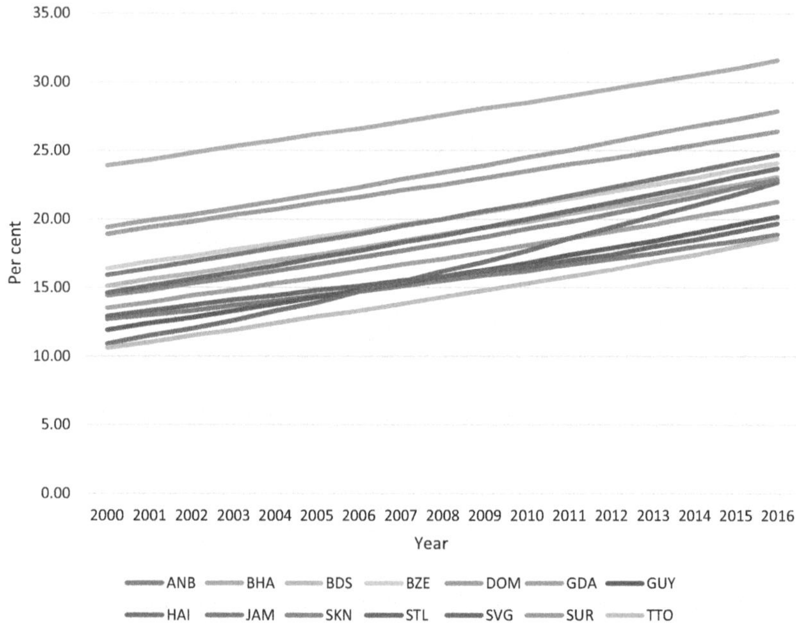

Fig. 6.1 Prevalence of obesity in adults in the Caribbean between 2000 and 2016 (*Source* FOFA dashboard database)

and Barbuda had the lowest (25.1%). The gaps between the sexes varied between 9 percentage points in Haiti and 18.1 percentage points in Jamaica. Moreover, in Antigua and Barbuda, Barbados, Grenada, Guyana, Jamaica, St Lucia and Trinidad and Tobago, the prevalence of obesity among females was more than twice that of their male counterparts (Fig. 6.2). The Regional Overview of Food Security and Nutrition 2022 (FAO/IFAD, UNICEF, WFP and WHO, 2023) further found that the differences between the sexes were attributable to socioeconomic factors since obesity rates were higher among women living in urban areas, but lower among women in the poorest quintiles as well as among women with only primary level education.

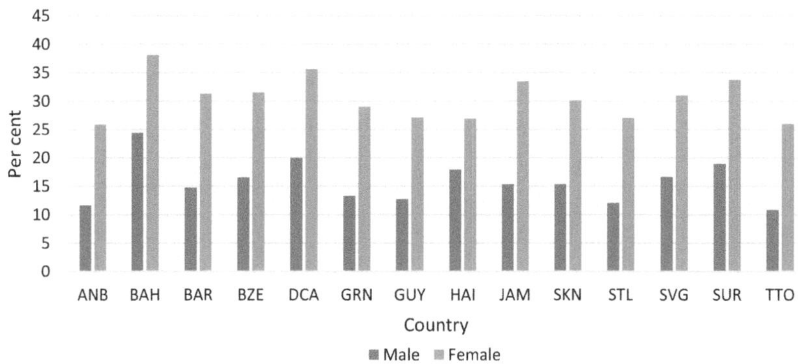

Fig. 6.2 Prevalence of obesity among adults in the Caribbean by sex and country (2016) (*Source* Regional Overview of Food Security and Nutrition 2022 [FAO/IFAD, UNICEF, WFP and WHO, 2023])

Even more troubling is the level of overweight and obesity among children. In 2022,[1] 4.2 million children (8.6%) under the age of 5 years in Latin America and the Caribbean were overweight. The corresponding rates in 2022 for South and Central America and the Caribbean were 9.7, 6.7 and 6.6% respectively. These figures are well above the global prevalence rate of 5.6% (Fig. 6.3).

The data further indicate that childhood obesity rates in the LAC region have increased markedly since 2000, when the rate was 6.8%. This increase is mainly attributable to the significant rise in South America (from 6.9 to 9.7%). The increase was not as marked in the Caribbean (from 6.1 to 6.6%), while in Central America, obesity rates actually fell from 6.9 to 6.6% between 2000 and 2016 and then increased marginally in 2022. The global prevalence rate in 2012 was 5.5% slightly lower than the rate in 2022.

When disaggregated by country, for the countries where data are available, Table 6.1 shows that there was an increase in the number of obese children in Haiti and Trinidad and Tobago between 2012 and 2022, while the number of obese children in the other countries declined. In terms of the prevalence of obesity, however, Fig. 6.4 shows that obesity

[1] UNICEF, WHO, World Bank Group Joint Malnutrition Estimates on child malnutrition of May 2023.

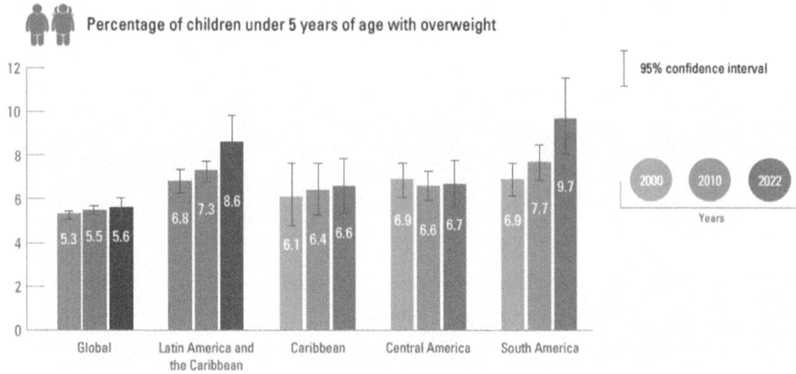

Fig. 6.3 Trend of overweight (including obesity) in children under 5 years of age in Latin America and the Caribbean from 2000 to 2022

rates in children under 5 years were highest in Barbados and Trinidad and Tobago. Obesity rates in Barbados, Haiti, Suriname and Trinidad and Tobago increased over the 10-year period. With the exception of Haiti and Suriname, all Caribbean countries exceeded the global rate of 5.5 and 5.6%, respectively, in 2012 and 2022. Barbados and Trinidad and Tobago also exceeded obesity rates for LAC and the Caribbean.

For children and adolescents between the ages of 5 and 19, Fig. 6.5 shows that among CARICOM countries, the Bahamas had the highest

Table 6.1 Number (thousands) of obese children under the age of 5 years in selected Caribbean countries in 2012 and 2022

Country	*2012*	*2022*
Barbados	2.0	1.9
Belize	3.2	2.2
Guyana	4.8	4.5
Haiti	42.4	47.2
Jamaica	14.5	9.4
St Lucia	0.7	0.6
Suriname	2.0	2.1
Trinidad and Tobago	10.8	12.6

NB. The most recent country data point (e.g. from household surveys) used to generate the modelled stunting and overweight estimates is from before the year 2000; interpret with caution
Source UNICEF WHO World Bank Group Joint Malnutrition Estimates, May 2023 edition

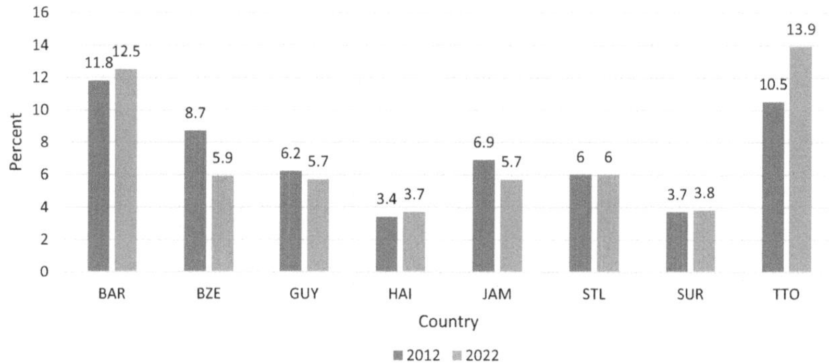

Fig. 6.4 Prevalence of obesity in children under the age of 5 in selected Caribbean countries (2012 and 2022)

prevalence of overweight and obesity at 38.5% and 17.3%, respectively, while St Lucia had the lowest with 23.4 and 8.8% in 2016. CARPHA indicates that these rates are among the highest in the Americas and two to three times higher than World levels (PAHO, 2016). They further portend a bleak future for the future generation because of the links between obesity and the incidence of chronic non-communicable diseases.

Links Between Overweight, Obesity, NCDs and Expenditure on Healthcare

The World Health Organization (2019) states that in 2009, NCDs, i.e. cardiovascular diseases (such as heart attacks and stroke), cancers, chronic respiratory diseases (such as chronic obstructive pulmonary disease and asthma) and diabetes were the leading cause of death in the world, accounting for 41 million deaths (74%) annually. Seventeen million of the deaths from NCDs occur before the age of 70. The majority of deaths (17.9 million) are due to cardiovascular diseases, followed by cancers (9.3 million), chronic respiratory diseases (4.1 million) and diabetes (2.0 million including kidney disease deaths caused by diabetes). Deaths due to NCDs are disproportionately high in low and middle income countries accounting for 31.4 million persons or 86% of the population.

In the Caribbean, deaths caused by NCDs ranged from 65% of the population in Haiti and Belize to 85% in Antigua and Barbuda (WHO,

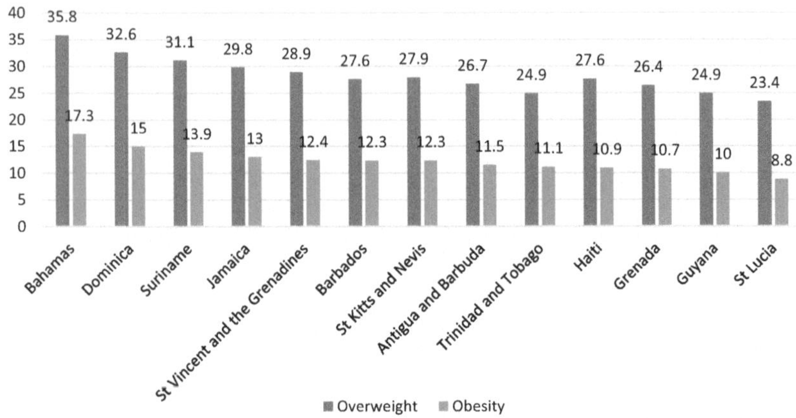

Fig. 6.5 Prevalence of overweight and obesity in children and adolescents aged 5 to 19 years (2016) (*Source* World Health Organization. Global Health Observatory)

2022) (Table 6.2). Moreover, the probability of premature mortality from NCDs varied from 16% in Barbados and Belize to 31% in Haiti.

Cost of NCDs to the Countries

The treatment of NCDs can be quite expensive and can put a considerable burden on a country's health services. Abdulkadri et al. (2021) reported that in Trinidad and Tobago, between 2010 and 2015, NCDs represented 53% of hospital admissions. Rising levels of NCDs, can therefore, result in increased government spending which may in turn affect the availability of funds for investment in other sectors of the economy.

Public expenditure on healthcare in the Caribbean currently averages 4.0% of GDP and ranges between 0.8% of GDP in Haiti to 4.4% in Barbados (ECLAC, 2020). It is anticipated that the increasing prevalence of NCDs and related risk factors, particularly among the youth and adolescents, will result in rising healthcare costs in the future not only to individuals, but also to the governments of the region. In Jamaica, the National Health Fund paid out individual benefits worth USD 30.65 million for subsidies to cover the cost of medication for persons with

Table 6.2 Percentage and number of deaths from NCDs and the probability of premature mortality from NCDs in the Caribbean

Country	*% deaths from NCDs*	*Number of deaths from NCDs*	*Probability of premature mortality from NCDs (%)*
Antigua and Barbuda	85	550	18
Bahamas	75	2000	20
Barbados	83	2800	16
Belize	65	1200	16
Grenada	83	840	23
Guyana	70	5600	29
Haiti	65	62,900	31
Jamaica	79	15,300	17
St Lucia	82	1200	18
St Vincent and the Grenadines	79	740	21
Suriname	79	3500	23
Trinidad and Tobago	83	7800	17

Source World Health Organization Non-communicable Diseases Progress Monitor 2022

NCDs (Abdulkadri et al., 2015). This amount represents 7.63% of the health budget in 2011.

RTI International (2016) undertook a rapid assessment of Economic Dimensions of NCDs for the IDB in Trinidad and Tobago. They found that the economic burden for diabetes, hypertension and cancer was approximately TT$8.7 billion annually or 5% of current GDP. The total cost for treating diabetes was highest (TT$3.5 billion) followed by hypertension (TT$3.3 billion) and cancer (TT$2 billion).

NCDs also have associated indirect costs due to loss of productivity, absenteeism, premature labour force exit and reduced work capacity. The WHO (2013) estimated that the global cumulative economic losses of premature deaths from NCDs was approximately US$7 trillion over a 15-year period. In the CARICOM countries, Abdulkadri et al. (2009) found that the estimated economic burden of diabetes and hypertension was 1.36% of GDP in the Bahamas, 5.34% of the GDP of Barbados; 5.87% of the GDP of Jamaica; and 8% of GDP in Trinidad and Tobago. Further analysis of the cost components for diabetes revealed that the indirect costs of mortality and morbidity were 39% and 73% of the total economic burden in the Bahamas and Trinidad and Tobago, respectively. In the case of Trinidad and Tobago, for treatment of hypertension, the indirect cost accounted for 47% of the total economic burden. In Jamaica, Mitchell-Fearon et al. (2017), found that the indirect cost of treating hypertension in older persons in that country accounted for 35% of all cost categories and was the largest share of all costs.

The COVID-19 pandemic also showed that persons with NCDs have a higher risk of contracting severe COVID-19 with longer periods of hospitalization and a higher probability of death. This will, undoubtedly, add a further burden to the national health cost of the countries.

Responsible Factors

The CDB FAO study conducted in 2019 attributes the nutritional challenges in the region to multiple causal factors which are compounded by "the scale of food imports and the related food import bill, vulnerability to natural disasters, and the high risk of fiscal crisis". The main factors which have contributed to this rising trend are the high prices of healthy, nutritious locally produced food, the limited availability of sufficient quantities of locally produced diversified food, poor nutritional food choices and consumption patterns, limited knowledge of what constitutes healthy eating and negative attitudes to healthy diets. The shelves of the supermarkets are also flooded with imported, ultra-processed food which are high in calories, fat, sodium, and sugar—all of which contribute to overweight, obesity and NCDs. Moreover, fast food outlets spend millions of dollars in advertising unhealthy foods. Frequently occurring natural disasters and the lack of risk management practices particularly at the household level also contribute to the unavailability of healthy food, after such disasters, thereby also contributing poor food utilization.

Figure 6.6 shows the progress of food price inflation in the three regions of Latin America and the Caribbean over the period 2001 to January 2023. The Caribbean subregion and Central America have shown a similar trajectory of food price inflation but with lower volatility in food prices than South American countries, since 2010. However, shocks related to the COVID-19 pandemic and the Ukrainian war led to lower increases in food prices for Caribbean and Central America than for South America.

The Caribbean Food Security and Livelihoods Survey Report *of August 2022 reported that o*n average, food inflation in the English and Dutch-speaking Caribbean has risen by 10.2% across 20 countries as of March

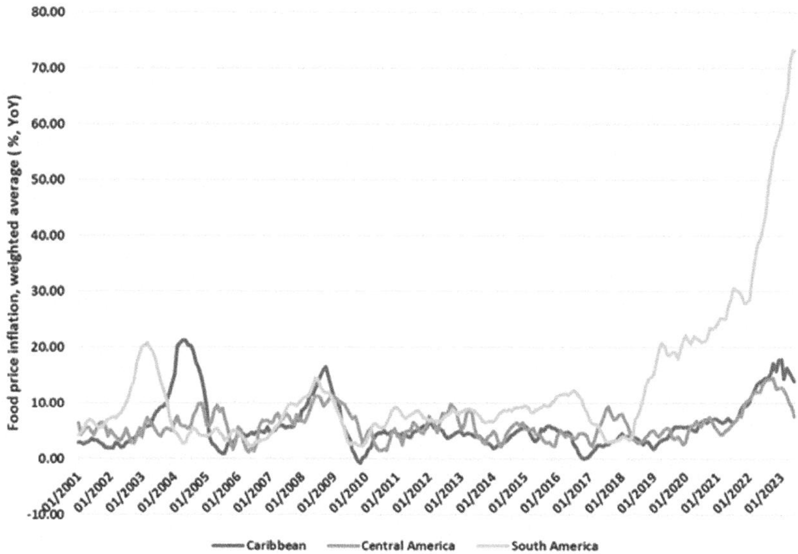

Fig. 6.6 Food price inflation, Latin America regions

2022. The report further noted that high energy prices are exacerbating the food price crisis.

Figure 6.7 shows a gradual rise in the consumer price index from 1990 to 2022. Between 2000 and 2006, the Consumer Food Price Index rose gradually from 44.2 to 68.2, an increase of 54%. The index then declined to 59.2 in 2007, but rose again from to 123.0 in 2018. Between 2018 and 2022, there has been a sharp rise in the index to 208.0, an increase of 69.1%.

A review of the different producer price indexes for four commodities (Fig. 6.8) shows a generally clear upward trends for producer prices in the period 2006–2021. Moreover, the surge in the prices of wheat, maize and sunflower oil poses challenges for food availability in the region. The data suggest that the Caribbean, where almost all cereals are imported, is vulnerable to international price hikes. Moreover, the cereals imported comprise ultra-processed foods which are high in sugar, salt and fat—all of which are linked to the high incidence of obesity and chronic non-communicable diseases.

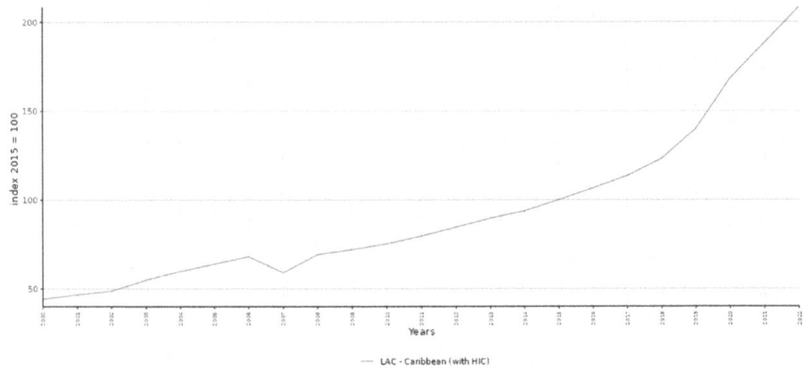

Fig. 6.7 Consumer price index for the Caribbean

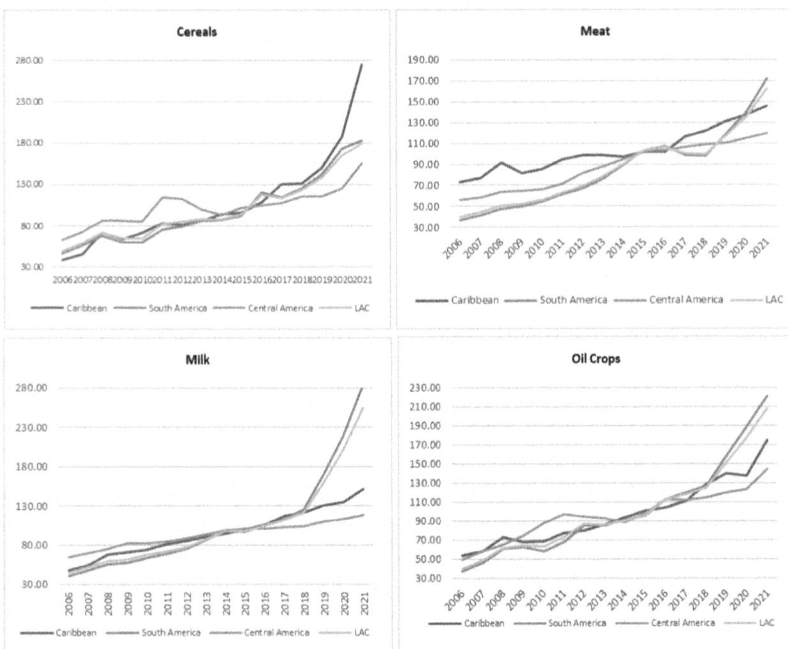

Fig. 6.8 Consumer price index of cereals, meat, milk and oil crops in Latin America and the Caribbean

In Chapter 2 it was shown that food imports to the Caribbean have increased over the years. Between 2016 and 2021, it rose from USD 3.4 billion to USD 4.1 billion. Despite the logistics and supply chain challenges during the COVID-19 pandemic, the bill increased by 19% between 2020 and 2021. Moreover, these imports comprised significant levels of cereals and fruit concentrates and purees, which are mainly ultra-processed foods, high in sugar, salt and processed carbohydrates. The advent of supermarket and fast food chains with their powerful advertising campaigns has also influenced consumer tastes and contributed in no small measure to the shift in demand for ultra-processed foods of poor nutritional quality instead of healthier, locally grown alternatives.

Regional and Global Frameworks to Address Obesity

In 2007, the Heads of Government of the Caribbean spearheaded the *Declaration of Port of Spain: Uniting to Stop the Epidemics of Chronic NCDs*, highlighting the need for response at the highest political level to the NCD epidemic. The Port of Spain Declaration comprises 27 commitments to action in key areas. These areas include risk factor reduction and health promotion; improving quality of care; the development of appropriate legislative frameworks and the establishment of NCD commissions or similar entities to provide oversight of NCD prevention and control efforts.

In October 2017, the Ministers of Agriculture of CARICOM signed the Declaration of St Ann: Implementing Agriculture and Food Policies to prevent obesity and non-communicable diseases (NCDs) in the Caribbean Community, acknowledging that region needed to address the causal risk factors as well as to strengthen the region's health and agriculture policies. In this declaration, they pledged their "full support for the initiatives and mechanisms aimed at strengthening regional health and agricultural institutions, to provide critical leadership required for implementing (their) agreed strategies for the reduction of the burden of Chronic, Non-Communicable Diseases". Some of the commitments of this declaration include:

- Support for the efforts to pursue fair trade policies in all international trade negotiations thereby promoting greater use of indigenous agricultural products and foods and reducing the negative effects of globalization on our food supply;
- Development of food and agriculture policies that explicitly incorporate nutritional goals including the use of dietary guidelines in designing food production strategies;
- Research and surveillance on the aspects of agricultural policy and programmes that impact on the availability and accessibility of foods that affect obesity and NCDs;
- Support for the establishment of formal planning linkages between the agriculture sector and other sectors (especially, health, tourism, trade and planning) in order to ensure a more integrated and coordinated approach to policy and programme development aimed at reducing obesity;
- The elimination of trans-fats from our food supply
- Mandating the labelling of foods or such measures necessary to indicate their nutritional content
- Advocacy for incentives for comprehensive public education programmes in support of wellness and increased consumption of fruits and vegetables and embrace the role of the media as a partner in all our efforts to prevent and control NCDs
- Support for CARICOM, CFNI/PAHO, FAO, IICA and CARDI as the entities responsible for leading the development of the regional Food Security Plan for the prevention and control of NCDs.

Also at the regional level, CARPHA has developed a regional Plan of Action for Promoting Healthy Weights in the Caribbean: Prevention and Control of Childhood Obesity (2014–2019). The aim of this plan is to halt and reverse the rise in child and adolescent obesity in the Caribbean by 2025, through the implementation of technical cooperation with Member States. The plan comprises four pillars:

(i) Socio-ecological Approach: assisting countries to implement impactful measures to reshape the environments where Caribbean children live, work and plan.

(ii) Lifestyle Perspective: to support the design and implementation of evidence-based interventions to bring about behaviour change of children, their families and their communities.
(iii) Care and Support: providing youth-friendly healthcare and psychosocial services for children who are already overweight or obese or for those who are at higher risk.
(iv) Capability and capacity development: to provide a platform of support to strengthen the countries' capacity to implement the activities identified in Pillars 1–3. The focus is on the delivery systems in key sectors of health, education and trade, as well as on developing capacity to foster and maintain strong partnerships among government, civil society and private sector organizations.

The call from the Caribbean Heads also led to the United Nations (UN) organizing a High-Level Meeting on non-communicable diseases in September 2011. During this meeting, a resolution titled "Political Declaration of the High-Level Meeting of the General Assembly on the Prevention and Control of Non-Communicable Diseases" was unanimously adopted. It emphasized the "urgent need for greater measures at global, regional, and national levels to prevent and control non-communicable diseases". This initiative elevated the fight against NCDs to the global level.

Two additional high level global meetings on NCDs were held by the UN General Assembly—one in July 2014 and the other in September 2018. The September meeting resulted in the political resolution entitled, "*Time to deliver: accelerating our response to address non-communicable diseases for the health and well-being of present and future generations*", which was a call for action by the countries to deliver on their commitments.

Other global initiatives which advanced the fight against NCDs were the Small Island Developing States (SIDS) Accelerated Modalities of Action (SAMOA) Pathway[2] in 2014 and the adoption of the Sustainable Development Goals in 2015. Coming out of these meetings, the Global Action Plan (GAP) for the Prevention and Control of NCDs 2013–2020 (WHO, 2013) was developed as a comprehensive plan for operationalizing the previous commitments made by Heads of State and Government

[2] UNGA resolution A/74/L.3.

in the Political Declaration on the Prevention and Control of NCDs. This GAP recognizes the role and responsibility of governments as well as the role of international cooperation to support national efforts.

Regional and National Policies

With the assistance of global and regional agencies such as CARPHA, CAHFSA, FAO, IICA, UNICEF and WHO/PAHO, countries in the region have been implementing a number of policies to address adult and childhood obesity. CARPHA has also developed a 6-point policy package. Policy actions include, but are not limited to:

- Food-based dietary guidelines and nutrition education;
- Mandatory front of package nutrition warning labelling to empower consumers to make the healthiest choices;
- Fiscal policies to reduce the cost of healthy options while increasing the cost of unhealthy foods;
- National school feeding programmes and regulation in school settings to ban the sale and marketing of ultra-processed foods;
- Food supply policies which support domestic production of healthy foods while disincentivizing the importation of unhealthy foods;
- Double and triple duty actions which improve food systems while also addressing related challenges such as climate change; and,
- Conflict of interest policies to protect policymaking spaces from vested interests.

At the National level, countries have been implementing specific plans tailored to their particular environments. Some examples include:

- The imposition of taxes on fast food and sugary drinks in Antigua and Barbuda and Dominica.
- The introduction of subsidies on local fruits and vegetables in Guyana and St Lucia.
- Mandatory physical education and nutritional guidelines in most Caribbean schools.
- Jamaica Moves led to the adoption by the other Caribbean countries as "Caribbean Moves" initiative was launched in 2018—as a result of this initiative, Barbados, Jamaica, Saint Kitts and Nevis and Trinidad

and Tobago have modified it and initiated their national versions of health promotion campaigns to raise awareness of and promote healthier lifestyles to reduce the incidence of NCDs.
- The promotion of school programmes such as "Water Wednesdays" to encourage the increased consumption of water as a healthier alternative to sugar-sweetened beverages and implemented "Fruit Fridays" to encourage the inclusion of more fruits and vegetables for a balanced diet instead of snacks high in sugar and salt.
- The introduction of public purchasing programmes where governments use local farmers to provide food for institutions such as hospitals, prisons and school feeding programmes. Policies to serve only local foods at government hosted events such as cocktail parties and high-level luncheons are also recommended.

School Feeding Programs

One of the initiatives that CARICOM countries have been using to address the problem of childhood obesity is the School Feeding Program. In these programs, the government provides free school meals to vulnerable children. FAO and UWI (2021) in their review of School Feeding Programmes in 14 CARICOM countries identified three main types of SFPs (Table 6.3):

(i) Decentralized school kitchen (DSK) model
(ii) Third-party caterer-based (CB) model: and the
(iii) Centralized school feeding (CSF) model.

Each type of SFP has its advantages and disadvantages. The choice of model depends on the circumstances in the particular country. Some of the recommendations for improvement of the SFP include:

- the improvement of the nutritional quality of the meal offerings;
- development of food and nutrition education programmes;
- expansion and promotion of school gardens;
- increased utilization of the food products and labour from local communities, e.g. through back yard gardens;
- enhanced efficiency of operations;
- a reduction of risks by enhanced food safety and quality;

Table 6.3 Summary of key details and characteristics of models of CARICOM school feeding programmes

SFP model	*Decentralized school kitchen (DSK) model*	*Caterer based (CB) model*	*Centralized school feeding (CSF) model*
Countries	Dominica, Grenada, Guyana (hinterland), Haiti, Jamaica, Nevis, Saint Lucia, Saint Vincent and the Grenadines, Suriname (proposed pilot Programme), Belize (Toledo district)	Bahamas, Belize, Trinidad and Tobago, Suriname (now ended)	Antigua and Barbuda, Barbados, Guyana (coastal), Saint Kitts, Jamaica (NPL)
Managed by	Ministry of Education, NGOs and international agencies (especially Haiti)	Ministry of Education	Ministry of Education
Food preparation	In kitchens on the school premises	By caterers on their own premises. Prepared meals (or snacks) are transported to schools	In large centralized industrial factories or meal production centers. Prepared meals (or snacks) are transported to schools
Inputs	Higher level of incorporation into the SFPs from parents and local communities of: • a limited range of food items (especially vegetables, seasoning herbs and root crops); and • voluntary or paid labor for meal preparation and the procurement of food items These inputs may lower the costs of the SFPs	Low level of incorporation into the meals of inputs of food and labor from the local communities	Very low level of incorporation into the meals of inputs of food and labor from the local communities

SFP model	*Decentralized school kitchen (DSK) model*	*Caterer based (CB) model*	*Centralized school feeding (CSF) model*
Portion sizes	Not fixed Food is served by the cooks or their assistants. This allows for control of meal portions and students can be served the quantities that they would normally like to eat. This reduces the problems of food rejection and food waste	Fixed	Fixed
Meal containers and cutlery	Meal containers (usually plates) and cutlery are usually washable and reusable, which avoids the use of Styrofoam, plastic and other one-use types of material which may be detrimental to the physical environment	Meal containers (usually boxes) and cutlery not usually re-usable	Meal containers and cutlery nor re-usable
Monitoring of operations and food quality standards	Less monitoring	Variably intensive monitoring	Rigorous monitoring

Source FAO and UWI (2021) Review of School Feeding Programmes in the Caribbean

- the linking of school feeding programmes to local farmers through public purchasing so that they provide healthy, local food for the programmes.

Other Initiatives

Other initiatives to encourage the production of healthy, nutritious local foods include the promotion of backyard gardening; Buy Local, Eat Local and Eat What you Grow campaigns, which have been promoted in countries such as Jamaica and Guyana and the support for peri-urban agriculture and community gardens.

In Guyana, for World Food Day, the FAO held a competition in which schools were challenged to produce healthy, nutritious meals for school feeding programmes and for business men's lunches on a specified budget. The recipes developed by the winning schools were used to prepare a Recipe Book of Healthy Nutritious School meals. In addition, the Carnegie School of Home Economics provided training for managers of tuck shops in Secondary Schools in Georgetown in the preparation of healthy alternatives by substituting unhealthy ingredients with healthy, local alternatives.

Food Safety

Food safety refers to the manner in which food is handled, prepared, transported and stored—at each stage of the value chain—to prevent contamination by potential hazards. These hazards may be biological (parasites, bacteria, viruses), chemical or physical in nature and can result in foodborne-related illnesses or injuries to both humans and animals. Food safety is, therefore, intimately linked with nutrition and health and by extension, food utilization and food security. For Caribbean countries, which rely heavily on tourism, food safety is important, not only for the health and well-being of its citizens, but also that of the tourists who visit or shores. A country's reputation and overall economy are at stake if the highest levels of food safety are not upheld.

The WHO (2022) estimates that 600 million persons (almost 10% of the global population) are affected by and 420,000 die from eating contaminated food every year, resulting in the loss of 33 million healthy life years (DALYs). Moreover, 125,000 children under the age of 5 years die annually from foodborne diseases and carry 40% of the burden of foodborne diseases. The WHO further indicates that in low and middle-income countries, US$110 billion is lost each year in productivity and medical expenses resulting from unsafe food.

In the Caribbean, CARPHA (2022) has noted that "diarrheal illness resulting from contaminated food or water (FBD) is the most common health problem faced by visitors to the Caribbean". The agency further indicated that between 2010 and 2016, they received reports of over 250 outbreaks of gastroenteritis from 23 countries, 15% of these occurred in hotels/resorts, accounting for over 25,000 cases. One outbreak in 2012 resulted in over 800 ill persons, hotel closure and a 20% decline in arrivals.

Climate change, increased global and regional food trade, antimicrobial resistance, increased food insecurity, changing food systems and food fraud are some of the main issues affecting food safety in the region.

At the country level in many countries there is duplication of roles by various agencies dealing with food safety and turfdom, it is often perceived that by ceding the roles to other agencies, there would be a loss of jobs in the affected agency, consequently, there is reluctance to implement institutional reform.

Conclusions

Food Utilization refers to the way the body uses the various nutrients in food. Food consumption, nutrition and food safety are essential elements of Food Utilization. With respect to Food Consumption, the Caribbean faces a double burden of malnutrition, with undernourishment coexisting alongside overweight and obesity. While undernourishment, particularly evident in Haiti with high prevalence of stunting and wasting, is a concern, there's also a significant rise in obesity rates across the region.

Obesity rates among adults have increased in all Caribbean countries from 2000 to 2016. The Bahamas had the highest prevalence of obesity among adults, while Trinidad and Tobago had the lowest. Obesity rates were generally higher in women compared to men.

The prevalence of overweight and obesity among children under 5 years of age in the Caribbean is higher than the global average. Rates have increased markedly since 2000, with South America experiencing a more significant rise compared to the Caribbean.

The high prevalence of overweight and obesity is linked to a higher incidence of chronic non-communicable diseases (NCDs) such as cardiovascular diseases, cancers, chronic respiratory diseases, and diabetes.

Deaths caused by NCDs are disproportionately high in the Caribbean, contributing to a significant burden on healthcare systems.

The treatment of NCDs can be expensive, putting a strain on healthcare systems and government budgets. Rising NCD prevalence can lead to increased healthcare costs, affecting investments in other sectors of the economy.

Factors contributing to the rising trend of obesity in the Caribbean include high prices of healthy, nutritious locally produced food, limited availability of diverse and affordable food, poor nutritional food choices, and consumption patterns influenced by the availability of imported ultra-processed foods.

Efforts to address obesity and NCDs include regional and national policies aimed at promoting healthy diets, improving food safety, implementing school feeding programs and increasing public awareness. Initiatives such as the Declaration of Port of Spain and the Declaration of St Ann highlight the commitment of Caribbean countries to address the issue.

Global initiatives and frameworks such as the United Nations High-Level Meetings on NCDs and the Sustainable Development Goals provide a platform for coordinated action against obesity and NCDs at the international level.

Food Safety on the other hand, refers to practices that prevent food contamination throughout the entire food supply chain, encompassing handling, preparation, transportation and storage. It is crucial for safeguarding public health, nutrition and overall well-being. In Caribbean nations heavily reliant on tourism, maintaining high food safety standards is vital not only for citizens but also for tourists, as it impacts the country's reputation and economy.

In the Caribbean, reports indicate numerous outbreaks, some resulting in significant economic losses and declines in tourism arrivals. Climate change, global food trade, antimicrobial resistance, food insecurity, changing food systems and food fraud exacerbate food safety challenges in the region.

Challenges at the country level include overlapping roles among agencies responsible for food safety, hindering effective coordination and implementation of reforms. Addressing institutional issues and fostering collaboration among agencies are crucial for enhancing food safety systems.

To address these challenges, the region must prioritize the collection, analysis and dissemination of accurate, up-to-date data to inform decision-making and plan appropriate responses to food safety-related outbreaks, especially considering the impact of climate change. Harmonizing procedures and legislation is essential to strengthen national food safety systems and facilitate trade. Collaboration among agencies and adoption of the One Health approach are vital for addressing health-related issues comprehensively.

There is urgent need for comprehensive and coordinated efforts to address the complex challenge of overweight, obesity and related NCDs in the Caribbean region, considering its significant health and economic implications. To address the challenges of food safety, Caribbean requires concerted efforts to address regional challenges, strengthen institutional frameworks, implement effective policies and foster collaboration among stakeholders to safeguard public health and support economic stability.

References

Abdulkadri, A., et al. (2015, September). WHO/ISH Total Risk Approach for Primary Prevention of Cardiovascular Disease Shows Greater Decrease in Costs for Women but Not the Elderly in Jamaica. *Journal of Clinical Epidemiology, 68*(9), 994–1001.

Abdulkadri, A., et al. (2021). *Addressing the Adverse Impacts of Non-communicable Diseases on the Sustainable Development of Caribbean Countries*. Studies and Perspectives Series-ECLAC Subregional Headquarters for the Caribbean, No. 100 (LC/TS.2021/4-LC/CAR/TS.2021/2). Santiago, Economic Commission for Latin America and the Caribbean (ECLAC).

Abdulkadri, A. O., Cunningham-Myrie, C., & Forrester, T. (2009). Economic Burden of Diabetes Andhypertension in CARICOM States. *Social and Economic Studies, 58*, 3–4.

CARPHA. (2022). https://carpha.org/THP/Food-Safety

ECLAC (2020). *The Caribbean Outlook: Forging a people-centred approach to sustainable development post COVID 19* (LC/SES.38/12), Santiago.

FAO. (2021). *Measuring Food Safety Indicators to Achieve Sustainable Development Goals*. Food Safety Technical Toolkit for Asia and the Pacific. https://www.fao.org/3/cb4111en/cb4111en.pdf

FAO, IFAD, PAHO, UNICEF and WFP. (2023). *Regional Overview of Food Security and Nutrition—Latin America and the Caribbean 2022: Towards Improving Affordability of Healthy Diets*. Santiago. https://doi.org/10.4060/cc3859en

https://www.worldobesity.org/resources/policy-dossiers/obesity-covid-19/frequently-asked-questions

Manikas, I., Ali, B. M., & Sundarakani, B. A. (2023). Systematic Literature Review of Indicators Measuring Food Security. *Agriculture & Food Security, 12*, 10. https://doi.org/10.1186/s40066-023-00415-7

Mitchell-Fearon, K., McKoy-Davis, J., Willie-Tyndale, D., Abdulkadri, A. O., & Eldemire-Shearer, D. (2017). The Economic Burden of Hypertension Among Older Persons: Lessons from a Developing Nation. *Journal of Public Health in Developing Countries, 3*(1), 347–357.

PAHO. (2016). *Economic Dimensions of Non-Communicable Disease in Latin America and the Caribbean. Disease Control Priorities* (3rd ed., Companion Volume). PAHO.

RTI International. (2016). *Rapid Assessment of the Economic Dimensions of Non-Communicable Diseases in Trinidad and Tobago.*

UNICEF, WHO World Bank Group Joint Malnutrition Estimates, May 2023 edition.

WHO. (2013). *Global Action Plan for the Prevention and Control of Noncommunicable Diseases 2013–2020.*

World Health Organization. (2016). *The Global Health Observatory. Prevalence of Overweight Among Children and Adolescents from 5 to 19 Years Old.* www.who.int/data/gho/data/indicators/indicator-details/GHO/prevalence-of-overweight-among-children-andadolescents-bmi-1-standard-deviations-above-themedian-(crude-estimate)-(-). Accessed 11 May 2023.

World Health Organization. (2019). *Global Burden of Disease Collaborative Network, Global Burden of Disease Study 2019 (GBD 2019) Results* (2020, Institute for Health Metrics and Evaluation—IHME). https://vizhub.healthdata.org/gbd-results/

World Health Organization. (2022). *Non Communicable Diseases Progress Monitor 2022.* World Health Organization. Licence: CC BY-NC-SA 3.0 IGO.

CHAPTER 7

Food Stability in the Caribbean

Introduction

Food stability refers to the extent to which food is available, accessible and appropriately utilized in an uninterrupted manner at the country, community and household level. The factors which impact the stability of food availability, access and utilization can be natural, man-made or economic. Natural phenomena include weather-related disasters, earthquakes, diseases, pests and pandemics. Wars and conflicts are important

---

Professor Donovan Campbell contributed the sections on Climate Change and Variability, as well as on Land Use Changes and Environmental Degradation.

Donovan Campbell is a Professor of Environmental Geography at the University of the West Indies. His main areas of expertise include climate change adaptation and food systems on small islands. He has contributed to several intergovernmental scientific assessments, such as the Intergovernmental Panel on Climate Change (IPCC), the Intergovernmental Science-Policy Platform on Biodiversity and Ecosystem Services (IPBES), and the Global Environmental Outlook (GEO). At the regional level, he works with communities and governments across the Caribbean to accelerate the adoption of innovative, climate-resilient strategies to secure a sustainable future.

D. Stanberry and L. Fletcher-Paul, *Food Security in the Caribbean*, Palgrave Studies in Agricultural Economics and Food Policy, https://doi.org/10.1007/978-3-031-66055-9_7

man-made conditions that can seriously impact agricultural production and physical movement of food. Other important man-made factors impacting food production include environmental degradation, land use changes, pollution and other human actions that can threaten the availability of natural resources required for food production—such as land and water. Economic factors include inflation and high food prices, devaluation, unemployment, factors that impede trade in food (high tariffs, quantitative restrictions and export bans), and indebtedness, which restrict the capacity of the State to invest in agriculture and the state of a country's social protection systems.

Factors affecting food stability can be inter-related. For example, natural disasters can wipe the food produced by a country, as well as its production capacity. This not only affects food availability, but also causes economic shocks to the system—negatively impacting Government's revenue, necessitating borrowing to restore production and creating fiscal deficits and increases in food prices, which in turn affects people's access to food. Food stability also has a spatial dimension. At the level of the country, food may be available in adequate quantities, but there may be limited economic access to food in specific communities and households because of their poverty level. The state of a country's social protection system is therefore critical in maintaining food stability.

Food stability also has a temporal dimension in terms of its duration, in that unavailability and lack of access to food can be short-lived or chronic. Short-term food insecurity relates to natural disasters which disrupt food production, but the short fall in food supply can be easily filled in the short term by increased imports, food aid or draw down from stocks.

At the household level, disruption in food access can be caused by loss of employment by the head of the household. The loss of household income caused by unemployment can be ameliorated by, inter alia, the State's social protection system, support from relatives and remittances. Long-term instability in food production and supply is often related to prolonged conflicts that can destroy production and production capacity and disrupt food aid and imports.

This chapter will examine the critical factors that impact food stability in the Caribbean, with a view to predict the likely behaviour of these factors in the future. The history of agricultural risk management in the Caribbean will also be reviewed and the available policy options to de-risk agricultural production and thereby attract the requisite private sector investment in the region's agriculture for enhanced food security will be discussed. The chapter will focus on those factors that constitute the greatest threat to the region's food security—climate change and variability, land use changes, economic shocks, conflicts and praedial larceny.

Factors Affecting Food Stability in the Caribbean

Climate Change and Variability

The climate crisis is negatively impacting food systems across the Caribbean, leading to crop losses, reduced yields, fluctuating food prices and decreased nutritional quality (Galli et al., 2023). By 2050, extreme climatic events such as heat, drought, flooding and saltwater intrusion from sea level rise are expected to reduce crop production by 10–25% (Annie et al., 2023; FAO, 2021). These events can disrupt food stability, leading to higher food prices and economic losses (Kumari & Bains, 2023). In general, the Caribbean is expected to experience a gradual decrease in precipitation through to the end of the century, with spatial variations in drying intensity across the region. Global Climate Models (GCMs) predict a reduction of up to 20% in annual rainfall for the central and southern Caribbean basin, while Regional Climate Models (RCMs) suggest a decrease of up to 25% to 35% by the century's end (CSGM, 2020). Additionally, GCMs indicate a decrease of up to 2% in annual mean rainfall by the mid-2020s, progressing to up to 6% drier conditions by the 2050s (Martin del Campo et al., 2023). These significant reductions in rainfall could severely impact agricultural productivity and food stability. Climate change is also expected to decrease agricultural productivity in the Latin America and Caribbean (LAC) region by 9.03% to 12.7% between 2015 and 2050, which translates to significant economic losses, ranging from $14.7 billion to $31.4 billion (Lachaud et al., 2021).

Slow-onset events, such as rising temperatures, changing precipitation patterns and increased frequency of droughts, significantly impact poverty and food security because the region's economies and societies are deeply reliant on environmental resources (Feher et al., 2023). Projected temperature increases of 0.48 °C–3.05 °C by the end of the century (CSGM, 2020) could shorten crop growing seasons and increase crop and livestock heat stress, thereby exacerbating food security challenges (Feher et al., 2023). In 2023, severe heat waves linked to climate change significantly impacted agricultural productivity and food security across the Caribbean.

The average temperature anomaly in Jamaica between June and August was 1.3 degrees Celsius higher than normal, leading to decreased crop production, limited water availability and livestock stress (Ewing-Chow, 2024). These impacts are far-reaching, affecting not only the quantity of food produced but also its nutritional quality and price stability. As posited by Alpino et al. (2022), climate change can negatively impact food and nutrition security by reducing crop yields, altering the nutritional content of food and creating unpredictable food price fluctuations. These conditions are expected to widen the productivity gap across the region in the coming decades.

The economic impact of extreme weather events, particularly hurricanes, is well-documented. According to data from the Overseas Development Institute, hurricanes cost the Caribbean an annual average of US$835 million in damages. The Caribbean Catastrophe Risk Insurance Facility (CCRIF) pay-outs surpassed US$50 million following the devastating 2017 hurricane season. Climate change disrupts every aspect of food security, affecting availability, stability, utilization and access to food (Feher et al., 2023). The impacts of hurricanes on Grenada, Dominica and Antigua and Barbuda have highlighted the urgent need for climate-resilient agricultural practices in these territories. In Dominica, category 5 Hurricane Maria caused $1.3 billion in damage, amounting to 226% of its GDP (Ewing-Chow, 2024; FAO, 2021). Lewis (2022) assessed the economic losses and damages from tropical cyclones (TCs) in the Caribbean from 1980 to 2019 and found a gradual rise from 1980 to 2009, followed by a sharp increase from 2010 to 2019. Predictive models suggest that climate change could lead to a doubling of annual cyclone-related losses, increasing from US$26 billion to US$53 billion by the year 2100 (Lewis, 2022).

The vulnerability of Caribbean food systems to climate impacts is closely connected to its economic fragility. Many Caribbean islands rely heavily on imported food (FAO, 2021), and extreme weather events can disrupt these imports, leading to food shortages and price volatility. In several Caribbean countries, imports account for more than 90% of total food consumed (Ewing-Chow, 2024). According to the FAO (2021), the region imports between 60 and 80% of its basic food needs—compared to a global average of 27.6%. This dependence on external sources increases susceptibility to disruptions caused by extreme weather events, trade fluctuations and global food price hikes.

Land Use Changes and Environmental Degradation

Land use changes and environmental degradation in the Caribbean significantly impact food security. These changes lead to reduced agricultural productivity, increased dependence on food imports and increased vulnerability to climate change. Environmental degradation, often driven by land use change, puts severe pressure on the biodiversity of foodscapes across the Caribbean and is projected to intensify by 2050 (IPBES, 2018). These interconnected challenges have serious implications for food security and related development goals. A significant portion of the Caribbean population relies on agricultural livelihoods; the loss of productive land directly affects food availability (Beckford & Campbell, 2013). Effective climate change adaptation and mitigation strategies are urgently needed to address land use and environmental degradation trends and their implications for food security across the region.

Since the 1950s, the Caribbean region has experienced significant changes in land use patterns, including urbanization, industrial development, tourism and agricultural expansion and intensification (Morgan et al., 2022). These changes have led to the conversion of agricultural land to non-agricultural uses, resulting in reduced agricultural productivity and loss of arable land. Environmental degradation, such as soil erosion, deforestation and biodiversity loss, further exacerbates the challenges to agricultural sustainability (Weis, 2007). Biomass flow accounting techniques can be used to assess the impact of land use change on food security in the Caribbean. For example, Rahman et al. (2022) utilized socio-metabolic research techniques to examine crop biomass flow data across the Caribbean. They found a decline in local food production since the 1960s in Caribbean nations (Barbados, Dominica, Grenada and Jamaica), and a simultaneous increase in net importation rates. This analysis provides evidence of a cumulative biophysical change in food production output and input across the region, and its implications for food security.

A long-standing challenge for the region is determining how to meet the ever-growing local needs for food while preserving the environment. In the region, continuous land use has occurred, causing significant soil organic carbon (SOC) loss (Jimenez-Castaneda et al., 2022). As agricultural land diminishes and productivity declines, dependence on imported food increases, making the region more susceptible to external shocks and price volatility (Beckford & Campbell, 2013). For example, the COVID-19 pandemic highlighted these vulnerabilities, with approximately 40.9% of the LAC population facing difficulties accessing food during the pandemic (Hernández-Vásquez et al., 2022). Currently, more than 50% of the population of the English-speaking Caribbean is either moderately or severely food insecure (Ewing-Chow, 2024; Mohammadi et al., 2022).

Table 7.1 shows that land degradation in the Caribbean varies in intensity and scale. Barbados experiences the highest percentage of degraded land at 56.50%, followed by the Dominican Republic at 31.25%. In contrast, countries like Cuba and Dominica report considerably lower degradation rates, at 0.47% and 0.40% respectively. The absolute area affected also shows vast differences, ranging from as little as 200 hectares in St. Vincent and the Grenadines to over 5 million hectares in Cuba. Suriname and Guyana exhibit substantial land degradation, with over 15% of their land areas affected, amounting to more than 2.5 million hectares each.

Across the region, sustainable land management practices, such as conservation agriculture, agroforestry and soil and water conservation techniques, have been identified as effective measures to combat soil

Table 7.1 Extent of land degradation in selected Caribbean countries

Country	*Date of the information*	*Degraded area (ha)*	*Degraded area as a % of total land area*
Antigua & Barbuda	2019	3800	10.33
Barbados	2015	24,000	56.50
Cuba	2015	5,015,200	0.47
Dominica	2019	300	0.40
Dominican Republic	2019	1,490,000	31.25
Haiti	2019	611,600	23.00
Jamaica	2019	83,800	7.71
St. Kitts & Nevis	2019	2800	11.20
St. Lucia	2019	500	0.85
St. Vincent & the Grenadines	2019	200	0.54
Trinidad & Tobago	2019	44,700	8.92
Guyana	2019	3,340,000	15.89
Suriname	2019	2,530,000	15.47

Source https://www.unccd.int/our-work/country-profiles

erosion, improve water retention and enhance agricultural productivity (FAO, 2017). Land use changes and environmental degradation significantly impact food security in the Caribbean by reducing agricultural productivity, increasing dependence on food imports and exacerbating vulnerability to climate change. Policies to support agricultural diversification and the preservation of agricultural land from non-agricultural development are essential to ensure long-term food security and have been advocated for several decades (Beckford & Campbell, 2013).

Programmes such as the Caribbean Small Island Developing States (SIDS) Multi-Country Sustainable Land Management Project and Jamaica's Rural Economic Development Initiative (REDI) are examples of promising efforts to promote sustainable land management and food security through the improvement of land and water resources management. By targeting issues such as soil erosion, land degradation and water scarcity, these programmes ensure that arable lands remain productive and capable of supporting agriculture. Jamaica's REDI focuses more broadly on rural economic development through sustainable agriculture, agrotourism and initiatives to improve market access for micro and small-scale rural producers. The REDI programme has had significant impacts on local agriculture and job creation, contributing to a 17% growth in the agricultural sector in 2016, the creation of approximately 1,300 jobs, and a US$6 million reduction in Jamaica's food import bill (Linton, 2020).

Economic Shocks

Economic shocks are random, unpredictable events, generally outside of the control of an economy, which when they occur, fundamentally change economic performance as measured by economic matrices such as unemployment, GDP, inflation and consumption. Although not a traditional economic variable, one of the variables that economic shocks can profoundly impact is the level of a country's food security. Apart from their vulnerability to adverse weather events, the Caribbean territories are characterized by their narrow economic base and openness to trade, which render them extremely susceptible to external economic shocks.

Since coming into nationhood with the wave of independence which started in 1962, the Caribbean faced its first major economic shock in 1973 with the Oil Crisis. This crisis started as an embargo on oil exports to the United States by Arab oil-producing countries in October 1973, with progressive cuts in production thereafter into 1974. This political response by Arabs to US support of Israel in the Yom Kippur War, precipitated a worldwide oil crisis, manifested in steep increases in the price of oil over a short period. Since oil is indispensable to the production of nearly all goods and services, increases in the price of oil resulted in increases in the prices of nearly all goods and services. In the case of food, Taghizadeh-Hesary et al. (2019), assert that 64.2% of the variability of food prices is attributable to movement in oil prices. There is therefore a strong positive correlation between energy prices and food prices.

With the exception of Trinidad and Tobago, Caribbean countries which were then solely dependent on imported oil, faced serious balance of payment problems, as their expenditure on oil imports increased by a factor far more significant than revenues from their commodity exports. This plunged many countries into a debt trap and resulted in serious fiscal challenges. The oil crisis further prompted many countries in the region to pay attention to energy conservation and diversification, as well as food security in the face of the food crisis precipitated by the energy crisis. It was out of this reality that the newly formed CARICOM set out to formulate the Regional Food Plan to replace expensive food imports, and in Jamaica for instance, self-reliance became a critical plank of public policy, under the banner of "Eat What You Grow, Grow What You Eat".

The next serious economic shock the region experienced was the erosion of its preferential access to the EU markets for its traditional exports of sugar and banana at the turn of the century, through the unrelenting forces of liberalization of agricultural trade. Jamaica, Guyana, Belize, Barbados, St. Kitts and Trinidad and Tobago, the region's largest sugar exporters were particularly affected. Sugar production ceased in St. Kitts and Trinidad and Tobago, and was significantly curtailed in Jamaica and Barbados. Guyana and Belize fared better, because they were more competitive in the production of sugar. The Windward Islands were similarly impacted by the erosion of access to the EU for bananas. In both instances, these crops were the main agricultural crops in terms of proportion of farm lands occupied, employment and involvement of small farmers and export revenue. Thanks to the diversification of these economies through tourism, manufacturing, non-tradition agricultural exports, services and mining, the economic fallout from the demise of export banana and sugar was somewhat mitigated at the macro level.

However, the social fallout through unemployment and the loss of livelihoods by small banana and cane farmers was considerable. According to data from the Sugar Industry Authority in Jamaica for instance, the number of small independent cane farmers who supplied sugar cane to factories declined from 6319 in 2005 to 2735 in 2020. This represents a significant economic fallout in terms of loss of livelihoods. Trotman et al. (2009) suggest that although agriculture's contribution to GDP in most CARICOM States is fairly modest, the sector employs a disproportionate share of the labour force. Hence, there is a significant risk to households' income, and by extension access to food, when agriculture is under stress. Further, in the case of sugar, the industry supported whole communities in terms of social amenities and other economic activities. Poverty therefore increased in sugar-dependent communities, negatively affecting access to food (Stanberry, 2022).

The next economic shock that the region faced, which negatively impacted its food security was the global financial crisis of 2007, which spiralled into a world food crisis in 2008. As outlined in Chapter 1, whereas in the pre-2008 period food crises were precipitated by weather-induced crop failures and conflicts, the 2008 world food crisis was not related to any significant curtailment in agricultural production. Instead, the crisis was more related to issues of speculation in futures markets for agricultural commodities and diversion of agricultural production from food to fuel in the face of high oil prices. This crisis was manifested in high food prices and such critical imported inputs as fertilizers and chemicals, many of which are by-products of the petroleum industry.

Examining the food import bill of CARICOM States, data from the CARICOM Secretariat show that the sharpest increase in the food import bill over the last 20 years occurred between 2007 and 2008, ranging from 14% in Belize to 26% in Guyana, with an average increase of approximately 20%. For the region's food import bill to increase by 20% in a single year is a major shock. The Caribbean lags behind the rest of the world in per capita food production (Trotman et al., 2009). Given the high level of dependence on imported food to satisfy the Caribbean's food demands, the region is highly vulnerable to high food prices and export restrictions. In 2008 therefore, the region's consumers faced high food prices, which negatively impacted their access to food.

Looking at food prices over a 60-year period, the FAO has identified a structural shift in the movement of food prices since the turn of the century. Between 1961 and 1987 (with the exception of the 1972–1976 period, associated with the Oil Crisis), global food prices declined by about one-third, then there was a level of stability up to 2000, and thereafter up to 2022, there was an almost doubling of the real food price index (FAO, 2022). According to FAO's Food Price Index, food prices are some 30% higher today than in the 1990s. The 2008 World Food Crisis marks the upward shift in real food prices, which differentiates it from previous food crises of the 1960s and 1970s (Chand, 2008). The prevailing high prices of food however do not take into account the negative externalities associated with food production globally, such as loss of biodiversity through habitat loss, land degradation, ground water pollution from inappropriate use of agricultural chemicals and saline intrusion due to over-pumping of ground water. Should these costs be internalized, then food prices would have been higher.

Based on linear trends from historical data, the prognosis for the future is for food prices to continue to rise, and to rise even higher if negative environmental externalities are captured in the prices of food (FAO, 2022). Factors such as climate change, continued diversion of food to fuel, financial speculation are all poised to impact food prices, to perhaps a greater degree than food availability itself. There are some mitigating factors that could halt rising food costs, such as greater utilization of precision agriculture technologies. For the Caribbean however, with a predominance of small subsistence farmers, these capital-intensive production technologies could be out of their reach and they could end up being overwhelmed and displaced if these technologies are employed on a wide scale to produce vegetables. As the Caribbean seeks to formulate its response to high food prices through import replacement, care must be taken to avoid the mistakes and missteps of the Green Revolution. A model needs to be found to incorporate small farmers, working in a sustainable and cooperative framework with the large private sector players, who must play a key role in the implementation of the "25 by 25" Initiative.

The most recent economic shock to have hit the CARICOM region and impacted its state of food security is undoubtedly the COVID-19 pandemic. Apart from the incalculable value of the human lives lost and the toll on the health of millions, the pandemic dealt a devastating blow to economic activities worldwide. Restrictions in the movement of goods worldwide had a significantly negative impact on cross-border trade. Restrictions in movement disrupted trade not only in finished goods, but raw material and inputs, which in turn impacted production of goods at the country level. For the Caribbean, deemed the most tourism-dependent in the world, (Simpson, 2022), tourist arrivals plummeted by approximately 70% in 2020 over 2019, according to data from the Caribbean Tourism Organization. This not only impacted the income of entities and individuals offering tourism services, but also affected employment in the sector through widespread lay-offs, thus compromising access to food. Farmers who supplied food to the tourism sector also suffered significant loss of income.

Given the high contribution of tourism to GDP across countries of the region estimated to be between 31.5% and 60.2% (Dukharan, 2020), the slowdown of overall economic activities as measured by decline in GDP over the period 2019 to 2020 was dramatic—ranging from 9.9% in Jamaica to 24.4% in St. Lucia. Economies which were more diversified had a lower percentage decline in GDP, but all CARICOM States experienced reduction, with the exception of Guyana, which saw GDP growth of 43.5%, due to its new found oil (Ali, 2023).

The marked reduction in economic activities and increase in unemployment warranted significant increases in public expenditure on social safety net programmes to assist affected people to cushion the impact of loss of income and to cope with a wave of higher prices for goods and services, ushered in by the impacts of the pandemic. The combination of reduced economic growth and government revenue on the one hand and the increased public expenditure on the other hand, increased fiscal deficits across the region and forced countries to borrow more to fight the pandemic and provide social support. Consequently, there was a general reversal of the gains made by many Caribbean countries in the pre-pandemic period in reducing their debts. Accordingly, the debt-to-GDP ratio for all CARICOM countries increased in 2020 compared with 2019, per data from the IMF.

Specifically in relation to food security in the region, the pandemic exacerbated the prevalence of undernourishment which was already on the rise in the pre-COVID-19 period. The impact of the pandemic on the proportion of undernourished people in the Caribbean, the percentage of food insecure people and the increases in the cost of a balanced diet due to inflation have been amply elaborated in Chapter 1.

Perhaps no other event has exposed the vulnerability of the region to external shocks and the fragility of the region's economic foundations than the COVID-19 pandemic. To lose up to 25% of GDP in a single year, as was the case in St. Lucia, is profound and speaks to the urgent need for economic diversification and sustainable import replacement for foods. Exports are concentrated, with all but 5 countries in the region, having their top five exports constituting more than 75% of export earnings, and in some countries as high as 90%, and the concentration has increased over time (Heger et al., 2008). While many Caribbean countries rank high on the UNDP's Human Development Index and boast of relatively high per capita income, this seeming prosperity is extremely fragile. In the case of Barbados, it is founded on "international beach tourism and a national service economy that is highly vulnerable to change in consumer taste and natural disaster impacts" (Pelling & Uitto, 2001). The deep integration of Caribbean economies in the global economic system and the region's openness to international trade continue to be a clear and present danger and significantly militate against its food security.

Conflicts

Conflicts have long surpassed crop failures and other natural disasters as the main driver of global food insecurity. There is a direct relationship between incidences of conflicts and the prevalence of malnutrition, famine and food insecurity. In fact, the FAO reports that the overwhelming majority of chronically food insecure and malnourished people reside in countries embroiled in conflicts (FAO, 2017). The genesis of most conflicts relates to control over natural resources, such as oil, minerals and water. However, recently many of the world's conflicts stem from growing radicalization, religious extremism, ethnic tensions and racism, political instability and criminal gangs in marginalized communities fighting for turf. The players in conflicts are also shifting from nations, to internal non-state actors, such as gangs and paramilitary and guerrilla groups; and many such internal conflicts are being internationalized, often drawing external nations into national conflicts. The nature of conflicts is also changing. In addition to armed combats involving violence, technological conflicts are now widespread, manifested particularly in cyber-attacks, threatening the democratic foundations of nations and destabilizing the operations of governments and businesses.

Conflicts of all types are set to continue to proliferate in the foreseeable future, driven by ever-increasing military spending. It is estimated that military expenditure was US$1820 billion in 2020, an increase of 9.6% over the 2010 expenditure (FAO, 2022). Post-World War II institutions set up to chart peace among nations are seemingly powerless to arrest growing militarization and resolve conflicts among nations. Multilateralism and diplomacy are no longer embraced as the framework within which conflicts are resolved, and the United States has seemingly in recent times, relinquished its leadership role in being a global 'policeman'. The emergence of China and its growing influence among developing countries is causing new geopolitical tensions. There is a pervasive distrust of governments and a lack of confidence in constituted authorities across the globe, giving rise to cynicism, increased demonstrations and an increased reliance on non-state actors to solve issues within countries. Growing disparity between the rich and the poor is also fuelling this distrust of Governments and national and international institutions. Food insecurity in and of itself is capable of sparking conflicts, as nations/territories vie for control of critical natural resources required for food production, such as water. Marginalized farmers are also fighting for control of their lands in the face of growing 'land grab' perpetuated by foreign interests and large developers. Food insecurity also breeds social discontent, which can spill over into demonstrations and conflicts, reminiscent of the 'Arab Spring', which was sparked by protests over, inter alia, high food prices.

The impact of conflicts on food availability, access and utilization is considerable. Violent conflicts physically destroy production and production capacity and seriously disrupt trade of agricultural goods. This disruption is most palpably demonstrated in the ongoing Russia/Ukraine War, where violent combat has been directly impacting the movement of grains from Ukraine through ports now largely under the control of the Russians. Wars and conflicts cause significant displacement of people, who abandon their productive activities as they flee for safety, and themselves become refugees requiring food aid and other humanitarian support. In many instances access to food aid is rendered difficult because of the armed conflicts, and aid agencies have resorted to pleading for cease fires between warring factions to distribute food aid. In fact, the FAO asserts that 80% of all humanitarian needs are attributable to conflicts (FAO, 2023). Military expenditure shifts resources from development of production capacity to enhance food security. In addition, the wanton loss of lives through violent combat robs nations of critical human resources required for development and production. In fact FAO asserts that death from famine and malnutrition caused by conflicts exceeds death by direct combat. The impact of human loss reverberates far beyond the conflicts, as war-ravaged countries could take a protracted time to restore production levels and capacity, with such widespread loss of lives.

The Caribbean region is relatively stable politically and armed conflicts between countries are rare, if not non-existent. Notwithstanding this relative stability, the region is not immune from the impacts of conflicts on its food security. With its economies fully integrated in the global economy and given its openness to international trade and high dependence on imported food, the region is highly vulnerable to the impact of conflicts, should they arise in countries and territories where it sources its food. Fortuitously, trade between Russia/Ukraine and the region is miniscule, hence the direct impact of the Russia/Ukraine War has been minimal (Ali, 2023). However, the region has not been spared from the impact of high food prices precipitated by the Russian/Ukraine conflict. Conflicts in the Middle East and attacks on vessels navigating the Red Sea and other waters around the Arabian Peninsula could portend danger for Caribbean food imports and imports of agricultural inputs, as these developments could cause increases in shipping costs and supply chain disruptions.

The Caribbean however, has to be mindful of the surge in gang violence and internal conflicts in Haiti and to a lesser extent Jamaica and Trinidad and Tobago. The situation in Haiti is particularly troubling, as internal conflicts and the overthrow of the rule of law are literally crippling production and the normal functioning of the economy. There is a burgeoning illegal trade of guns from Haiti into Jamaica in exchange for meat, which in itself has been fuelling the theft of animals in the Southern parishes of Jamaica. Refugees from Haiti fleeing to the Bahamas and Jamaica, though not at crisis proportion at this time, remains a matter of concern. In the Southern Caribbean refugees from the politically tense Venezuela into Trinidad and Tobago have also become an issue of concern. Recently renewed claims by Venezuela of two-thirds of Guyana's territory must also be closely monitored for any possible escalation into an armed conflict. The widespread poaching of conch and other pelagic resources from Jamaican territorial waters has been a longstanding source of tension between Jamaica and fishers from Honduras. Not only is this a latent source of conflict, but the illicit fishing robs the country of significant resources that could otherwise enhance Jamaica's export earnings as well as its food security.

Praedial Larceny

While the FAO in its 2022 report on the divers and triggers of food insecurity in the world in the foreseeable future identified growing geopolitical tensions and conflicts as a major driver, no specific mention was made of praedial larceny as a critical factor influencing the stability of food supply and access in the future. The report however, points to the concerning trend of "unprecedented levels of militia and gang violence … linked to politics and the economic benefits of conflict" (FAO, 2022, p. 91). Praedial Larceny or theft of agricultural produce falls squarely within this sphere of activity, motivated largely by economic gains to the perpetrators. This is one of the factors that negatively impacts the stability of food supply and access that is entirely internal to a country, unlike the impact of climate change, high food prices, changes in external market conditions, diseases, pests and pandemics. The impact however, is no less devastating on agricultural production, and is considered one of the biggest deterrents to agricultural production in the region. Moreover, it is not limited to the Caribbean.

Praedial Larceny is often under-reported and categorized as a mere rural crime for which there is often considerable empathy for the perpetrators, who are deemed poor and engaged in this activity to address their own food insecurity. (Graham, 2014). However, recently praedial larceny has moved from the realm of petty crime to major organized crime on a commercial scale, often involving violence. In fact, there is a growing body of literature focusing on the impact of the theft of agricultural produce (crops, livestock and fish), farm machinery and implements, as well as agricultural inputs, on food production, the livelihood of farmers (victims), the increased cost of production to secure agricultural production and the overall impact on countries' food security. These studies examine the extent and impact of praedial larceny in the United States, Europe (Britain and Scotland), Africa and as far as Australia. The scholarship on praedial larceny seems to be more advanced with respect to the situation in Australia, with scholarly work from Barclay (2001), Barclay and Donnermeyer (2001), Anderson and McCall (2005), Cardach (2002), and Hedyeh (2008). Swanson et al. (2000) estimate that the global loss of agricultural production to praedial larceny could be as high as US$5 billion, while Barclay (2001) quantified the prevalence of praedial larceny in Scotland and Australia, impacting 32% and 54% of primary producers respectively over a two-year period. Gbigbi (2021) indicates that 68% of farmers in a survey of farmers in the Delta State of Nigeria was impacted by farm pilferage. Bunei (2016) and Bunei et al. (2013) have written extensively of the magnitude of farm theft, particularly of livestock, becoming a highly organised enterprise in Kenya and serving as a major disincentive to investment in agricultural production.

The Caribbean region is particularly impacted by praedial larceny, and given the predominance of small players in the region's agricultural landscape, its impact not only affects food availability on a national scale, but compromises access to food by the very victims, who sometimes lose a considerable portion of their livelihood and production capacity. Also, given the relatively small scale of production in the Caribbean, employing measures to secure agricultural production will have a greater impact on unit cost of production, than obtains for farmers in developed countries, where the scale of production tends to be larger. The region has recognized the impact of praedial larceny on agricultural production, food security and rural livelihoods and has therefore been placing appropriate emphasis on the matter. In 2010 the CARICOM Secretariat commissioned a study on the extent and nature of praedial larceny in member countries. That study indicated that 98% of producers/farmers surveyed were victims of this crime, with a then conservative estimate of the value of losses to praedial larceny covering crops and livestock at US$385 million, constituting between 6 and 18% of annual agriculture output across member countries (CARICOM, 2010). This report identified praedial larceny as particularly chronic in Jamaica and Trinidad and Tobago, with losses of US$55 million and US$22.6 million respectively.

Other studies have focused on the matter of praedial larceny at both the individual country level and the region as a whole. In 2014 the Ministry of Agriculture and Fisheries in Jamaica commissioned its own study on the scope and impact of praedial larceny. This study examined the extent of losses by the agricultural sector, with details in specific areas such as domestic food crop production, livestock (cattle and dairy), export crops (coffee, cocoa, banana and citrus), non-traditional exports (ackee) and aquaculture, as well as across value chains. In summary, the study concluded that primary producers are disproportionately impacted by praedial larceny compared with players higher up in the value chain, with an overall estimate of crop losses in excess of US$700 million over the period 2008–2012, loss to 12 livestock farmers in the survey amounting to US$2 million over the 2010–2014 period and a per hectare loss of US$11,000 in aquaculture (Graham, 2014). The study further confirmed the frightening development of a burgeoning transhipment trade in livestock (meat and live animals) to Haiti from Southern Jamaica, in exchange for guns, and the deadly violence accompanied by the theft of animals, as well as the extent to which said guns fuel crime in Jamaica.

Ganpat and Isaac (2018) showed the significant impact of praedial larceny in Trinidad and Tobago from a survey of two sets of farmers, confirming the high impact of praedial larceny in Trinidad and Tobago outlined in CARICOM's 2010 study. Isaac et al. (2017) give a comprehensive treatment of praedial larceny in the Caribbean in terms of its scope, nature, impact and the weakness of existing measures to combat this crime.

In summary, the impact of praedial larceny on food security is significant and multifaceted. It affects supply of food both directly and passively. It discourages investment in production, so that without its existence food production would have undoubtedly been higher, and consequently income from production activities and export earnings. Graham (2014) for instance points to significant attrition from livestock farming and aquaculture due to impact of praedial larceny, as well as losses amounting to as much as 25% of primary production. It is not unusual for livestock farmers or orange farmers to have truckloads of their produce pilfered overnight. Given the small scale of production typical in the region, few farmers can recover from such losses under conditions where insurance is absent. Consequently, Graham (2014) highlighted the reduction of acreage under cultivation and change in the mix of crops cultivated as typical responses of victims of praedial larceny.

Increasingly, acts of praedial larceny are accompanied by gun violence, which hardens the resolve of many victims to exit production in order to preserve life. Apart from loss of production capacity, these victims lose their livelihoods, threatening their own access to food. The high cost of security including fencing, electronic monitoring and armed security guards is prohibitive to the typical farmer, and where this is done, it pushes up the cost of agricultural goods, hence, restricting access to affordable food. Farm theft also carries with it food safety risks to consumers, as often recently sprayed vegetables are stolen and introduced into the retail trade and stolen animals are slaughtered under unsanitary conditions and offered for sale.

The response to praedial larceny must of necessity be multifaceted to be effective, as it is not solely the responsibility of the farmer to secure his production. The State has a responsibility to protect its citizens' lives and livelihoods. In a sense therefore, praedial larceny has to be taken as seriously as murder, rape, corruption or any other serious crime. In this regard legislation must be amended to increase fines and penalties under various legislation addressing praedial larceny to signal a recognition of the importance of this crime. Similarly, at the operational level, police departments must treat praedial larceny as a serious crime in terms of their attitude to reports, the thoroughness of their investigation and their agility in responding to reported incidence. The State similarly has to establish adequate traceability systems and use legislation to force producers, distributors and all handlers of agriculture produce to operate within the ambits of these systems. The construction of abattoirs, proper public health inspection of meats, tagging of animals and establishment of DNA repositories for all tagged animals and frequent inspections/checks of motor vehicles transporting agricultural produce are some of the actions that need to be taken. New technologies such as electric fences, the use of drones for surveillance are currently being introduced to assist farmers to deal with praedial larceny.

Overall, legislation and inspection activities must make it difficult for stolen goods to enter the legitimate trade. Therefore the burden must be placed on retailers and end users to establish the legitimacy of the sources of the produce they sell and distribute. The State has to bolster its capacity to monitor its shoreline and maritime space to stem illegal, unregulated and unreported fishing and other nefarious activities on the high seas involving illicit trade, such as the meat for guns trade between Jamaican and Haiti. Agriculture insurance is also an imperative, and must cover farm theft alongside weather-related losses. Farmers also have a responsibility to be as vigilant as possible and work in community groups to monitor their production and passing intelligence to the police.

See Box 7.1 for Jamaica's response to the praedial larceny challenge.

Box 7.1 Institutional Arrangement for Praedial Larceny Management and Prevention in Jamaica

Against the background of the prevalence and heavy losses associated with praedial in Jamaica, the Government of Jamaica established the Praedial Larceny Prevention Programme on May 2, 2015, a joint initiative between the Ministry of Agriculture and the Jamaica Constabulary Force. According to a brief from the Ministry of Agriculture, Fisheries and

Mining, dated December 28, 2023, The mission of this programme is "to develop a framework for addressing praedial larceny and protecting Jamaican farmers through initiatives aimed at partnering with stakeholders, sharing information, effective enforcement and coordinating activities using innovation and technological advancement".[1] Within this framework, praedial larceny is first and foremost considered a crime for which the police has primary responsibility for managing. Within each Police Division therefore a praedial larceny team is operationalized to enforce the major anti-praedial larceny legislation—The Agriculture Produce Act and the Praedial Larceny Prevention Act, through stop and search of vehicles, responding to and investigating reported incidences with a view to arrest and prosecute perpetrators, patrolling of farms and farming districts and liaising with farmers to set up community farm watch groups. This concentrated focus on praedial larceny has yielded good results with over 1103 reports of praedial larceny incidences since its inception, with a reasonable percentage of arrests and conviction.

Within the Ministry of Agriculture is established a 5 person unit responsible for coordinating legislative and policy initiatives for praedial larceny prevention, as well as partnering with other State agencies, whose work impinges on praedial larceny. This Unit has worked on revamping and harmonization of legislation dealing with praedial larceny, resulting in increases in fines and prison terms for farm theft, and bringing all players in the agriculture value chain (primary producers and dealers) under a registration system to ensure traceability of agricultural goods. The Unit works closely with the Public Health Department of the Ministry of Health and Wellness to coordinate efforts at inspection of abattoirs and slaughter houses to trace the source of animals handled in these facilities. The Ministry's database of registered farmers is shared with the police to easily establish the bona fide of people stopped in patrols. The Unit also partnered with the National Spatial Data Unit to map praedial larceny hotspots across the island using GIS, based on reports from the police, and to focus resources for the fight against praedial larceny in the areas that matter. Work is also done with the Judiciary to sensitize their members on the impact of this crime, so that the Judiciary can take this crime more seriously. The Unit also works with the police and prosecutors in case preparation to increase the likelihood of successful prosecution in the courts.

A significant part of the Unit's work is public education, sensitizing farmers how to safely conduct their farming endeavours and the public at large about the economic and social impact of praedial larceny. Related public sector entities are also sensitized about the Ministry's traceability systems. Other initiatives the Unit is working on include designing a course in collaboration with the national training agency HEART, for the certification of Agricultural produce valuators, which is indispensable for adjudication of loss/damage in the court system. An agricultural warden programme is also being developed to augment the field personnel to deal with patrolling and monitoring of praedial larceny hotspots, complementing the work of the police.

In addition to the above institutional arrangements, the Ministry also established a fairly elaborate traceability system to track agricultural goods to prevent praedial larceny and support food safety. A critical element of this architecture is the National Animal Identification and Traceability System (NAITS), under which all cattle are supposed to be tagged and a database with the DNA of all tagged animals established. Each tagged animal is provided with a passport containing vital information about the animal and recording the movement of animals through change of ownership. Under NAITS over 75,000 heads of cattle have been tagged up to December 2023, representing approximately 60% of Jamaica's cattle population.[1] The Ministry through its extension agency RADA, manages a database (Agricultural Business Information System) of registered farmers and under the Agriculture Produce Act, farmers and dealers of agricultural produce are obliged to use specially designed receipt books for all transactions involving produce.

The above institutional framework and partnership among the major stakeholders in the fight against praedial larceny reflect the complexity of the phenomenon and the multifaceted approach required to address it. This level of deliberateness is critical to combat praedial larceny.

Main Challenges in Addressing Issues Relating to Food Stability in the Caribbean

As small island states, the carbon footprint of the Caribbean is relatively small in comparison to the disproportionate impact of climate change on the islands. The region lies in a tropical cyclone zone, impacted by extreme weather events for 6 months of the year. In the last 20 years, there have been considerable increases in the number and intensity of hurricanes, floods and droughts. These events have a direct impact on food production, resulting in loss of livelihoods and production capacity and therefore threaten access to food. A number of Caribbean territories also lie in an earthquake zone. These natural occurring phenomena, compounded in intensity and severity by climate change, which the region contributes little to, place the region in an extremely vulnerable position. Although the prevention of these natural challenges is beyond the control of regional governments and institutions, they nevertheless require creative responses to mitigate their impact and adapt to their impacts.

Given the region's vulnerability to the impacts of these hazards as well as the relative scarcity of good agricultural lands in most territories, public policies are required that ensure the most prudent utilization and management of the region's natural resources. In addition, proper attention must be paid to physical planning and the built environment. However, the region has fallen into the trap of having its major infrastructure and economic activities concentrated along its coasts, where the impact of sea level rise and flooding are greatest. Mining, without proper restoration of mined-out lands is also a major challenge. The use of agricultural lands for housing and commercial developments is a major threat to food security, particularly in those territories which have abandoned or significantly scaled down sugar and banana production, in the wake of loss of preferential markets in the EU. Competition for water resources as urbanization increases is also a potential threat to food security, as is the pollution of rivers and the marine environment through improper disposal of sewage, solid waste and agricultural run-offs. Unsustainable fishing practices, such as the use of dynamite, spear fishing and small-sized nets and general overfishing of near reefs are affecting the replenishment of fish stocks. These issues require robust regulatory, policy and institutional frameworks, as well as strict enforcement mechanisms to ensure the most sustainable use of natural resources for food security and to mitigate the impact of climate change.

Apart from the appropriate policy, institutional and regulatory framework required to address the challenges of climate change, natural resources and environmental management, considerable investments are required to respond to the challenges that threaten the stability of the region's food stability. The reality of climate change and variability demands an alternative to rain-fed agriculture as a sustainable means of conducting agricultural production. Chapter 4 speaks to the low coverage of irrigation in the region. Irrigation is however a public good, and no attempt to seriously expand agricultural production and strengthen the stability of food production can be sustained without massive expansion of irrigation infrastructure, and in some instances drainage. Given the predominance of small-sized players in the agricultural sector, operating basically at a subsistence level, it is equally important that irrigation service is not only available but affordable. In this regard, irrigation systems must be powered by cheap, renewable sources of energy, such as solar power, and appropriate investments must be made in water saving on-farm irrigation equipment, to ensure access, improve water use efficiency and reduce the region's carbon footprint.

The traceability systems described above to combat the scourge of praedial larceny, and assist with proper surveillance of the marine spaces of the region's island states to prevent poaching of fisheries resources and illegal transnational trafficking of stolen agricultural goods, will also require significant state investments.

Critical to the rapid restoration of food production in the aftermath of a disaster is the availability of planting material for critical crops. This shortage of planting material has proven to be a limiting factor to expansion of production generally, and more so in times of disaster. The unfortunate situation relates to insufficient attention being paid in the region to the preservation of plant genetic resources for food security and an over-reliance on imported seeds. Important indigenous plant species are becoming extinct, and a number of varieties require cleaning because they are disease-riddled. Seed banks of critical varieties of the region's food need to be established so that seeds are readily available for distribution in times of disasters. Similarly, urgent attention needs to be paid to preserving and improving critical breeds of livestock and rapid multiplication techniques available to small holders to expand their stock and boost animal productivity.

The major investment that the State is required to make is to de-risk the agricultural sector. Agricultural risk management has traditionally not been the focus of public policy, as Governments in the past tended to simply respond to the impacts of natural disasters through re-organizing current budgets, relying on international aid and borrowing. However, as the frequency and severity of natural disasters increased in the last 20 years or so, the focus has changed from recovery involving the restoration of public infrastructure and the provision of social welfare to affected communities, to the whole disaster risk management cycle encompassing prevention, preparedness, response and recovery rather than just response.

Consequently, a priori arrangements for risk management have taken centre stage in economic policy and planning.

Moreover, risk management must be seen as the responsibility of all stakeholders—the state, private sector, farmers and processors. It encompasses, inter alia, the preparation of disaster risk management plans with roles and responsibilities of all actors, the construction of infrastructure such as sea defences and tanks for rainwater harvesting, the establishment of data and information systems for accurate forecasting, building capacity in climate smart technologies and agricultural insurance.

However, except for a few export crops, such as coffee, banana and coconut in Jamaica and bananas in Grenada, Dominica and St. Lucia, crop insurance has largely been non-existent in the region. This lack of insurance coverage is directly related to the predominance of subsistence farmers operation on small plots (less than one hectare), as outlined in Chapter 4 and the practice of multiple cropping on those small plots. This system of production renders crop insurance extremely difficult, particularly as it relates to assessment of losses/damages in a disaster. Furthermore, given the subsistence nature of production, these small holders can ill-afford insurance premiums.

Risk management and insurance, however, are not restricted to the mitigation of natural hazards. Caribbean economies are open and deeply integrated into the global economy, with the region's high dependence on imports, dependence on a narrow band of exports for survival, as well as on tourism. This openness of their economies renders the region highly susceptible to external economic shocks. These shocks include global inflation and volatility in commodity prices, the economic performance of those countries from which tourists come to the region, as well as geopolitical tensions. The region therefore has to pursue economic diversification, particularly in services (entertainment and the orange economy), the blue economy and greater value addition in agriculture. Sustainable replacement of some food imports is also a critical strategy in reducing the region's vulnerability to external shocks. Analogous to the thrust to find insurance solutions against natural disasters, creative solutions must also be found to manage the risks associated with economic shocks, such as hedging.

The capacity of the State to manage the various issues and risks that threaten food stability is largely a factor of its indebtedness, that is, the degrees of freedom or fiscal space a State has to invest in infrastructure, institutions, regulatory mechanisms, etc., against the background of the pre-eminence of debt payments within national budgets. The region has traditionally been characterised by high, unsustainable levels of debt, with debt-to-GDP peaking in Barbados in 2016 at 151.2% and in Jamaica at 140% in 2008/2009 (First Citizens, 2022). At these high levels of indebtedness a significant portion of the country's revenue is allocated to debt servicing, leaving little fiscal space to invest in critical infrastructure to support agricultural development. In recent years however, thanks to IMF and World Bank sponsored reforms, the indebtedness has been on the decline due to fiscal consolidation and two bouts of debt restructuring in Jamaica. However, with the onset of the COVID-19 pandemic, the downward trajectory of debt-to-GDP was reversed, with average debt-to-GDP in the Caribbean moving from 75% in 2019 to 99% in 2020 (Rosenblatt et al., 2023).

Debt-to-GDP levels have returned to its downward trend and stood at an average 77% in the Caribbean in 2023, with Guyana and Jamaica experiencing the sharpest declines with debt-to-GDP at below 30% and 73%, respectively, in 2023 (Rosenblatt et al., 2023). Guyana's position is highly favourable due to massive GDP growth attributable to its booming and new-found oil industry. Guyana is therefore in a favourable position to not only enhance its own food security through investments in expanding agricultural production, but to lead the '25 by 25' Initiative.

Notwithstanding the resumption of the downward trend in the level of indebtedness in the region after the pandemic, at an average of 77% in 2023, the region is still above the 60% threshold that economic studies deem critical for sustainable economic growth (CAPRI, 2023). In fact, notwithstanding Jamaica's admirable performance in reducing public indebtedness, 17% of its expenditure is still devoted to interest payment on debts in 2023, compared with 8.4% in upper-middle-income countries (CAPRI, 2023). The situation is still dire in Barbados and Suriname, where indebtedness is still over 100% of GDP. Coupled with the low levels of investments in the agricultural sector, as measured by the share of domestic credit attributable to agriculture (Ali, 2023), and the decline in multilateral support to the sector, the region is at risk of not realizing the objective of reducing its food import bill by 25% by 2025, which requires private sector investments of US$7.5 billion. The stability of the region's food security is therefore stymied by the impairment in the capacity of State to invest in agricultural infrastructure, as well as limited private sector investment.

Agricultural Risk Management

The dependence of most Caribbean territories on agriculture and tourism makes them particularly vulnerable to natural and environmental disasters. (Heger et al., 2008). Being small island states means that most Caribbean islands concentrate all their production and other economic activities over a small land space, and without sufficient hinterlands to spread production and economic activities. One single disaster has the capacity to affect an entire country's production capacity in one swoop. Although always subject to tropical cyclones between June and November of each year, the region has experienced a marked increase in the number and intensity of weather-related natural disasters since the 1990s. In 2004 for instance, a particularly active year for hurricanes, damages resulting from hurricanes is estimated at US$3.1 billion, with losses ranging from 10% of GDP in Jamaica to over 200% in Grenada. In fact between 1988 and 2005, the impact of hurricanes/floods on various Caribbean territories ranged from 59% of GDP in Guyana in 2005 to 365% of GDP in St. Lucia in 1988 from Hurricane Gilbert (Heger et al., 2008). The region has also been experiencing more frequent and prolonged droughts, resulting in dramatic declines in crop and animal productivity.

The economic impact of natural disasters is direct in terms of the value of production, production capacity and infrastructure destroyed or damaged, or indirect in terms of loss of revenue and increased cost of production and transportation resulting from the disaster. These loses impact both the State and individuals. No country in the Caribbean experiences the level of economic growth and diversification, or possesses the kind of reserves to be sufficiently resilient to cope with such levels of disruption of economic activities without resorting to heavy borrowing and reliance on aid to restore production capacity and infrastructure after disasters. The fact of one adverse weather episode affecting multiple states or the same state being impacted multiple times in a given year by natural disasters only exacerbate the vulnerability of Caribbean States. In 2004 for instance, Hurricane Ivan impacted Jamaica, Haiti, and Grenada, while in 2007 Hurricane Dean impacted St. Lucia, Dominica, Jamaica and Belize. Haiti in 2008 was impacted by multiple hurricanes over a very short time period (Trotman et al., 2009). Against the background of the increasing frequency and intensity of natural disasters, agricultural risk management must become central to economic planning and policy if Caribbean nations are to ensure the stability of its food supply.

The reality however is that the region has had limited experience in agricultural crop insurance. Only two insurance companies have offered agricultural insurance in the recent past in the Caribbean—Windward Island Crop Insurance Limited (WINCROP) in the Eastern Caribbean and AGRODOSA in the Dominican Republic (Carballo & Reis, 2013; World Bank, 2012). WINCROP, owned by banana growers, was established in 1987 in Dominica to cover banana farmers, with St. Vincent and the Grenadines and Grenada joining in 1996 and 2000, respectively. The pooling of the risk among these three countries was a significant factor in making the premiums affordable. Some 2767 farmers or 63% of banana farmers were covered in 2013, representing some 62% of acreage under banana (Carballo & Reis, 2013). WINCROP successfully paid out EC$8 million in claims in 1989 after Hurricane Hugo and EC$15.5 million in the 1995 hurricane season (World Bank, 2012). AGRODOSA on the other hand is a public private partnership in the Dominican Republic, under which the Government provides legislative underpinning, some of the capital, and subsidizes some farmers' premiums. The company however is run along private sector principles and offers multi-peril crop insurance, covering some 7% of cultivated area in the Dominican Republic in 2013 (Carballo & Reis, 2013).

Apart from these 2 companies offering agricultural insurance coverage, Jamaica has some experience in crop insurance for banana, coffee and coconut. The banana and coffee schemes collapsed in the early 2000s due to the frequency of adverse weather events. In the case of banana, the Banana Insurance Fund was set up by statute in 1946. Under this statute all farmers involved in the export of banana were obligated to pay a cess, collected by the Banana Board, which was responsible for arranging exports and the shipping logistics for of all banana exported from Jamaica to the UK. The cess was computed for each exporter based on volume of banana exported the previous year and was extracted at source from the export proceeds of each farmer. The cess was then used to buy insurance from Lloyds of London. With the frequency of hurricanes, the arrangement with Lloyds ceased and the Government was thereafter self-insuring until 2007 when the funds were depleted after a pay-out of J$33.7 million after Hurricane Dean (Alert, 2012). Banana exports to the UK ceased in 2008 due to back to back devastations from hurricanes in 2007 and 2008.

The collapse of the Banana Insurance Fund in 2007 coincided with the establishment of the Banana Catastrophe Fund in 2007, seeded with a grant of $31 million from the European Union Banana Support

Programme. The aim of the Fund was to improve the resilience of banana industry to weather-related damages. In addition to the EU grant which constitutes the unallocated portion of the Fund, subscribing farmers pay an annual registration fee, plus a one-off 12% of the value of inputs they received in the aftermath of Hurricanes Dennis and Emily. This registration fee and one-off amount paid, constitute the allocated portion of the Fund. The Fund is managed through an Oversight Committee with administrative support from the Banana Board. Some 700 banana growers registered at the inception of the Fund. The Fund grew to $50 million by 2010, when $9 million was paid out to 250 farmers for damages associated with Tropical Storm Nicole. Another $13 million was paid out in 2012, for damages incurred by Hurricane Sandy (Alert, 2012).

The coffee industry in Jamaica had an analogous arrangement as banana for crop insurance. Part of the cess coffee exporters were mandated to pay to the Coffee Industry Board under the Coffee Industry Board Act, was used to buy insurance from Dyoll Insurance Limited, a local underwriter. This arrangement collapsed in 2007 however, due to protracted delays in assessment of losses from the 2004 Hurricane Ivan, legal disputes associated with Dyoll being placed in receivership and difficulties finding re-insurers in Europe.

The crop insurance scheme managed by the Coconut Industry Board, like the schemes for banana and coffee, is similarly underpinned by statute, obligating registered coconut farmers to pay a cess to the Coconut Industry Board. This cess is used in part to fund the insurance scheme. Due to astute management by the Coconut Industry Board, this scheme is still functional.

The general absence of agricultural insurance to cover crop and livestock production is related to the structure of agricultural production across the region, that is, the predominance of small holdings cultivating a multiplicity of crops, rendering assessment of losses of individual crops difficult. The small scale of production and the frequency of adverse weather events render premiums expensive and outside of the reach of small farmers. Re-insurers in Europe also became reluctant to do business in the Caribbean, because of the region's heightened vulnerability to natural disasters. When they do engage, premiums are extremely high. The general dearth in the quality and quantity of agro climatic data so critical for the design of agricultural insurance instruments, is also an inhibiting factor. The propensity of Governments to dole out aid to the farmers after disasters events for political gain, also does not incentivise farmers to pay insurance premiums. In Jamaica for instance, Government's support to the sector in the aftermath of natural disasters between 2000 and 2010 stood at J$1.2 billion (World Bank, 2012). It is interesting that the only crop insurance schemes that survive for any appreciable period in the Caribbean are those associated with export crops, where the Commodity Boards through which all exports pass, collect premiums at source from farmers' export proceeds.

Notwithstanding the limited availability of agricultural insurance in the Region, in the last 15 to 20 years Governments have been actively exploring the feasibility of increasing agricultural insurance coverage and more generally promulgating comprehensive risk management strategies in the face of increased natural disaster episodes and their catastrophic impact on national economies. The challenge in agriculture has been how to design instruments that take cognizance of the realities of the sector in terms of its structure and allow for rapid release of funds after an event to facilitate quick restoration of production activities and capacities. Indeed, one of the drawbacks of conventional insurance schemes has been the protracted time it takes to assess damages and losses and adjudicate claims. In an effort to better manage agricultural risks, several Caribbean countries have sought the assistance of multilateral funding and technical cooperation agencies to develop ex-ante contingent financing strategies. The World Bank reported that between 2009 and 2012 six Caribbean countries sought assistance in developing country-specific weather risk management strategies for their agricultural sectors. These countries are Jamaica, Guyana, Haiti, Dominican Republic, Grenada and Belize (World Bank, 2012). The objective was to design market-based instruments for small and medium-sized farmers/producers, with a high level of private sector participation.

In addition to the aforementioned support of the World Bank to design country-specific ex-ante contingent financing strategies for agricultural risks, countries have focused efforts on creating the enabling environment for agricultural insurance. In this regard the FAO in 2020 conducted a study in Jamaica (similar study carried out in Grenada and St. Vincent) in determining the enabling environment for the development of agricultural insurance. The study recommended the establishment of a comprehensive framework for agricultural risk management for agricultural insurance to be viable, rather than focusing on the design of crop-specific schemes (FAO, 2020). Within this framework, a public private partnership model is highly commended involving Government, insurance providers/underwriters and re-insurers and farmers.

Government's role is critical in creating the enabling environment including policy, legislation, regulation, provision of meteorological data and data on crop yields, as well as facilitating the registration of farmers and general public education. It is not recommended that Government takes a major stake in the capitalization of these schemes, but limits its financial participation to instances of market failure. Organizing farmers around value chains, larger commercial farming, development of farming clusters such as agro parks and the increased use of contract farming between end users and primary producers would considerably enhance the viability of agricultural insurance. Opportunities also exist for governments to underwrite a portion of the risk and thereby share the risk with the private sector.

In the search for solutions to the challenge of agricultural crop insurance, parametric models of agricultural insurance have emerged as viable models to address the issue of difficult and protracted damage assessment and allow for quick pay-out, and hence, rapid restoration of productive activities. A parametric insurance scheme is an index-based scheme that facilitates an automatic pay-out once a predetermined parameter (index) of hazard (wind speed, rainfall, earthquake magnitude) has been attained and independently verified. This arrangement therefore obviates the need for cumbersome and protracted assessment of damage after an event, as is associated with indemnity-based schemes, such as Named Peril Crop Insurance (NPCI) and Multiple Peril Crop Insurance (MPCI).

Jamaica rolled out its first parametric insurance scheme for small farmers in 2022. This scheme is underwritten by a local insurance company GK General Insurance Limited. The scheme covers three types of hazards—rain, drought and wind. The Ministry of Agriculture was instrumental in providing critical historic agro climatic data, as well as data on crop yields, farmer registration and the location of farms of registered farmers, to assist the insurance company to set the parameters and design the scheme. The products are sold in buckets of J$50,000 (minimum pay-out for each hazard) and farmers can purchase coverage of up to $1 million dollars. Therefore the maximum coverage any one farmer could have is $3 million for all three hazards. The premium is $3000 for $50,000 coverage of rainfall and drought and $2000 per $50,000 of hurricane coverage. The products are sold in 2 seasons—April to June and August to November. The objective of the scheme is not to replace losses or damages, but to place small farmers in a position to quickly restore production.

GK Insurance Limited indicated that so far only 970 farmers have subscribed to the scheme,[1] which is miniscule compared to well over 200,000 farmers registered with RADA, the Ministry's extension agency. However, in the aftermath of flood rains in Jamaica in November 2023, some 28 farmers received pay-outs between $25,000 and $200,000, representing some 50% of their sum insured. Emanating from this small demonstration of the tangible benefit of crop insurance, the company has advised of an uptick in application for the April 2024 season. The company is collaborating with the Ministry of Agriculture to promote this scheme. This is an excellent example of public private partnership, so crucial for the success of agricultural insurance schemes within the Caribbean context.

The Ministry of Agriculture in Jamaica has also partnered with SAGICOR Life Insurance Company to design an insurance scheme for farmers and fisherfolk, dubbed SAGICOR Agri-care Plan. This scheme is offered to farmers and fisherfolk registered with RADA and the National Fisheries Authority respectively, and covers life, health, critical illness and personal accident. The over 200,000 farmers registered with RADA forms a critical mass to make this unique insurance scheme for farmers viable and sustainable. Membership in the scheme currently stands at 1474 farmers, down from 2630 farmers who subscribed at the inception of the programme on March 1, 2021.[2] This initiative will ameliorate the widespread scenario in which small farmers die, become ill or rendered disabled and their families are left without income, which impairs their food security.

Although the parametric insurance model for agricultural insurance seems attractive to small farmers, from the stand point of quick pay-out, there are concerns that pay-outs bear no relation to actual loss. Therefore, while this model assists small farmers to quickly re-engage the productive process after a disaster, it is not conducive for large commercial operations required to significantly expand agricultural production and appreciably move the region's food security. In this regard, there are

[1] Interview with General Manager of GK General Insurance Limited, January 12, 2024.

[2] Data from Ministry of Agriculture, Fisheries and Mining.

some initiatives underway in Jamaica to revisit indemnity-based agricultural insurance schemes. These schemes, are designed to more efficiently and objectively compute losses and damages after a disaster. Moreover, these initiatives will require better quality data not only to determine baselines, but to more accurately, quickly and dispassionately compute losses. In this regard new technological tools such as drones and satellites are being used to capture critical data, required to properly assess and price risk. Local operatives work in collaboration with Governments and multilateral organizations to access resources available from various international Climate Change Funds. The same kind of data will be required to design meso level or macro level parametric schemes.

Agricultural insurance is critical to the well-being of farmers in terms of their continuity of production. However, at the national level, Governments also need quick budget support to: (i) restore critical infrastructure to get the economy going again, (ii) provide social support to the most vulnerable who would have temporarily lost employment and livelihood and (iii) import food supplies in the short run. All of these actions are imperative in a scenario where export earnings and taxes from trade are cut off abruptly. Indeed, efforts at restoring production at the farm level can be stymied if critical national infrastructure such as irrigation systems, farm roads and electricity are destroyed. Agricultural insurance therefore must be pursued within the broader framework of comprehensive risk management strategies. With the increasing frequency and intensity of weather-related disasters occasioned by climate change, Governments in the region have been seeking means of transferring the risks associated with low frequency, high impact disasters, even as they put in place mechanisms for self-insurance in relation to high frequency, low impact events (see Box 7.2 for Jamaica's comprehensive risk management strategy). This approach became necessary given the history of natural disasters significantly impacting Caribbean economies, destroying production capacity and infrastructure, cutting off revenues abruptly and plunging economies into fiscal crises, necessitating heavy borrowing.

Box 7.2 Jamaica's Comprehensive Strategy for Financing Risks

Jamaica's comprehensive risk management strategy is encapsulated in the National Natural Disaster Risk Financing Policy, approved by the Parliament of Jamaica on June 27, 2023. The overarching objective of the

Policy is to shield the national budget from the adverse impacts of natural disasters. The Policy calls for a layered approach to disaster risk financing, clearly establishing mechanisms for the Government to absorb certain risks through self-insurance and to transfer other risks to third parties through the purchase of a variety of insurance instruments. The Policy also makes provision for an asset register and building capacity within Government for disaster preparedness, prevention and mitigation.

With respect to the financing of risks, the Government will retain certain levels of risks, associated with high frequency, low impact disasters through the following mechanisms:

1. **Continuous topping up of the Contingency Fund**. The Contingency Fund is provided for by the Constitution of Jamaica and established under Section 13 of the Financial Administration and Audit Act to deal with emergencies. In 2019 the limit of this Fund was increased from J$100 million to J$10 billion, specifically to accommodate response to natural disasters. The Contingency Fund is capitalised by the Consolidated Fund and Government pledges to make periodic transfers to it from the Consolidated Fund. The Contingency Fund is managed by the Accountant General's Department and as at December 31, 2023 stood at $5.13 billion.
2. **The National Disaster Fund**. This Fund was established under Section 37 of the Disaster and Preparedness and Emergency Management Act, 2015. Its purpose is to deal with disaster mitigation, promotion of disaster prevention and preparedness, as well as to provide relief and recovery after a disaster. It was capitalized by the Consolidated Fund and receives periodic allocations from the national budget, as well as a percentage of the building fees collected by the local authorities. The funds are managed by the Office of Disaster Preparedness and Emergency Management, and now stands at J$465 million.
3. **IDB Contingent Credit Facility**. The Government of Jamaica has secured from the IDB a contingent credit facility in the amount of US$285 million to be drawn down in disasters relating to tropical cyclones and earthquakes. For this facility to be drawn down the disaster has to be of a certain magnitude and the Governor General of Jamaica has to declare a state of national emergency.

In relation to risks that the Government will transfer, the following has been put into place:

1. CAT Bond—the Government with the assistance of the World Bank in 2021 issued a Catastrophe Bond in the amount of US$185 million. These funds remain with the World Bank to be drawn down with the occurrence of a tropical cyclone of a particular magnitude. The Government pays interest quarterly to bond holders, and this facility matured in December 2023. The Government is currently in dialogue with the World Bank for the re-launch of the Bond in 2024.
2. CCRIF—the Government of Jamaica remains a member/subscriber of the CCRIF (see details below on CCRIF) with coverage of over $36 billion for hurricanes, earthquake and excess rainfall.

This multi-layered risk financing strategy provides a certain level of predictability, certainty and structure in relation to the country's response to the impact of natural disasters and ensures that the country's budget is not overwhelmed in times of disasters.

The most important initiative in the Caribbean to provide Governments with quick budget support in the immediate aftermath of a disaster to restart economic activities and maintain functionality of Governments, is the Caribbean Catastrophe Insurance Facility (CCRIF), formed in 2007. CCRIF is said to be the world's first macro level multi-country risk pool parametric insurance facility. It was developed with technical support from the World Bank and capitalized through contributions from a number of bilateral and multilateral donors. The original members of CCRIF are Anguilla, Antigua and Barbuda, The Bahamas, Belize, Bermuda, Cayman Islands, Dominica, Grenada, Haiti, Jamaica, St. Kitts and Nevis, St. Lucia, St. Vincent and the Grenadines, Trinidad and Tobago and Turks and Caicos Islands. CCRIF started by offering insurance coverage for hurricanes, earthquakes and excess rainfall, and over time its structure has been adjusted to admit countries of Central America to join. In addition to the original members, Nicaragua, British Virgin Islands, Montserrat and St. Marteen have joined the facility. The pooling of risk among so many countries has had the effect of reducing premiums by 45% to 50% (World Bank, 2012). Between 2007 and 2017, CCRIF has made pay-outs amounting to US$130.4 million (FAO, 2020). These pay-outs cover high-impact, low-frequency events and are in the form of budget support to Ministries of Finance. Conceivably some of these funds may have gone to the agricultural sector. However the sector needs insurance for high-frequency, low-impact events. The search therefore continues for a version of CCRIF more tailored to the needs of the agricultural sector in the region.

Apart from CCRIF, countries in the region have been exploring other financial instruments to cover climate-related risks. Belize and Barbados, for instance, have issued blue bonds and utilized the fiscal space created from debt for nature swaps to make nature conservation investments in coastal areas (Georgieva et al., 2022). The International Monetary Fund has also been working with some of its highly indebted borrowing members in the use of State-contingent debt instruments to provide automatic reductions in a country's sovereign debt burden in instances of natural disasters. This reduction in debt servicing allows for fiscal space during natural disasters to make critical expenditure for restoration of production and infrastructure, as well as on disaster relief. Barbados and Grenada have made use of this novel instrument (Guerson et al., 2023). Although there is a plethora of climate funding available within the United Nations system and otherwise, the Caribbean has only been able to access only approximately US$800 million from these sources, which is far from being commensurate with the needs of the region in terms of recovery of loss from natural disasters, as well as for adaptation (Guerson et al., 2023). The fact is many small States do not possess the range of technical competencies required to successfully prepare proposals to apply for these grants, and the transaction costs to prepare these grants are high.

Caribbean States in the last 40 years experienced the greatest loss and damages in the world as a percentage of GDP from natural disasters (Guerson et al., 2023). Yet these States have not been accessing green and climate funds in the measure required, neither are they qualified for concessionary financing, being middle- and upper-income developing countries. This dilemma has forced Caribbean States to advocate for special consideration in relation to funding climate change mitigation, adaptation and more agile response to disasters, without plunging into further debt. Foremost among these advocates has been the Prime Minister of Barbados, who has been pushing the Bridgetown Initiative. This initiative proposes the reform of the global financial system to assist developing countries to better respond to climate disasters and other crises. This Initiative also advocates for changes in loan and repayment arrangements to give countries hit by disasters temporary breathing space from debt payments. The initiative also calls for the establishment through multilateral development banks, a fund of US$1 trillion to assist developing countries with climate resilience. A lowering of lending rates for climate-vulnerable developing countries borrowing for investment in resilience projects is also being advocated. The initiative further calls for the establishment of a Global Climate Mitigation Trust, funded by both private sector and the IMF, as well as a new loss and damage fund to make pay-out to countries suffering from a major disaster.

Conclusion

The Caribbean Region has been identified as the most vulnerable region in the world in relation to natural disasters, being exacerbated by climate change, to which the region contributes little. The impact of natural disasters on the economies, livelihoods and the food security of the region has been considerable in the last 20 years, amounting to losses multiple times the individual countries' GDP in some instances. The openness of the economies of countries in the region to the global economy has also exposed them to significant economic shocks, which similarly impact the region's food security. Unfortunately, the major triggers and drivers of the major factors that impact the stability of the region's food security (climate change, environmental degradation, land use changes, economic shocks, conflicts and praedial larceny) are poised to worsen in the short, medium and long terms. This portends danger for the attainment of the objective of the region's 25 by 25 Initiative, to increase food security by expansion of regional food production to lower the region's food import bill by 25% by 2025.

Against the background of these realities, measures to climate proof agricultural production in the region must not only be accelerated, but mainstreamed in agricultural policies, production and practice. These measures must include investments in irrigation systems, seed banks for rapid restoration of production and the establishment of a comprehensive ex-ante risk financing mechanism to allow for adequate compensation of losses and quick restoration of productive activities. The development planning framework must also be overhauled to preserve and better manage agricultural lands. A more robust environmental management regime, inclusive of strict enforcement is also essential to reduce the region's carbon footprint and arrest and discourage actions that negatively impact the natural environment and agricultural production and food security. Given the chronic nature of praedial larceny in the region and its massive impact on food stability, consistent and multifaceted measures must be instituted to combat it. All of the measures are best implemented within a regional integration framework for greater impact and sustainability.

References

Alert, G. (2012). *Case Study of Banana Production in Jamaica.*

Ali, M. (2023). *Post COVID-19 Ukraine—Russia Crises Ticking Time Bomb for CARICOM.*

Alpino, T. et al.(2022). *The impacts of climate change on Food and Nutritional Security: a literature rewiew.*https://doi.org/10.1590/1413-81232022271.05972020

Anderson, K., & McCall, M. (2005). *Farm Crime in Australia.* A Monograph by the Australian Institute of Criminology.

Annie, M., Pal, R. K., Gawai, A. S., & Sharma, A. (2023). Assessing the Impact of Climate Change on Agricultural Production Using Crop Simulation Model. *International Journal of Environment and Climate Change, 13*(7), 538–550. https://doi.org/10.9734/ijecc/2023/v13i71906

Barclay, E. (2001). *A Review of the Literature on Agricultural Crime.* Report on the Criminology Research Council, Armidale, Institute for Rural Futures.

Barclay, E., & Donnermeyer, J. (2001). *Crime in Regional Australia.* Paper Presented at the 4th National Outlook Symposium on Crime in Australia, New Crimes on New Responses Covered by the Australians Institute of Criminology, pp. 21–22.

Beckford, C., & Campbell, D. (2013). *Domestic Food Production and Food Security in the Caribbean: Building Capacity and Strengthening Local Food Production Systems.* Palgrave Macmillan. ISBN 9781137296993.

Bunei, E. (2016). Farm Theft in Kenya and Farmers' Experiences and Responses. *African Journal of Education and Social Sciences.*

Bunei, E., Rono, J., & Chessa, S. (2013). Factors Influencing Farm Crime in Kenya: Opinions and Experiences of Farmers. *International Journal of Rural Criminology, 2*(I), 27–100.

Cardach, C. (2002). *Farm Victimization in Australia* (Trends and Issues in Crime and Criminal Justice, No. 235). Australian Institute of Criminology, Canberra.

CAPRI. (2023). *Budget Breakdown 2023: An Analysis of the Proposed Revenue.*

Carballo, D., & Reis, L. (2013). *The Agricultural Insurance Market in the Caribbean.* World Bank.

CARICOM. (2010). *Analysis of Extent and Nature of Praedial Larceny in CARICOM States.*

Chand, R. (2008). The Global Food Crisis: Causes, Severity and Outlook. *Economic and Political Weekly, 43*(26/27), 115–122. https://www.jstor.org/stable/40278908

Climate Studies Group Mona (CSGM) (Eds.). (2020). *The State of the Caribbean Climate*. Produced for the Caribbean Development Bank.

Dukharan, M. (2020). *COVID-19 Caribbean Economic Impact Report*. https://marladukharan.com/wp-content/uploads/2020/03/MD-COVID-9-Caribbean

Ewing-Chow, D. (2024). *Caribbean Food Systems Are Among the Most Climate Vulnerable Globally*. Forbes Business Food & Drink. Caribbean Food Systems Are Among the Most Climate Vulnerable Globally (forbes.com).

FAO. (2020). Insurance for Agricultural Risk Management in Jamaica: Context and Way Forward. FAO Technical Cooperation Project "*Creating an Existing Environment for Agri-Insurance Provision in THREE CARIBBEAN COUNTRIES*". Final Report for Jamaica.

FAO. (2021). *Latin America and the Caribbean—Regional Overview of Food Security and Nutrition 2021: Statistics and Trends*. Santiago, FAO. https://repositorio.cepal.org/server/api/core/bitstreams/13ca87a7-82f8-4c86-820f-85514fe63fb2/content

FAO. (2022). *The Future of Food and Agriculture: Drivers and Triggers of Transformation* (The Future of Food and Agriculture, No. 3). Rome. https://10.4060/cc0959en

FAO. (2023). *The future of food and agriculture: Drivers and triggers for transformation*. Food and Agriculture Organization of the United Natiuons. Rome.

FAO, IFAD, UNICEF, WFP and WHO. (2017). *The State of Food Security and Nutrition in the World 2017. Building Resilience for Peach and Food Security*. Rome, FAO.www.fao.org/3/a-17695e.pdf

Feher, L., Osland, M., & Swarzenski, C. (2023). Estuarine Salinity Extremes: Using the Coastal Salinity Index to Quantify the Role of Droughts, Floods, Hurricanes, and Freshwater Flow Alteration. *Estuarine, Coastal and Shelf Science, 291*, 108445.

First Citizens. (2022). *Caribbean Debt*. firstcitizensgroup-com//tt/news-insights/caribbean-debt/

Galli, N., Govoni, C., & Rulli, M. (2023). *Assessing Food Security Disruptions in the Aftermath of Extreme Events*. ESS Open Archive [Preprint]. https://doi.org/10.22541/essoar.167751603.31304821/v1

Ganpat, W., & Isaac, W. (2018). Facing Boldly the Scourge of Praedial Larceny on Food Production in the Caribbean. *Journal of International Agricultural and Extension Education, 25*(4), 52–62. https://doi.org/10.519/jiaee.2018.25409

Gbigbi, T. (2021). The Nexus Between Pilfering Menace and Crops Farmers' Income Stock Evidence from Nigeria. *Journal of Agriculture and Nature, 24*(1), 200–2011. http://doi.org/10.18016/Ksutarimdoga.ni.700483

Georgieva, K., Chamon, M., & Thakoor, V. (2022). *Swapping Debt for Climate or Nature Pledges Can Help Fund Resilience*. IMF Blog.

Graham, L. (2014). *Determining the Impact of Praedial Larceny on Sustainable Development in Jamaica*. ECLAC-Project Documents Collection.

Guerson, A., Morsink, J., & Munoz, J. (2023). *Caribbean Climate Crisis Demands Urgent Action by Governments and Investors*. IMF Blog.

Hedyeh, H. (2008). *Commercial and Farm Vehicle Theft in Urban and Rural Australia*.

Heger, M., Julca, A., & Paddison, O. (2008). *Analysing the Impact of Natural Hazards in Small Economies: The Caribbean Case* (Research Paper No. 2008/25—UNU-WIDER).

Hernández-Vásquez, A., Visconti-Lopez, F., & Vargas-Fernández, R. (2022). *Factors Associated with Food Insecurity in Latin America and the Caribbean Countries: A Cross-Sectional Analysis of 13 Countries, MDPI*. Multidisciplinary Digital Publishing Institute. https://www.mdpi.com/2072-6643/14/15/3190

IPBES. (2018). The IPBES Regional Assessment Report on Biodiversity and Ecosystem Services for the Americas. In J. Rice, C. Seixas, M. Zaccagnini, M. Bedoya-Gaitán, & N. Valderrama (Eds.), *Secretariat of the Intergovernmental Science-Policy Platform on Biodiversity and Ecosystem Services* (656 pp.). https://doi.org/10.5281/zenodo.3236252

Isaac, W., Ganpat, W., & Joseph, M. (2017). Farm Security for Food Security; Dealing with Farm Theft in the Caribbean Region. In W. Ganpat, R. Dyer, & W. Issacs (Eds.), *Agricultural Development and Food Security in Developing Nations*. IGI. Global. https://doi.org/10.4018/978-1-5225-0942-4.ch013

Jimenez-Castaneda, M., Lal, R., Mello, F., Witkowski, K., St. Martin, C., & Villarreal, F. (2022). An Overview of Carbon Sequestration in Agricultural Soils of Latin America and the Caribbean. *Critical Reviews in Plant Sciences, 41*(6), 391–405. https://doi.org/10.1080/07352689.2022.2148923

Kumari, S., & Bains, G. (2023). Agrifood and Climate Change: Impact, Mitigation, and Adaptation Strategies. In M. W. Ansari, A. K. Singh, & N. Tuteja (Eds.), *Global Climate Change and Plant Stress Management* (1st ed., Chapter 7). [online] https://doi.org/10.1002/9781119858553.ch7

Lachaud, M., Bravo-Ureta, B., & Ludena, C. (2021). Economic Effects of Climate Change on Agricultural Production and Productivity in Latin America and the Caribbean (LAC). *Agricultural Economics, 53*(2), 321–332. https://doi.org/10.1111/agec.12682

Lewis, C. (2022). *Climate Change and the Caribbean: Challenges and Vulnerabilities in Building Resilience to Tropical Cyclones, MDPI.* Multidisciplinary Digital Publishing Institute. https://www.mdpi.com/2225-1154/10/11/17

Linton, L. (2020). *PM Launches Rural Economic Development Initiative Phase II.* Jamaica Information Service. https://jis.gov.jm/pm-launches-rural-economic-development-initiative-phase-ii

Martin del Campo, F., Singh, S., & Mijts, E. (2023). The Resource (In)sufficiency of the Caribbean: Analyzing Socio-Metabolic Risks (SMR) of Water, Energy, and Food. *Frontiers in Climate*, [online] 5. https://doi.org/10.3389/fclim.2023.1085740

Mohammadi, E., Singh, S., McCordic, C. et al. *Food Security Challenges and Options in the Caribbean: Insights from a Scoping Review.* Anthr. Sci. 1, 91-108 (2022). https://doi.1007/s44177-021-00008-8

Morgan, P., McNeill, J., Mulcahy, M., & Schwartz, S. (2022). Conclusion: Caribbean Environmental History Since 1850. In *Sea and Land: An Environmental History of the Caribbean* (pp. 253–C4.T2). https://doi.org/10.1093/oso/9780197555446.003.0005

Pelling, M., & Uitto, J. (2001). Small Island Development States: Natural Disaster Vulnerability and Global Change. *Environmental Hazards, 3*(2001), 49–62.

Posen, P., Beraud, C., Jones, C., Tyllianakis, E., Joseph-Witzig, A., & St. Louis, A. (2023). *Vulnerability of Coastal Infrastructure and Communities to Extreme Storms and Rising Sea Levels: An Improved Model for Grenada and its Dependencies.* SSRN. https://ssrn.com/abstract=4355055 or https://doi.org/10.2139/ssrn.4355055

Rahman, S., Singh, S., & McCordic, C. (2022). Can the Caribbean Localize Its Food System?: Evidence from Biomass Flow Accounting. *Journal of Industrial Ecology, 26*(3), 1025–1039. https://doi.org/10.1111/jiec.13241

Rosenblatt, P., Clayton, K., & Mooney, H., et al. (2023). Regional Overview Dealing with Debt in the Caribbean. *Caribbean Economic Quarterly, 12*(3). https://doi.org/10.18235/0005372

Simpson, J. (2022). *Travel and Tourism in the Caribbean: Prospects for Growth.* https://wttc.org/Portals/0/Documents/Reports/2022/Travel-and-tourism-in-the-caribbean-pdf

Stanberry, D. (2022). *How Trade Liberalizations Affects a Sugar—Dependent Community in Jamaica: Global Action, Local Impact.* Palgrave Macmillan.

Swanson, C., Chamelin, N., & Territo, L. (2000). *Criminal Investigations.* McGraw Hill.

Taghizadeh-Hesary, F., Rasoutinezhou, E., & Yoshino, N. (2019). Energy and Food Security: Linkages Through Price Volatility. *Energy Policy, 138*, 796–806.

Trotman, A., Gordon, R., Hutchinson, S., Singh, R., & McRae-Smith, D. (2009). Policy Responses to G.E.C Impacts on Food Availability and Affordability in the Caribbean Community. *Environmental Science and Policy, 12*, 529–541.

United Nations Convention to Combat Desertification (UNCCD). (2020). *Country Profile for Selected Caribbean Countries.* https://www.unccd.int/our-work/country-profiles

Weis, T. (2007). Small Farming and Radical Imaginations in the Caribbean Today. *Race & Class, 49*(2), 112–117. https://doi.org/10.1177/03063968070490020607

Wilkinson, E., & Campbell, D. (2022). 'Building Back Better' in the Caribbean: An Introduction. *Disasters, 46*, S3–S9. https://doi.org/10.1111/disa.12538

Wilkinson, E., Twigg, J., & Few, R. (2018, January). *Building Back Better: A Resilient Caribbean After the 2017 Hurricanes* (Briefing Note). Overseas Development Institute.

World Bank. (2012). *Agricultural Risk Management in the Caribbean: Lessons and Experiences 2009–2012.* World Bank Group.

CHAPTER 8

Recommendations for Action

Introduction

Food security has been a concern of nations dating back to the earliest civilization. The Caribbean by virtue of its colonial antecedence, specializing in the production of a narrow band of export crops and importing most of its food for domestic consumption from the colonial masters, has been historically conditioned and structured to be reliant on others for its food. The long neglect and even conscious undermining of domestic agriculture in the colonial period reinforced this dependency. As Caribbean nations attained independence starting in the early 1960s, attention began to be paid to domestic agriculture and a level of diversification of the economy was attained with the emergence of tourism, manufacturing and mining as important economic activities. Domestic agriculture responded positively to the challenge of food self-sufficiency in the 1970s and 1980s. However, with World Bank and IMF-sponsored structural adjustment programmes in the 1980s, Caribbean states were told to focus on services such as tourism and rely on the developed world for 'cheap food'. The growing trend of liberalization of international trade since the 1990s quickly and significantly eroded the gains of the domestic agriculture and ushered in a flood of food imports. With global liberalization of trade, the region lost preferential markets in the EU for its traditional exports, resulting in significant loss of revenue and increased poverty among

D. Stanberry and L. Fletcher-Paul, *Food Security in the Caribbean*, Palgrave Studies in Agricultural Economics and Food Policy,
https://doi.org/10.1007/978-3-031-66055-9_8

producers of those export commodities. Small island states, therefore, require special and differential treatment in international trade, through longer periods of adjustment and protection of sensitive industries, to bolster their food security as well as ensure sufficient linkages between domestic agriculture and the tourism and manufacturing sectors.

The Caribbean region is now characterized by high dependency on imported food, with only Belize and Guyana producing more than 50% of the food consumed locally. Undernourishment in the region was on the decline up to 2018, but increased with the COVID-19 pandemic, and the incidence of severe food insecurity at the beginning of the pandemic was three times the world's average. While there has been some abatement in the incidence of stunting and wasting since the end of the pandemic, the region is facing a quiet epidemic of obesity and overweight, which is contributing to rising levels of non-communicable diseases and overwhelming the public health system. The region also has the highest cost of procuring a healthy meal per day at US$4.23. Moreover, 52% of the region's population cannot afford it. The region is also the most vulnerable in the world in terms of annual losses and damage from weather-related disasters. This is due to the impacts of climate change, manifested in more frequent and intense adverse weather events, and the dominance of agriculture and tourism in the economies of the region, which are sectors most vulnerable to natural disasters. The absence of adequate agricultural insurance against these risks is a clear and present danger to the stability of the region's food security.

The region however has had a long history of building institutions, programmes and policies to increase its food security, within the framework of regional integration. However, these efforts have not had the desired effect for many reasons, and primary among them is the lack of political commitment to the regional integration movement. As a result of this lack of commitment, policies and rules governing the application of the Common External Tariff and other safeguards are frequently ignored by CARICOM States. Additionally, the CARICOM Secretariat has been ineffective and regional institutions created to promote regional agriculture and trade have been starved of funds.

The COVID-19 pandemic, which exposed the level of food insecurity in the region, has however provided an impetus for the region to revisit the issue of food security and specifically food sovereignty, with the formulation of the '25 by 25' initiative, to reduce the region's food import bill by 25% by 2025. This initiative has the buy-in of the region's private sector and is a credible plan if all the relevant actors—CARICOM Secretariat, governments, private sector, farmers and citizens/consumers, play their respective part in its implementation.

The Overarching Framework

Given the state of food insecurity in the Caribbean, a quantum leap is required in the level of regional food production and a commensurate reduction in the region's food import bill. Major inroads also have to be made to reduce the levels of overweight and obesity as well as improve the resilience of the region to the impacts of climate change and economic shocks. In this regard, the '25 by 25' Initiative must focus on the following areas to reduce the food import bill: SPS and Trade related Policies, Increased Production and Productivity, Market-Driven Production and Intelligence, Cross-Border Production and Investments, Climate Smart Agriculture, Regional Food and Nutrition Security Status, Coordination and Governance Mechanism, Digitalization of the Sector and De-risking and Financial Literacy of the Regional Agriculture Sector. It also complements the Regional and National Food and Nutrition Policy and Action Plans which were formulated by the countries of the region in 2010 to provide a comprehensive framework for addressing the challenges of Food and Nutrition Insecurity in the region.

The following sections will outline the policy recommendations under the four pillars of Food Security, including specific actions which need to be taken by the various actors—Regional and National Policymakers, Private Sector, Civil Society, Consumers, Farmers and Development Agencies. Because of the interrelated nature of the pillars, policies identified under one pillar will also contribute to the other pillars. For example, policy recommendations to support increased production may also contribute to increased incomes, employment and poverty alleviation—all of which may improve food access.

Food Availability

The main objective of policy interventions under this pillar is to increase domestic and regional agricultural production and productivity, with special attention to the commodities which can be grown to increase exports, substitute imports and improve trade. However, because of the diversity of production systems involving different farm sizes, levels of technology, capacities of farmers and farmer organization and infrastructure, recommendations and strategic options vary. Policy recommendations include:

- Identification of priority commodities and value chains based on assessments of market opportunities, production and agro-processing capacity, availability of land, water and other inputs, and land capability. At the regional level, the CPSO has already identified the priority commodities for expanded production—beef, dairy, goat meat and fish production, animal feeds, cereals, raw material for manufacturing of drinks (puree and concentrates), and in the case of Barbados and Trinidad and Tobago—fresh vegetables. Such assessments should be continued on an ongoing basis to identify new opportunities.
- Based on comparative advantage in terms of availability of lands, water and cheap energy, production of the identified livestock and animal feed production should be concentrated in the larger territories, particularly Guyana. Private investors can engage in cross-border investments in Guyana, Suriname and Belize, facilitated by bilateral agreements. The current arrangement between Guyana and Barbados is an example of such an investment.
- All countries can increase production of vegetables and fruits, which require smaller outlay of lands. In Barbados and the OECS, where lands are relatively scarce, intensive systems (such as greenhouses, hydroponics and other protected agriculture systems) can be used to grow vegetables. This does not preclude the use of intensive systems in the larger islands to augment their national production capacity.
- Land reforms should be promoted to make more lands available to farmers. In this regard, gender disparities need to be considered to ensure that female farmers have equal access to production inputs such as land and capital.
- The establishment of land banks should also be considered as a means of making state owned lands available for agricultural production—especially to youth.
- Improvement of infrastructure such as irrigation systems and rain-water harvesting systems would also go a long way to open up new lands for production as well as increasing productivity.
- Seed banks must be created to facilitate expansion of crop production, and the capacity must be created to repatriate the supply of

seeds to the region. Similarly, there is need for expanded artificial insemination, embryo transfer and other rapid multiplication techniques in order to quickly increase livestock production. For the medium to long term, serious work needs to be done to improve local breeds of goats and cattle.

- Opportunities for export offered by existing and potential trade agreements, new consumer preferences and consumption trends must be fully exploited. While the region cannot compete on volume because of its size, opportunities exist for niche markets for herbs, spices and value-added products of coffee, cocoa, jams, jellies, sauces and primary products demanded by the Caribbean diaspora in North America and Europe such as yams, mangoes, ackee, etc.
- Governments need to create policies, programmes and incentives to promote agri-tourism linkages between local production and the hotel sector, since a critical portion of imported foods is destined for the hotel sector. Jamaica's Tourism Linkage Network serves as a good template for other countries to follow. Incentives such as tax rebates on agro-processing equipment should be considered.
- Public purchasing policies in which local farmers are contracted to provide food for state institutions such as jails, hospitals and school feeding programmes would also promote local production.
- Development of institutional capacity in agrifood trade and use of international trade databases which also provide opportunities for South-South and triangular cooperation with Latin America, Africa and other SIDS.
- Capacity building of farmers to work better in clusters and to engage in contract farming.
- Strengthening of extension and advisory Services to assist farmers and agro-processors in all aspects of the value chain—agribusiness, credit and financing—not just production.
- Strengthening leadership and governance capacities through wider education reforms—working in collaboration with the Ministries of Education.
- Promotion of innovation by supporting research and development
- Promotion of public-private partnership through the improvement of the ease of doing business and the promotion of fair and enforceable financial measures.

Food Access

Policy interventions related for food access are primarily aimed at poverty reduction and income and employment generation to improve the lives and livelihoods of farmers and farm families as well as to promote equal opportunities particularly for vulnerable groups such as rural women, indigenous peoples, small farmers and youth. The policies and strategic options include:

- Investment in the expansion and upgrading of the network of rural and farm roads to improve the movement of agricultural goods, and hence physical access to food. This measure will also assist in reducing post-harvest losses of food, which is estimated to be as high as 40% in the Caribbean.
- Improving the network of markets in rural areas, as well as the creation of more electronic platforms for marketing, which not only increase physical access to food, but economic access to the extent that direct sales of food through electronic platforms eliminate middlemen, reduce mark-ups and hence lower food prices.
- Governments also need to carefully assess the extent to which they can provide subsidies for production of critical food items to reduce price, and hence access. These subsidies must however be consistent with WTO rules. In this regard, the WTO allows subsidies, so long as they are not trade-distorting. These subsidies should relate to research, extension and infrastructure which have the capacity to increase productivity and lower cost of production.
- Agencies such as the CARICOM Secretariat and UWI can raise awareness, provide information and build capacities in the Ministries of Agriculture and Trade on policy spaces and options available to them under the WTO for actions to promote local production.
- Critical food items can also be exempted from sales taxes to promote greater access and consumption.
- Backyard gardening, urban container gardens and community gardens should be promoted by governments, by providing vulnerable people especially, with seeds and instructions (YouTube videos and printed material) on how to grow basic foods. Such programmes can be made part of social safety net mechanisms which may be supported by NGOs and civil society.

- Given the disproportionate representation of indigenous people, rural women, small farmers and youth among the poor, these groups must be targeted in social safety net programmes to improve their access to food.
- The abovementioned groups should also be targeted for programmes to improve their access to land, land tenure and natural resources rights and finance.

Food Utilization

The objective of policy interventions that support food utilization is to promote the consumption of safe, nutritious foods. These interventions help to stem the increasing trend in overweight and obesity and the attendant increase in chronic non-communicable diseases. They also prevent outbreaks of foodborne diseases which not only affect the well-being of the citizens but also the tourists, which could hurt the reputation and overall economy of many Caribbean countries for which tourism is the mainstay of their economies.

Policy Recommendations Include:

- Procurement policies to support the consumption of locally grown nutritious food in government institutions such as jails, hospitals and school feeding programmes, by contracting local farmers to provide food for those institutions. Locally grown food should also be offered at all government functions.
- Formulation and promulgation of standards for imported foods, regulating content of sodium, refined sugars and unhealthy fats.
- Institution of bans of the sale of unhealthy foods in schools not only in tuck shops but also by food vendors who ply their trade in the vicinity of the schools.
- Promotion and harmonization of food standards and legislation including taxes on sugar-sweetened beverages, control of advertisements targeting school children, elimination of transfats and the use of bold front of package labelling of food to help consumers easily identify unwholesome foods. NGOs and Civil Society must sustain their advocacy in this regard. (It should be noted that the private sector in the Caribbean has resisted this use of front of label

packaging. This is because as net food importers, it will incur an additional cost to change the labels of all items to include labels with food warnings and dietary information. This will contribute to an increase in cost of the food item as the additional cost will be passed on to the consumer.)

- Design and implementation of plans and programmes and the implementation of fiscal policies and incentives including subsidies that favour the sustainable production and consumption of healthy foods such as locally grown fruits and vegetables, as opposed to imported unhealthy foods such as cereals and sugar-sweetened drinks.
- Promotion and implementation of Food-Based Dietary Guidelines
- Promotion of collaboration and dialogue among producers, consumers, processors, traders, retailers and other service providers, to foster the production, promotion and practices of healthy diets, particularly for the nutrition of vulnerable households and individuals.
- Provision of support to Small and Medium Enterprises and producer associations in the agrifood industry to develop, distribute and market healthier food products.
- Development of targeted and sustained public education programmes aimed at effecting behaviour change and promoting the benefits of consuming healthy food. This campaign must be driven by governments with strong support from civil society and local private sector. For greater impact, social media channels and influential bloggers should be co-opted as partners. Innovative communication strategies including competitions and the promotion of recipes involving local foods can also be explored.
- Increased investment in food safety infrastructure, such as modern abattoirs, to reduce the incidence of foodborne illnesses and promote the consumption of safe foods.

Food Stability

The main objective of policy recommendations related to Food Stability is to ensure that food is available to ***all*** people at ***all*** times—even in times of natural disasters, conflict or economic shocks. Recommendations and strategic options include:

- Formulation of comprehensive risk management strategies in all countries of the region, focusing on disaster prevention, preparedness, response and recovery, and with clear indication of which risks will be retained and which will be transferred.
- Creation of the necessary enabling environment to design and roll out market-based agricultural insurance instruments. Critical elements of this enabling framework for the private sector to develop these instruments include governments facilitating the registration of farmers, with geo-referencing of farmers' holdings, strategic deployment of weather stations, supply of agro-meteorological data and data on crop yields, as well as joint promotion of agricultural insurance schemes.
- Given the region's openness to international trade and vulnerability to increasing commodity prices, geopolitical tensions and economic shocks, governments must explore means of transferring these risks through hedging and other appropriate measures.
- Life, health and peril insurance for farmers should be pursued to ensure their continued access to food in times of illness and disability, and the same for their families upon their demise.
- Comprehensive strategies must be formulated to combat praedial larceny, using a multifaceted approach involving police action, traceability systems, legislation with heavy penalties and active surveillance by public health authorities of food establishments.
- At the regional level sustained advocacy for more of the region's middle and high income countries to be able to access the same concessionary financing terms that are accorded to least-developed countries for investment in resilience and disaster recovery.
- Greater collaboration among countries of the region to access climate and green funds, given the dearth of skills in the regions to prepare proposals for these funds.
- Greater collaboration among countries of the region in pooling their risks to access more affordable insurance instruments.
- Promotion of innovative risk management schemes such as the establishment of a special disaster fund within saving and loans by farmer organizations. This fund would provide farmers groups with ready cash soon after a disaster.
- Public-private partnerships in which government underwrites a small percentage of the risk of insurance companies also need to be explored.

- Promotion of and building capacity in climate smart agriculture, agroecology and regenerative agriculture and sustainable land management practices.
- Strengthening monitoring and surveillance systems to prevent and detect outbreaks of pests and diseases.
- Promoting a One Health approach to address and understand risks at the human-animal-plant-environmental interface.

Cross-Cutting Issues

In the implementation of the abovementioned policies, a number of cross-cutting issues which are common to all pillars of food security will have to be addressed. These issues include, but are not limited to, education and awareness, coordination and collaboration, creation and innovation, gender and the criticality of data collection for proper analysis and sound evidence-based decision-making. These issues are elaborated below.

Coordination and Collaboration

The relatively small size of the Caribbean countries, their extreme vulnerability to natural disasters, climate change and external economic shocks and the complexity and multifaceted nature of the phenomenon of food security warrant coordinated actions both at the national and regional levels. The Revised Treaty of Chaguaramas, with its goal of full regional integration, through the creation of a single market and economy, provides an appropriate framework for the collaborative actions required to increase the region's food security. There are sufficient policies, regulations and institutions to facilitate the attainment of the treaty's objectives. The analysis shows however, that the policy and institutional framework, though necessary, is not sufficient. The efforts of increasing regional trade in food and promoting regional food security are being stymied by lack of commitment to follow the rules. The widespread suspension of the CET and other safeguards to allow for extra-regional importation of foods is not merely a result of unwillingness to follow the rules, but a failure to coordinate the efforts of farmers and regional manufacturers.

Global trade liberalization has also presented opportunities for trade in agricultural goods, but these opportunities must be exploited in a coordinated and collaborative manner. Few Caribbean countries can produce at the scale, consistency and level of competitiveness required to survive in these global markets. Therefore, the concept of concentration of production in the larger territories through cross-border investments makes perfect sense. This concentration of production however requires considerable coordination to create the enabling environment to make it a reality.

The region similarly needs to speak with one voice in its advocacy for better terms in negotiations of international agreements on food trade and development within the multilateral system. Many countries simply do not have the range of technical personnel and expertise to attend and effectively participate in the plethora of international meetings dealing issues such as sanitary and phytosanitary measures and Codex Alimentarius that impact food security and trade with the rest of the world. In this regard, the CARICOM Secretariat has a pivotal role to play in preparing delegations and coordinating regional participation in these fora. Similar coordination and collaboration are required in pooling regional risks and searching for innovative and cost-effective solutions for risk insurance. Likewise, in mobilizing investment to solve the regional transportation problem for the efficient movement of goods and services across the region, coordination and collaboration are absolutely indispensable.

At the national level, coordination and collaboration are equally critical to increase agricultural production, reduce importation of food, boost agricultural exports, increase access to food, achieve better utilization of food and increase the stability of food supply, access and utilization. Governments, farmers, the private sector, civil society, international partners and consumers all have unique and distinct, yet complementary roles to play.

Governments must establish the institutional, policy and legal framework to achieve the goal of increased food security. The physical infrastructure required for sustainable and efficient agricultural production must also be provided. Moreover, the private sector needs to invest in all aspects of the value chain, in response to government's policies. Governments also have a role in building the capacity of small farmers, providing research and extension services, assisting farmers to work in clusters and facilitating linkages between farmers and agro-processors (both large and small scale) and hotels, restaurants and manufacturers, through contract farming and marketing contracts. Jamaica has excellent experience with farmers working collaboratively with manufacturers in the broiler industry, and with hotels through the Tourism Linkage

Network. Jamaica's Irish potato import substitution programme is to be commended as a good example of collaboration among farmers, importers/distributors, government and financial institutions, coordinated by the government through RADA.

The creation of appropriate agricultural insurance instruments will also require coordination between governments, the private sector, farmers and re-insurers at the national level. The lessons learnt from WINCROP, statutory insurance schemes in Jamaica and the current parametric scheme described in Chapter 7, can be applied in designing similar schemes in other countries of the region.

Many government-sponsored school feeding programmes are being used to procure imported foods, because of ease of logistics and costs. The magnitude of expenditure on imported food makes a strong case for food to be supplied from local agricultural production. In this regard, coordination is required to mobilize local farmers to produce the foods that schools procure and consume through these school feeding programmes. Appropriate arrangements must be made to move produce from the farms to the schools or the kitchens where the school meals are prepared, appropriately sorted and packaged. This linkage with local farmers will increase rural incomes, reduce food imports and contribute to the consumption of healthier, more nutritious local food in schools.

Education and Awareness

The high dependence on imported food to satisfy the consumption needs of the Caribbean (over 80% of regional food consumption) is not only fiscally unsustainable, but represents on assault on the region's sovereignty and has radically changed the region's taste preferences, resulting in unprecedented levels of non-communicable diseases. While the flood of imported food has primarily been a result of global liberalization of agricultural trade, the proliferation of foreign cable television stations in the region since the early 1990s, followed by the invasion of the internet and social media, has played a significant role in creating an alien taste and preference for food in the region. Unfortunately, the region is yet to mount an effective counter-assault on this foreign taste. In a democratic society consumers have freedom of choice, and governments cannot arbitrarily ban importation of food by legislation, except in demonstrably justified circumstances, such as on sanitary and phytosanitary grounds. The countries of the region subscribe to international trading agreements and must abide by the rules of engagement. In the circumstances therefore, a sustained public education and awareness campaign is required to effect over time behaviour change with respect to people's food purchase choices.

The counter-messaging required must emphasize the seriousness of the epidemic of obesity and NCDs and the urgency for good nutrition. It must also stand up against the current messages of fat shaming and body pride by influencers in the movie industry who are, themselves obese. Allies have to be co-opted from NGOs, consumer groups and even the private sector. Studies need to be conducted to determine the factors that are likely to get buy-in and influence tastes for healthy, nutritious, local food among all age groups. The education campaign must also use the very tools that created the foreign taste in the first place—social media, internet and all forms of mass communication. Bloggers and influencers should be used strategically to obtain the desired effect. Assessments also need to be conducted to determine the effectiveness of the campaigns and identify areas where they can be tweaked to be more impactful. Additionally, targeted campaigns have to be run over extended periods to ensure that the impact is sustained.

Public education and awareness however should not be limited to reversing the taste for imported foods, but also to influence the region's private sector, distributors, food retail chains, hotels and foreign-based fast food franchises to use more local inputs and form alliances with primary food producers for their supplies. Farmers need to be educated to use more efficient methods and technologies to produce food in a more efficient and competitive manner, and to form clusters which will enhance their efficiency. Overall, the issue of food security is everybody's business and the awareness must be created and sustained for a new ethos to be created with respect to peoples' relationship with food.

Gender

Men and women play separate and distinct roles in all four pillars of food security. Gender roles in food security in the Caribbean vary depending on factors such as culture, socioeconomic status and geographic location. However, there are some commonalities.

With respect to **Food Availability**, and specifically agricultural production, traditionally, men have often been the primary participants in commercial agricultural production in the Caribbean, particularly in larger-scale farming operations and cash crop cultivation. This may include activities such as land preparation, planting and harvesting. However, women also play significant roles in agriculture, especially in subsistence farming, backyard gardening and small-scale farming of staple crops. Women's contributions to agriculture are often critical for household food security, providing nutritious food for their families and generating income through the sale of surplus produce.

Women typically bear the primary responsibility for food processing, preparation and meal planning in Caribbean households. This includes activities such as cleaning, sorting, cooking and preserving food. Women's knowledge of traditional food preservation techniques, such as drying, smoking and fermenting, is often passed down through generations and plays a crucial role in ensuring food security, particularly during periods of scarcity or economic hardship.

Women are often involved in informal food markets. Outside of farm families, women, dubbed higglers, in most Caribbean territories play a critical role in the distribution of food, purchasing farm produce at the farm gate in bulk and taking the produce to urban centres and municipal markets. Women are also involved in small-scale food processing enterprises in the Caribbean, contributing to local food systems and livelihoods. However, they may face barriers to accessing formal markets, such as limited transportation options, lack of market information and discriminatory practices. Promoting women's entrepreneurship, access to market infrastructure and training in business skills can enhance their participation in agricultural value chains and improve their economic opportunities in the food sector.

With respect to Food Access, Chapter 5 showed that unemployment and poverty rates are higher among women than men, and hence, they are more challenged with respect to access to food. Given the relatively high percentage of female-headed households across the region, it is important that social protection systems target vulnerable women and female-headed households to improve their access to food.

Also of concern is the issue of youth unemployment. In the study conducted by UNICEF of Barbados and the OECS (2017), it was found that in all countries studied, youth unemployment rates were double those of the total population and in the case of St Lucia, and it was 49.2% in 2021, according to the ILO Statistics. Such high levels of unemployment are linked with the incidence of crime and violence in the society, and it calls for the need for specially targeted programmes for youth in Agriculture, particularly among the males.

Gender disparities in access to land, credit, agricultural inputs and extension services can affect women's ability to engage in agricultural production and contribute to food insecurity. In many Caribbean countries, cultural norms and legal frameworks may restrict women's rights to land ownership and control over productive resources, limiting their economic empowerment and autonomy. Efforts to promote gender-sensitive land reform, access to credit and extension services are essential for addressing these disparities and empowering women in agriculture.

On the subject of Food Utilization, Caribbean women often have primary responsibility for meal preparation and ensuring that family members receive adequate nutrition. However, gender disparities in education and decision-making power may affect women's knowledge of nutrition and their ability to make informed choices about food and dietary practices.

For food stability, women are key agents of resilience in Caribbean communities, employing various coping strategies to mitigate the impacts of natural disasters, climate change and economic shocks on food security. Women's social networks, knowledge of local ecosystems, and adaptive capacity are critical for food production, distribution and food-sharing practices during times of crisis. Engaging women as active participants in disaster risk reduction, climate adaptation and community-based food security initiatives can enhance the resilience of Caribbean communities and promote sustainable development.

Integrating gender perspectives into policy, programming and research on food security can help ensure that the unique needs, priorities and contributions of both men and women are recognized and addressed effectively. There is also need for comprehensive gender-disaggregated data sets to better inform decision-making. Equally important is the need for disaggregation of data by age, to ensure that the concerns of youth are considered so that targeted interventions which attract youth and promote youth entrepreneurship programmes are developed. These programmes should include access to land and finance, training and capacity building.

Criticality of Data

The formulation of programmes and policies for food security must be evidence based, requiring data which are current, accurate and disaggregated along gender, age and spatial lines. It is also important that as a region comprising several countries, there is uniformity in terms of how data are collected, processed and presented to allow for spatial and temporal comparisons.

In relation to several critical variables required for analysis, there is a severe lack of data. Countries of the region have not kept apace in terms of the frequency of conducting agricultural censuses. Data on the number, distribution and structure of agricultural lands and farmers are dated. Admittedly, censuses are huge and expensive undertakings. However, extension services can do more to collect data on the farming population in terms of numbers, acreage, demographics and location of farms. This can be achieved through a system of farmer registration, as obtained in Jamaica through RADA's Agricultural Business Information System (ABIS). Farmers can also be incentivized to register, by making registration a prerequisite for obtaining benefits from the government. Rich and relevant data can be mined from farmers' registration. It is data from RADA's farmer registration database that supported the design of the current parametric insurance scheme in Jamaica and which the police use in their stop and search exercises in the fight against praedial larceny.

Under the auspices of CARICOM, countries of the region need to urgently agree on the critical indicators required to analyse and track progress on food security, as well as to formulate appropriate policies and programmes in support of food security. Common methodologies of data collection, processing and presentation must also be agreed upon. This endeavour can be supported by technical assistance from development partners. Monitoring of progress in achieving the SDGs has presented an opportunity for standardization of some key targets and indicators of Food Security, Poverty Alleviation and Climate Change. The Annual SDG Progress reports also provide useful information for stocktaking, monitoring as well as methodologies for data collection, analysis and presentation.

More recently, the advent of high-speed super computers, digital technology, data analytics and artificial intelligence has assisted in improving the efficiency of many aspects of the agrifood system. These include in disease control, supply chain management, the use of drones to name a few. Big data platforms are also used in agrifood systems to acquire data to improve processes such as the marketing of agricultural produce. However, there are concerns that the data and analytic capabilities are controlled by a few countries and big companies thereby leading to polarization of the control and use of the data. The CARICOM Secretariat therefore has an important role to play in assisting countries to develop legislation and regulations to protect their data—particularly financial data and avoid further polarization of Caribbean countries in the global context, as well as the exclusion of poor and unskilled workers at the national level.

Conclusion

The magnitude of the food security challenge facing the region, with over 80% of its food demand satisfied by imports, and the silent epidemic of overweight, obesity and non-communicable diseases, requires urgent action. Thankfully, over its fifty years of existence, the region through CARICOM has spent much time and resources to establish the requisite institutional, policy and legislative framework to enhance its food security. The recent COVID-19 pandemic and the ongoing Russia/Ukraine war have exposed the region's vulnerability and helped to refocus attention on the critical issue of food security. The increasing frequency and intensity of weather-related disaster events in recent years has also heightened awareness of the region's vulnerability and lent some impetus to the urgency to act. The '25 by 25' Initiative adopted by CARICOM and its endorsement by the region's private sector, forms a good basis for action. Outlined in this chapter are some of the other critical actions required by both state and non-state actors to enhance the food security of the region.

Given the plethora of plans, programmes and initiatives that have been formulated and articulated by the region in the past to improve its food security, only to fade over time, what will make the difference this time around? Without a doubt there needs to be a new commitment to the regional integration movement by governments and the private sector, who must now see the regional market as an extension of their domestic (country) market. Success will depend on all stakeholders buying into the vision of increased agricultural production, reduced importation of food extra-regionally, increased exports and increased consumption of local foods. A broad coalition of interests for food security is required, involving governments, private sector, farmers, academia, civil society, development partners and consumers. The criticality of the issue of food security requires that it becomes everybody's business and public education must create and sustain this awareness, change behaviour over time and impel all stakeholders to action.

Index

D. Stanberry and L. Fletcher-Paul, *Food Security in the Caribbean*, Palgrave Studies in Agricultural Economics and Food Policy,
https://doi.org/10.1007/978-3-031-66055-9

D

SPRINGER NATURE

GPSR Compliance

The European Union's (EU) General Product Safety Regulation (GPSR) is a set of rules that requires consumer products to be safe and our obligations to ensure this.

If you have any concerns about our products, you can contact us on ProductSafety@springernature.com

In case Publisher is established outside the EU, the EU authorized representative is:

Springer Nature Customer Service Center GmbH
Europaplatz 3
69115 Heidelberg, Germany

The manufacturer's authorised representative in the EU is Springer Nature Customer Service Centre GmbH, Europaplatz 3, 69115 Heidelberg, Germany. If you have any concerns regarding our products, please contact ProductSafety@springernature.com

Printed and bound by CPI Group (UK) Ltd, Croydon, CR0 4YY
01/10/2026
02225854-0007